Three Methods of Ethics

Great Debates in Philosophy
Series Editor: Ernest Sosa

Dialogue has always been a powerful means of philosophical exploration and exposition. By presenting important current issues in philosophy in the form of a debate, this series attempts to capture the flavour of philosophical argument and to convey the excitement generated by the exchange of ideas. Each author contributes a major, original essay. When these essays have been completed, the authors are each given the opportunity to respond to the opposing view.

Three Methods of Ethics: A Debate

Marcia W. Baron
Philip Pettit
Michael Slote

 Blackwell Publishing

BLACKWELL PUBLISHING

350 Main Street, Malden, MA 02148-5020, USA
108 Cowley Road, Oxford OX4 1JF, UK
550 Swanston Street, Carlton, Victoria 3053, Australia

The right of Marcia Baron, Philip Pettit, and Michael Slote to be identified as the
Authors of this Work has been asserted in accordance with the UK Copyright,
Designs, and Patents Act 1988.

First published 1997
Reprinted 1998, 1999, 2000, 2001, 2002, 2003, 2005

Library of Congress Cataloging-in-Publication Data

Baron, Marcia
   Three methods of ethics: a debate/Marcia Baron, Philip Pettit, Michael Slote.
       p.   cm.—(Great debates in philosophy)
   Essays presented at a conference by the Dept. of Philosophy,
Monash University, June 1995
   Includes bibliographical references and index.
   ISBN 0–631–19434–7 (hardback: alk. paper).—ISBN 0–631–19435–5
(pbk: alk. paper)
   1. Ethics—Congresses. 2. Consequentialism (Ethics)—Congresses.
   3. Virtues—Congresses. 4. Kant, Immanuel, 1724–1804—Ethics—Congresses.
   I. Pettit, Philip, 1945– . II. Slote, Michael A. III. Title. IV. Series.
   BJ1031.B27   1997
   171—dc21   97–10143
                                                                    CIP

A catalogue record for this title is available from the British Library.

Set in 10.5 on 13 pt Melior
by Pure Tech India Ltd, Pondicherry
Printed and bound in the United Kingdom
by MPG Books Ltd, Bodmin, Cornwall

The publisher's policy is to use permanent paper from mills that operate a sustainable
forestry policy, and which has been manufactured from pulp processed using
acid-free and elementary chlorine-free practices. Furthermore, the publisher ensures
that the text paper and cover board used have met acceptable environmental
accreditation standards.

For further information on
Blackwell Publishing, visit our website:
www.blackwellpublishing.com

Contents

Introduction

Philosophers have been occupied with the task of thinking about moral issues for a very long time. Ever since Socrates (if not before) they have sought a general criterion or criteria for distinguishing between right and wrong and between good and evil, and have applied philosophical techniques of analysis and argument to this task.

In recent years, three ways of thinking about morality have come largely to dominate the landscape of ethical debate. These three are consequentialism, which emphasizes good results as the basis for evaluating human actions; Kantian ethics, which focuses on ideals of universal law and respect for others as the basis for morality; and virtue ethics, which views moral questions from the standpoint of the moral agent with virtuous character or motives. Although there has, over the past few years, been a great deal of important work on all three approaches to ethics, the present book is the first to bring them into sustained critical dialogue.

The present volume was in fact originally supposed to have the format of other volumes in this series: it was to be a debate just about the merits of virtue ethics. But almost from the first it seemed a good idea to broaden its mission, because in very recent moral philosophy virtue ethics has in fact had two main competitors: consequentialism and Kantian ethics. Each would have very different things to say about virtue ethics, and since both the alternatives are in some sense better established than virtue ethics, it seemed a good idea to occupy a larger terrain. So the book turned into a debate about and among what many take to be the three most prominent contemporary approaches to ethics.

We believe that the closest predecessor of the present book –
in spirit, if not in actual substance – is Smart and Williams's
Utilitarianism: For and Against. That classic is, well, a classic.
But some of the debate in ethics has moved beyond the possibilities and assumptions envisaged in that work. Some of the most
important work that has been done in Kantian ethics has occurred
subsequent to that volume, and the present importance of that
approach was in no way anticipated in the Smart and Williams
volume.

Then too, consequentialism has moved beyond what it was
when Smart expounded it – in part by way of response to the
criticisms of consequentialism Williams made and, in part, by
further development of the framework for consequentialist theorizing that Smart so clearly and boldly constructed. Finally,
virtue ethics, after a long slumber, has emerged as a genuine self-
standing alternative to consequentialism and Kantian ethics, and
although Williams himself has had some influence on this revival,
the revival itself, once again, is not anticipated in the earlier book.

The present book makes some assumptions that not everyone
will share. It assumes that substantive ethics should proceed
analytically: by argument, example, and distinction-making. It
also assumes that the three approaches it discusses are the most
important in today's substantive ethical theorizing. The essays
include some discussion, e.g., of contract theory and intuitionism, but the main focus is on Kantianism, consequentialism, and
virtue ethics. Of course, the debate among *all* approaches is likely
to go on long after the appearance of this book, but we hope that
the present debate will at least have a significant effect on the
course and character of that future debate.

In June 1995, the Department of Philosophy at Monash University organized a conference at which the three of us were given
an initial opportunity to air our views. We found that conference a
wonderful stimulus to our thinking and writing and would like to
thank those who organized it, in particular Rae Langton and
Michael Smith.

Marcia Baron
Philip Pettit
Michael Slote

Kantian Ethics

Marcia Baron

1 Introduction

The term "Kantian ethics" is used rather loosely to refer not only to Kant's ethics but also to an array of contemporary ethical theories that rely on key ideas in Kant's ethics. My aims in this essay are not primarily interpretive and so I will not be offering a full summary of Kant's ethics. But I want to understand "Kantian ethics" as more than just inspired by Kant's ethics. What I propose to do is to develop and evaluate themes of Kant's ethics that are most central to contemporary debates in ethics.

The approach I take is informed by a view of the history of philosophy according to which it is most interesting, when we look at the writings of Kant or Aristotle or Hume or other figures in philosophy, if we view what they have to say not as frozen doctrine, but as an ongoing ·project. The philosopher's views are thus not of merely antiquarian interest, i.e. of interest just insofar as they help us to understand our past and the history of our current views. As Christine Korsgaard puts it, when they're understood as a project (or even, she suggests, as a method), they "become something living, and...usable" (1995: 1166). This approach, she observes, frees us to develop Kantian views on matters that Kant never addressed, and more boldly, to claim that Kant shouldn't have said what he did – meaning that on Kantian grounds, something that Kant asserted should be rejected. This is the spirit in which I shall discuss Kant's ethics. When we take this approach, the distinction between Kant's ethics and Kantian ethics blurs. Of course there is plenty of room for disagreement as to whether something counts as a Kantian ground, and for suggestions that the bit that we are claiming should be rejected is in fact more central to Kant's ethics than the Kantian ground on which we are claiming that it should be rejected. But such disagreement is itself salutary. It is part of what is involved in working out the Kantian project.

Kantian Ethics as an Alternative to Consequentialism and Virtue Ethics?

Our three-way debate suggests that consequentialism, virtue ethics, and Kantian ethics form three distinct and competing ethical theories. This is problematic for two reasons. First, it is difficult to see what all three are theories of. Are they theories of what makes an action right? That would not be an accurate way to characterize virtue ethics. (Nor would it aptly characterize Kantian ethics.) Are they theories about how one ought to act? That is more promising, but still rather forced. The fit with consequentialism is clumsy at best, since that theory is primarily not about how to act, but about what makes actions (or policies) right; and the fit with virtue ethics is also a poor one. I doubt that there is anything that all three are theories of.[1]

Perhaps it is more apt to think of them as competing approaches to ethics. "Approaches" leaves room for their not all being theories, or theories of the same thing. Their disagreements may thus be, in some instances, disagreements about what ethics is about, and about what the focus of our attention should be. This mitigates but doesn't fully address the problem, though, because the points of agreement and those of disagreement are not plain to view. (The problem is all the more acute because the term "virtue ethics" is used in so many different ways.) With this problem in mind, I will be explicating and defending Kantian ethics by reference to consequentialism and later to virtue ethics, bringing Kantian ethics into dialogue with each of them. This will help us to see what the disagreements are between Kantians and consequentialists, and will also separate out those aspects of virtue ethics that are at odds with Kantian ethics from the positions that are shared by virtue ethicists and most Kantians. Kantian ethics is, it seems to me, much closer to virtue ethics than is usually supposed; indeed, it may be only a minority of virtue ethicists who hold positions that are at odds with Kantian ethics. But to this later. The contrast between consequentialism and Kantian ethics is reasonably sharp, and is a good place to begin.

2   Consequentialism versus Kantian Ethics

The core idea of consequentialism is that what makes an action (or a policy) right is that it brings about better consequences than any of its alternatives. "Right" is ambiguous between "obligatory" and "permissible," so let's clarify: what makes an action (or policy) obligatory is that it brings about better consequences than any of its alternatives. What makes it permissible is that it brings about consequences that are at least as good as any of its alternatives. "Better" or "better consequences" can be cashed out in a variety of ways, but we needn't concern ourselves with that now. And the item whose consequences determine its moral status is typically an action, but could be a policy or, on some versions of consequentialism, a motive or trait. I shall generally suppose that it is an action, and shall signal when I do not.

Kantians (and many others, as well) take issue with two tenets of consequentialism, which are:

1 It is morally obligatory to do whatever will produce the best consequences.
2 It is always morally permissible to do whatever will produce the best consequences.

Kantians (and others) also question whether one can judge well enough what the consequences will be to base rightness on that judgment. Consequentialists deflect that criticism by pointing out that they are not committed to holding that the way to decide what it is morally obligatory (or permissible) to do is to determine whether what one is proposing to do will bring about the best consequences. Thus, consequentialists need not hold that their theory is action-guiding. But critics may reply: how useful is an ethical theory if it isn't action-guiding? I share the sentiment of such critics but will not press the point here.[2]

In challenging (1) and (2), critics of consequentialism challenge the notion that rightness – either moral permission or moral obligation – is a matter of bringing about the best result or maximizing the good. Rightness, they insist, involves *acting on principle*. Their objection points to a sharp difference in approach to ethics: consequentialists focus on goals; non-consequentialists (of various stripes) do not. An example will help here.

An administrator once told me about the following dispute. A speaker had been invited to campus. The point of his lecture would be to oppose free speech. Some of the faculty objected strenuously to having him to campus and favored "uninviting" him. Free speech is a great value, and they did not want to see it undermined by this or any other speaker. Others defended the plan to bring him to campus – and they did so in the name of free speech.

How could both parties appeal to free speech – and only free speech – in defense of their respective views? Those who opposed the speaker's visit saw free speech as a goal, a goal which would not be advanced and might well be hindered by a speaker who spoke against it. Those who supported the speaker's visit saw free speech as a matter of principle, imposing a side- constraint on our conduct.[3] In the view of the former, what is desired is that free speech flourish, and to that end it might occasionally be necessary to squelch (what would otherwise be) free speech. In the view of the latter (those who supported the speaker's visit), free speech is a value not in the sense of a goal to be promoted, but a value never to be violated. It would be a violation of free speech to prevent a speaker from speaking on the ground that his or her views were considered noxious, outrageous, or dangerous. That allowing the speaker to speak might undermine the cause of free speech by winning over some impressionable college students to the speaker's side is irrelevant, in the supporters' view. Those who opposed the speaker's campus visit viewed free speech as a goal to be promoted or advanced. Those who opposed the attempt to uninvite the speaker saw free speech as a matter of principle: as constituting a side-constraint on our conduct. Side-constraints work this way: they tell us that no matter how worthwhile the goal, there are things which we may not do even if they are crucial for that goal.[4]

A different example may help to bring out what is at issue. Suppose that Leigh and Kim, a monogamous couple, are fairly trusting of one another, although the trust is somewhat fragile. Kim engages in a lengthy but (he is fairly sure) non-serious flirtation with someone and at one point lies to Leigh about his whereabouts to reduce the chance that she will come to be aware of this flirtation. Lying to her in this way is (let's assume) a violation of her trust in him. (Perhaps the flirtation is too, but that is another matter.) Yet lying far better promotes *the goal* of furthering her trust in him, since if he told her the truth, she would have less trust in him than she now does. (I am assuming of course that in this particular scenario there is extremely little risk that he will be caught in the lie; if he is caught lying, she will trust him even less than if he had told the truth. I am also assuming that the situation is such that he cannot avoid telling the truth except by lying.) Insofar as trust is a goal, lying would seem to be the right choice (given that the flirtation is already in place); but if trust is a value to be honored, lying to her would be wrong.

Act-consequentialism versus Rule-consequentialism

Now we must complicate things somewhat. Contemporary philosophers distinguish act-consequentialism from rule-consequentialism.[5] What I have been presenting as consequentialism is act-consequentialism, the position that an act is obligatory insofar as it promotes better consequences than any of its alternatives, and permissible insofar as it promotes consequences that are at least as good as any of its alternatives. For simplicity, let's say: an act is right insofar as it promotes better consequences than any of its alternatives. Rule-consequentialism, by contrast, holds that an act is right insofar as it conforms to a rule, conformity to which promotes better consequences than would conformity to a different rule. The idea is to look not at the particular act under consideration, but at a general policy – or rule – of performing such acts.

The opposition to consequentialism that I have been describing is more sharply at odds with act-consequentialism than with rule-consequentialism. According to the act-consequentialist, it is always permissible – indeed obligatory – to do whatever will promote the best consequences. The rule-consequentialist takes a different stand: it is always permissible – indeed obligatory – to act according to a rule general adherence to which would promote the best consequences. If cheating on an exam will promote the best consequences, it is what I should do, according to the act-consequentialist. But the rule-consequentialist asks, Would general conformity to a rule of cheating on exams (in circumstances such as the agent's) promote the best consequences, or would general conformity to a rule of never cheating on exams promote the best consequences? Only if the answer is that general conformity to a rule of cheating (in such circumstances) would promote the best consequences is it permissible for the agent to cheat.

Rule-consequentialists can, in their own consequentialist way, recognize side-constraints. If adhering to a particular side-constraint promotes better consequences than not adhering to it, then it is obligatory to adhere to it. By the same token, they can recognize rights and the value of acting on principle. To see this, consider a question which at first may seem very puzzling. In *Utilitarianism*, John Stuart Mill develops and defends utilitarianism – a (and the most influential) form of consequentialism. The whole point of the work is to articulate and defend the view that "actions are right in proportion as they tend to promote happiness; wrong as they tend to produce the reverse of happiness" (Mill 1979: 7). Yet the thesis of another work by Mill, *On Liberty*, is that the sole legitimate basis for coercively interfering with the liberty of an individual is to stop or prevent that individual from harming others. The "only purpose for which power can be rightfully exercised over any member of a civilized community, against his will, is to prevent harm to others. His own good, either physical or moral, is not a sufficient warrant" (Mill 1978: 9). This principle governs absolutely, thus trumping utility. How can the principle advanced in *On Liberty* be consistent with Mill's utilitarianism? To many this is deeply puzzling. It is puzzling because we would expect Mill, as a utilitarian, to say that interfering with the liberty of others is permissible – indeed obligatory – insofar as it promotes the greatest happiness of the greatest number. Or rather: we would expect him to say that if he were an act-utilitarian. But if he is a rule-utilitarian (and here I should note that the distinction is a fairly recent invention, and certainly did not exist in Mill's time), there is no puzzle at all.[6] Happiness is maximized, Mill can hold, not by interfering with the liberty of others any time a calculation of utility shows that the particular instance of interfering will maximize utility (happiness), but rather by adhering steadfastly to a rule which says: never interfere with the liberty of others except to prevent harm to others. (Note that it does not say: and interfere whenever doing so does prevent harm to others.) What Mill is saying, in effect, is that recognizing and abiding by a side-constraint sometimes produces the best consequences, better than those produced by performing an individual action which (considered without regard to rules or principles) would produce the best consequences.

Act-consequentialism is not incompatible with the idea that at times – indeed, much of the time – one should not calculate which of the available options can be expected to promote the best consequences. Act-consequentialism can hold that although the right action is the one that brings about the best consequences, the time taken to calculate the consequences, the risk of error (and tendency to self-deception) and the loss of spontaneity are "costs" that may outweigh the good of calculating the consequences. So the act-consequentialist has no problem with the idea that one may – indeed, should – stick to what are sometimes called "rules of thumb," for example, don't cheat people, always stop at red lights and stop signs, and so on. However, the act-consequentialist holds that if for some reason it really is clear that sticking to the rule of thumb in a particular case will produce worse consequences than breaking it, the right thing to do is to break it. By contrast, the rule-consequentialist favors sticking to it, as long as it is the case that a policy of sticking to the rule can be expected to produce better consequences than abiding by a different rule (e.g. a meta-rule which says to stick to the rule in question except in special circumstances). Another way to make the point is to say that what act-consequentialists treat as

mere rules of thumb (rules that can be broken) rule-consequentialists treat as side-constraints.[7]

To illustrate, recall the free speech example. The rule-consequentialist will ask, Which will bring about better consequences? Adhering to a rule of restricting speech (including
uninviting speakers) if the view that the speaker puts forth is
one which, if widely held, would bring about bad consequences?
Or, adhering to a rule of not so restricting free speech? A rule-
utilitarian could take either view, for there is room for disagreement on what the consequences in each instance are most likely
to be. In his famous and eloquent defense of free speech in *On
Liberty*, Mill took the latter position. But whatever conclusion
they reach, they would arrive at it by comparing the (likely)
consequences of adhering to one rule or policy with the (likely)
consequences of adhering to a different rule or policy.

Now if rule-consequentialists recognize and value adherence to
some side-constraints, how do they differ in their view of side-
constraints from the critics of consequentialism? The difference is
that for rule-consequentialists, a side-constraint is valid (and thus
to be adhered to) only if sticking to it promotes the best consequences. For Kantians (among others), we are morally obligated
(or, it is virtuous) to adhere to the side-constraints even if doing so
doesn't promote the best consequences. "How can this be?", someone with consequentialist intuitions will ask. How can adhering to
the side-constraints be anything but irrational unless general
adherence (or, adherence in this particular case, anyway) promotes the best consequences? There are various ways of answering
the question, all of which rely on the idea that what makes a course
of conduct right needn't be only its consequences. Since my concern is with Kantian ethics, I will focus on the Kantian response.[8]

Kantian Adherence to Principles

The reason why certain principles are to be adhered to is, in a
word, humanity. We are to respect humanity as an end in itself. In
a famous passage Kant proclaims that "man, and in general every
rational being, *exists* as an end in himself, *not merely as a means*
for arbitrary use by this or that will: he must in all his actions,

whether they are directed to himself or to other rational beings, always be viewed *at the same time as an end*" (*G* 428).[9] It is crucial here that "end" doesn't mean "goal." The end must be conceived "not as an end to be produced, *but as a self-existent* end" (*G* 437). (See Wood 1995.)

What, more precisely, is it that we are to respect? And what does this respect entail? We are to respect humanity or rational nature. (Kant generally uses these two words interchangeably, since humans are, if not the only rational beings, the only ones we know about.) More specifically, it is our capacity to set ends – any ends whatsoever – for ourselves. This capacity allows an individual to resolve to swim for at least thirty minutes daily, or to adhere to a particular moral principle; it makes it possible to refuse to do something, no matter how tempting it is, if we judge it to be wrong. On a Kantian view, we are not governed by our impulses. There are some people who may seem to be, but what is really happening is that they are choosing to act impulsively. If I claim "I just couldn't help myself; I was overcome by desire," what I claim is, on a Kantian view, not strictly speaking true. What has really happened is that I've let desire determine how I'll act. That we can say "No" to any impulse or desire is brought out dramatically in the following passage in Kant's *Critique of Practical Reason*:

> Suppose that someone says his lust is irresistible when the desired object and opportunity are present. Ask him whether he would not control his passion if, in front of the house where he has this opportunity, a gallows were erected on which he would be hanged immediately after gratifying his lust. We do not have to guess very long what his answer would be. But ask him whether he thinks it would be possible for him to overcome his love of life, however great it may be, if his sovereign threatened him with the same sudden death unless he made a false deposition against an honorable man whom the ruler wished to destroy under a plausible pretext. Whether he would or not he perhaps will not venture to say; but that it would be possible for him he would certainly admit without hesitation. He judges, therefore, that he can do something because he knows that he ought, and he recognizes that he is free – a fact which, without the moral law, would have remained unknown to him. (*PrR* 30)[10]

Respecting persons means respecting them as rational agents, as beings who set ends for themselves, beings who act on reasons. ("Everything in nature works in accordance with laws. Only a rational being has the power to act *in accordance with his idea* of laws – that is, in accordance with principles" (*G* 412).) We are to respect humanity in ourselves and in others and respect it both positively and negatively. Respecting it negatively means recognizing that various types of action are wrong: deceiving, manipulating, assaulting (except in certain instances, such as self-defense), mocking, and so on. Respecting it positively does not mean treating it as a goal – there is no duty to try to create more of it – but placing a positive value on it and acting accordingly. To place a positive value on it is to have as ends one's own perfection and the happiness of others. Having these ends entails that one is to develop one's talents and seek to improve oneself morally and promote others' happiness, but there is no requirement that one do all of this as much as possible.

Before discussing these ends and duties in greater detail, let us – partly by way of summary, partly in anticipation of things to come – go over the contrasts between consequentialism and Kantian ethics. We have seen that consequentialism differs from Kantian ethics in the role it allows for side-constraints, and since different consequentialisms allow different roles for side-constraints, some consequentialisms differ more from Kantian ethics than do others. Kantian ethics is much closer to rule-consequentialism than to act-consequentialism. Rule-consequentialists can recognize side-constraints: if binding oneself to a particular side-constraint promotes better consequences than not binding oneself to it, then it is obligatory to bind oneself to it. But side-constraints are only justifiable, on a consequentialist view, if adhering to them promotes the best consequences, and this of course is not the Kantian view.

Related to this difference are two others. First, consequentialism is concerned to produce some good; this is not a central concern of Kantian ethics.[11] To invoke an Aristotelian distinction: the Kantian focus is not on *poiēsis* (on producing something), but on *praxis* (on how one acts). Second, consequentialists typically are concerned to maximize. If it is good to help others, it is best to help others as much as one possibly can. Kantian ethics has very little concern with maximizing. This will become clearer shortly, as we explore the Kantian notions of obligatory ends and imperfect duties.

Obligatory Ends

The notion of an obligatory end may seem odd to contemporary ears. We are used to hearing of obligatory actions, but obligatory ends? The idea, which plays a central role in Kant's ethics but tends to be neglected in the classroom, is that we are morally required to have certain ends. We are obligated to act accordingly, but the duty to act in certain ways is secondary, and is based on our duty to have certain ends. The ends that we are obligated to have are the happiness of others and our own perfection. We are to promote others' happiness and improve ourselves. Promoting others' happiness means helping them to realize their ends. Self-improvement has two dimensions: developing one's talents and improving oneself morally.

Others' happiness

"Promoting others' happiness" can be thought of in either of two ways: promoting what we, who seek to help, take the other person's happiness to be; or promoting what the other person takes her happiness to consist in. With some qualification, the second option is the one that Kant takes. The duty to promote others' happiness is the duty to help them to realize their ends.

But, a critical reader will ask, surely I am not to aid the embezzler in figuring out the surest way to embezzle without being caught! Surely I am not to aid the stalker by learning, and then disclosing to him, the daily routine of the woman he is stalking. Indeed Kant does build in a qualification: we are to promote only their permissible ends. In helping others, we are of course not to aid and abet crime, or even less serious vice. We are not to "give a lazy fellow soft cushions so that he [can] pass his life away in sweet idleness," nor "see to it that a drunkard is never short of wine and whatever else he needs to get drunk" (*MM* 481). Furthermore, Kant does not require (or even recommend) that we help others to achieve their permissible ends without regard to which ones we think most worthwhile. What is ruled out is ignoring their ends and imposing on them what we think their ends should be. In seeking to help them, we seek to promote their (permissible) ends; but we may choose to help to promote those which we think are most worthwhile. "It is for them to decide what they count as belonging to their happiness; but it is open to me to refuse them many things that *they* think will make them happy but that I do not, as long as they have no right to demand them from me as what is theirs" (*MM* 388). So, the duty to promote others' happiness leaves room for discretion but does not leave room for heavy-handed paternalism. It doesn't allow for deciding that while his ends are *w*, *x*, *y*, and *z*, really he should care much more for *a*, and so I'll seek to promote his happiness by providing him with, or promoting as if it were his end, *a*.

In Kant's insistence that it is others' ends that (with the quali-fications noted) define how we are to understand what it is that we are to promote, we see his opposition to paternalism. This is a reflection of his emphasis on autonomy, a value that is also evident in the following asymmetry: we are to promote our own moral perfection, but not that of others. Why is this? Why aren't we to promote human perfection in general? Why aren't we to seek to perfect others as well as ourselves? The basic idea is that it is not our business to try to transform or even reform other people. One's relation to oneself is special: we are responsible for our own conduct (and to some extent, our characters), not for that of others.

Three comments are in order. First, we are of course talking about adults here. Parents bear some responsibility for the con-duct of their children, and certainly have an obligation to help them to be and become good people. Second, while we are not to seek to perfect others, helping them to perfect themselves is a different matter. Recognizing that friends may be able to help each other to become more virtuous, Kant says that "it is . . . a duty for one of the friends to point out the other's faults to him" (*MM* 470). This is, he says, "a duty of love" (*MM* 470). Pointing out a friend's faults, we hope, helps him to improve himself. Furthermore, we should bear in mind that our conduct (whether or not intention-ally) may facilitate or pose obstacles to their self-improvement.

And so in addition to having a duty to point out our friend's faults to him, we should take care not to facilitate vice by, for example, keeping the drunkard supplied with wine.[12]

Third, it would be a mistake to think that the point about responsibility – that we are responsible for our own conduct but not that of others – carries over to responsibility for the *fate* of others. Each individual bears a special responsibility for his or her character and conduct, but we "share fate." We have a duty to promote others' happiness; there is no notion that their problems are theirs, not for us to be concerned with. "Minding one's own business" means not trying to manage other's characters or decide for them what their ends should be; it does not mean ignoring them when they are suffering. We are very much obligated to try to alleviate suffering.[13]

Self-improvement

It might be thought that the duty to improve ourselves – or, as Kant often puts it, to perfect ourselves – would allow us to improve ourselves in any way we like, with no further specification. In fact, it splits into two parts, one of which has more latitude than the other. The part that is quite open-ended is the duty to develop our talents. But whatever talents we choose to develop, we are also required to perfect ourselves morally. In his brief discussions of this duty, Kant spells it out in terms of moral motivation: it is a duty to make "the thought of duty for its own sake...the sufficient incentive of every action conforming to duty" (*MM* 393; see also 387). In other words, it is a duty to see to it that duty is a sufficient incentive for us. Elsewhere, however, he offers a lengthy discussion of qualities that we are to cultivate in ourselves – most notably, sympathetic feeling – and of other qualities that he says are vices. This provides yet more content to the duty to improve ourselves. Envy, ingratitude, and malice are vices, as are contempt, arrogance, and servility.[14] And there are vices that fall under these headings; one form of malice – the sweetest, Kant says – is the desire for revenge. Part of moral self-improvement would thus be ridding oneself as much as possible of vices such as envy and the desire for revenge, detecting in oneself tendencies in those directions and attempting to check them. The duty to improve oneself morally will clearly involve considerable self-scrutiny. So it's not surprising to find Kant saying that the first command of all duties to oneself is "*know* (scrutinize, fathom) *yourself*" (*MM* 441).

Further details about the obligatory end of self-improvement will emerge in the course of the next section, as we examine the latitude inherent in imperfect duties. I turn now to two features of obligatory ends that are particularly important. The first is the fact that there are two and neither trumps the other. The second concerns the nature of the duties that they generate, more specifically, the fact that they involve considerable latitude. I'll address these in reverse order.

Imperfect duties

The duties generated by the obligatory ends are imperfect duties. These are duties to help others and to develop one's talents. Exactly what one does – whom one helps, how and how often – is not specified. This is not a gap in Kant's ethics; this is the way it is supposed to be. The imperfect duties leave a lot of latitude. We do not have a duty to help others as much as we possibly can and whenever we can; we do not have a duty to do as much good for others as is possible for us. Likewise, we do not have a duty to develop all of our talents as much as we can, nor to pick one or two talents and develop them maximally. How we go about helping others and developing our talents is left open.

Imperfect duties contrast, not surprisingly, with perfect duties. (The labels, which have a history that predates Kant, are misleading; there is nothing "imperfect" in the usual sense about imperfect duties.) Perfect duties are reasonably clear-cut. Though they sometimes leave us latitude as to how we discharge them (if I owe you $20, I can discharge my duty by paying by mail or in person, today or tomorrow, by cash or by check) they don't leave us anything like the latitude entailed by the imperfect duties. I shall have little to say about them. It is the imperfect duties that give Kant's ethics a distinctive flavor.

There are, to be sure, limits to how we may go about helping others and developing our talents. Some of these are imposed by the perfect duties: I may not help my friends by cheating others, or help the needy by robbing the wealthy.[15] The limits that are harder to spell out are those entailed by the obligatory ends. If I decide to help others only when it will be rewarded, this indicates that I have not really adopted the end of others' happiness. It indicates that I regard their happiness as worth promoting only when I can reap some benefit from doing so. So it will not do to have the following sort of attitude: "I want to be moral, and to be moral I have to help people sometimes, since helping others is obligatory. I might as well do this in a way that will best promote my own interests, so I'll help people only when the fact that I'm helping is amply noticed and appreciated. This way, I can kill two birds with one stone: I can meet the moral requirement of helping others and enhance my reputation." The person with this attitude has not really embraced the end of others' happiness. He is just trying to meet a requirement. He is thinking of ethics as if it were simply a set of rules to follow. But for Kant, there is far more to ethics than that. One has to care, not just act a certain way.

There are limits to how we may go about helping others and developing our talents, but there is latitude, as well. We are not required to help others at every opportunity, and there needn't always be a compelling reason for not helping (such as that one is exhausted and needs to rest if one is to be able to go on helping others in the future). At the same time, there are instances where a failure to help would indicate that the agent has not really embraced the end of others' happiness. Suppose, for example, Joe is taking a stroll and sees someone grab his chest and collapse. There is no one else around and there is a telephone within easy reach. It would be inexcusable not to dial the emergency number to get help for the unfortunate man. "I do care about the welfare of others, but this is not my way of helping; I contribute money to charity and help my friends fix their cars, and I am great at lending an ear to a friend who wants to tell me his woes, but in instances like this, where someone I don't know is in trouble, I keep my distance" would be unconvincing. Joe could not be said, on a Kantian view, really to care about the welfare of others. He may well care about the happiness of certain others and be prepared to try to further it, and he may also like the idea of helping those he doesn't know now and then, when it suits him, but he doesn't regard the needs of others as making a normative claim on him. He doesn't accept Kant's position that "the maxim of common interest, of beneficence towards those in need, is a universal duty of people, just because they are to be considered fellow humans, that is, rational beings with needs, united by nature in one dwelling place so that they can help one another" (*MM* 453, translation altered).

It is clear from the example of Joe that the latitude in Kant's imperfect duties does not extend so far as to allow us to help only those near and dear to us, and neglect to help everyone else. ("To *do good* to others insofar as we can is a duty, whether one loves them or not" (MM 402; "other men" replaced by "others").) But are we then required to help others without regard to our personal ties to them? Must we select whom to help without any regard to our history with them, how well we know them, and the like? No. I have a duty of non-indifference towards others; the needs of others make a claim on me even if they are strangers to me. But it is part of the latitude in the duty to promote others' happiness that I don't have to help everyone equally, or help without regard to my personal ties to certain others.

So how much latitude is there in imperfect duties? This cannot be spelled out very exactly. The most we can say is that one's maxim must be consistent with, and indeed must reflect, a genuine commitment to the obligatory end.[16] A maxim of helping only when it is convenient, or only when it seems likely to reap some reward, does not. Indeed, it suggests that the agent is trying to qualify in a very superficial way as moral: trying to meet the letter of morality but not the spirit. (On a Kantian view this makes no sense; one can't count as moral unless one is genuinely committed to acting morally and being moral.)

A word about the use of "maxim" here. To say that we have a duty to embrace the happiness of others and our own perfection is equivalent to saying that it is obligatory to have among one's maxims, "Promote the happiness of others" and "Perfect thyself." A maxim is basically a personal policy, a principle that guides one's conduct. We shall have more to say about maxims later.

The notion of embracing an end and acting accordingly is rather different from the understanding of promoting an end that we find in consequentialism. The idea is that we care about the end and act accordingly; we take it very seriously, and both honor it and seek to further it. But this cannot be cashed out as seeking to bring about a state of affairs in which there is as much as possible of the end in question. While it is very common among consequentialists to speak as if what matters most is bringing about certain states of affairs, it is alien to Kantian ethics. And as has been noted, the idea of maximizing plays a key role in consequentialism (though there are some consequentialists who see it as inessential to their theory) but virtually no role in Kantian ethics. This is evident from the latitude involved in the imperfect duties. They require us to embrace the obligatory ends and act accordingly, but do not require that we do as much as possible to help others and perfect ourselves.

Now it might be thought that even though the obligatory ends do not require that we maximize, Kant would nonetheless hold that the more we do by way of helping others and perfecting ourselves, the better we are. Although Kant's writings are not unambiguous on this point, this seems not to be his view.[17] And this brings me to the second feature of imperfect duties that I want to highlight.

Two obligatory ends

A very common view, both within academic moral philosophy and outside of it, is that the people who are ethically most admirable are those who are most committed to improving the welfare of others. Except among those who are too troubled by her opposition to abortion and contraception to overlook it, Mother Teresa is regularly cited as a moral exemplar: about as good a person as one finds. And thus one might expect that Kant ranks promoting others' happiness higher than perfecting oneself. But in fact this is not the case. Neither obligatory end is ranked higher than the other. This, conjoined with the latitude accorded the imperfect duties, has an interesting implication: it precludes a unitary conception of moral excellence. Moral excellence comes in considerable variety, on a Kantian view. Although there is room for some ranking, there isn't the clear "best" that we find on views which see ethics as strictly other-directed and regard altruism as the most important virtue.

The importance of the pluralistic conception of moral excellence entailed by Kant's ethics is evident in the fact that it prevents his theory from some pitfalls that have received a lot of attention in contemporary moral philosophy.

The first pitfall is what might be called the "excessive demands" problem. Morality, as understood on some moral theories, is said to make excessive demands on people, in particular, to require us to give up our pet projects and possibly even what gives our lives meaning. To the extent that this problem has a foothold, it is a problem for theories that ask us, as consequentialist theories often do, to maximize the good. If the good to be maximized is a general good, such as human happiness, rather than a personal good, such as one's own happiness, the injunction to maximize happiness may leave little room for pursuing one's own project. The entomologist who is fascinated by the habits of a certain type of insect and devotes much of her time to studying it probably is not maximizing the general happiness. Her research skills could be put to a more humanitarian use. Yet do we want to say that she is acting immorally in pursuing her research in entomology? Or even that her choice of career shows a lack of virtue? Presumably not, and this suggests that the conception of morality in theories which require us to maximize human happiness may be faulty.

Kantian ethics is not open to this charge. We are not morally required to maximize human happiness, but only to take it very seriously, see it as making a normative claim on us, and seek (in some ways or other) to promote it. There are many ways in which a commitment to promote the welfare of others may be expressed. The entomologist is not deficient for having allowed her fascination with bugs to shape her career choice rather than selecting a line of work solely on the basis of what would best promote human welfare. Kant's ethics allows us to pursue our own projects provided that we abide by the perfect duties and the principles of imperfect duty.

A related pitfall that Kantian ethics avoids is the "moral saints" problem. Developed in an influential essay by Susan Wolf (1982), the problem is that the sort of person we think of as morally best is someone we would never aspire to be, never hope our children might become, never would enjoy as a friend. Moral saints, Wolf claims, are dull, lacking in interests other than promoting the welfare of others. They cannot appreciate a Munch painting or enjoy an off-color joke; they work single-mindedly to better the lot of humanity. It would seem, then, that a moral theory which regarded as morally ideal the sort of people Wolf calls "moral saints" would be flawed.[18] While on some theories as well as in ordinary extra-theoretic moral thinking such a person counts as morally ideal, this is definitely not the case on a Kantian view. There is no premium placed on being single-mindedly devoted to improving the lot of others. We have two obligatory ends, not one. A Kantian "moral saint" would not work single-mindedly to better the lot of humanity. Still, it might be thought that Kant's ethics places a premium on being single-mindedly (double-mindedly?) devoted to the two obligatory ends (whatever that might mean). But this is not the case, for there is no notion in Kant's ethics that we are to lack ends other than the obligatory ones. Indeed, the obligatory ends require that we have other ends in order for the obligatory ends to have content. I cannot very well develop my talents if I have no interest in music, storytelling, drawing, athletics, the arts and sciences, cooking, sewing, etc.[19]

The Consequentialist Rejoinder

All this will be very puzzling to the consequentialist. Why shouldn't we seek to promote an obligatory end as much as possible? If the development of talents is a great good, shouldn't I be concerned to promote it, rather than just developing my own talents? And if humanity is the value on which the two obligatory ends rest, shouldn't the point be to promote it, and thereby respect it? One reply to these questions would be a baffled "Why?" But since looks of bafflement and replying to "Why" questions with a "Why?" do not tend to advance a discussion, let's see if we can do better than that. Let's try to figure out what is behind the questions.

The suggestion appears to be that value in general is such that the right or best thing is to promote as much of it as possible. This is the position taken by Philip Pettit. Indeed, he defines consequentialism as "the view that whatever values an individual or institutional agent adopts, the proper response to those values is to promote them" (Pettit 1991: 231). Other responses to value are appropriate only as a means to, or a part of, promoting them. "The agent," Pettit continues, "should honour the values only so far as honouring them is part of promoting them, or is necessary to promote them" (p. 231). I find the position wholly unpersuasive. Value comes in many varieties, even if we limit ourselves (as I mean to, and imagine the consequentialist also would) to non-instrumental value, and it doesn't appear that all value calls for the same response. Some are such that the best response is to exemplify or instantiate them; others are such that the best response is to promote them; still others call for producing as much of them as possible; others call for honoring them by refraining from doing anything that would violate them. A mixture of these responses will often be called for, a mixture whose proper proportions may differ, depending on the value and the particular situation. (Not that there will typically be only one appropriate response or blend of responses; there will be some inappropriate ones, but often more than one appropriate response.) This is not the place to try to work out the varieties of value and the proper responses to them. My aim is only to establish that there are other appropriate responses to value and valuable things besides that of seeking to promote them. To do so, I'll borrow from Christine Swanton's groundbreaking essay, "Profiles of the virtues" (1995).

Swanton's project is to outline and defend a value-centered virtue ethics. Of particular interest to my topic is her claim that there are various appropriate responses to value, and that virtues "can be classified in different ways according to the responses to value which are characteristic of those virtues." Thus "the virtues of connoisseurship specialize in appreciation, friendship is characteristically manifested in expression, benevolence in promotion, justice in respecting or 'honoring'" (1995: 48). There are two crucial points here: Pettit to the contrary, *promotion is not the only appropriate response to value*; and *honoring is not the only plausible alternative*. An appropriate response to such value as the value of a redwood forest is to appreciate it, and one appropriate response to some values is to express them.

Calling the various types of appropriate responses to value "profiles of the virtues," Swanton notes that many virtues have more than one profile. It is not hard to see that this is the case. Consider friendship, understood as a virtue. Imagine someone who visits a friend in the hospital not because he wants to, but because this is, he believes, what a good friend does. It is, in his view, a duty of friendship. He *honors the friendship.* (Swanton imagines that the hospitalized friend "considers himself the life and soul of the ward, is flirtatious with the nurses, talks loudly and boastfully," and knowing this, his friend is not at all looking forward to visiting him. Indeed, his friendly feelings dissipate as he pictures how his friend conducts himself when hospitalized.) By contrast, someone who visits his friend out of friendly feelings *expresses* friendship (1995: 52–3).

Nor are honoring and expressing the only appropriate responses to the value of friendship. Two friends who haven't seen each other in years delight to be together. Here the valuable object is the friend (*qua* friend) and the response is *appreciation*. *Promotion* also has its place in the virtue of friendship, and it can take several objects: a friend seeks to promote her friend's welfare, but also seeks to promote the friendship. She may also seek to promote the virtue of friendship in herself (Swanton 1995: 61).

Reflection on friendship and other virtues discloses what a mistake it is to suppose that the only appropriate response to value is promotion (honoring being worthwhile only as a means to, or instance of, promoting).

Consider another virtue, justice. Justice has as its characteristic profile respecting or honoring it by being just oneself. Imagine someone who sought to promote justice but did not hesitate to act unjustly if he thought this the best way to promote it. This is not, I take it, someone we would consider just. (Honesty has a profile very similar to that of justice, except that even more than in the case of justice, promoting has to take a backseat to honoring.)

Of course the consequentialist could (Pettit notwithstanding) acknowledge the position that promotion is not the only appropriate response to value but still maintain that the proper response to Kant's two obligatory ends is to promote them, and that the best way to respect humanity, the value that underlies these obligatory ends, is to promote it.

To determine whether promotion is the only, or at least the primary, appropriate response to the value of humanity, it will help to have some examples before us. Reflection, via the examples, on how we respond to the loss of items of different sorts of value, and in particular, on what expressions seem appropriate in response to instances in which we find, with regret, that we must harm or destroy bearers of such value will lend support to my claim that promotion is not the only or the primary appropriate response to the value of humanity.

Suppose I love trees, and determine that I have to cut down a dogwood. I don't shrug and say, "A tree is a tree; I'll just plant a new one." It isn't at all the same to plant a new one; I'd prefer (and for reasons beyond those of cost) to keep the old one. Nevertheless, it *is* an expression of my love for trees that I make a point of replacing any tree that I have to cut down.

To transpose this slightly: imagine that a landlord decides that he has to cut down numerous trees to clear the area for an apartment building he has decided to build. Suppose that he regrets having to cut them down but feels that he makes up for it to some extent by planting as many trees as he cut down. (I'm imagining that there isn't room on the property for as many new trees as were there before the apartment building was built, and that he finds some other suitable place(s) to plant the rest of the trees.) It is a sign of love (or perhaps respect) for trees that he takes care to replace them.[20]

Now imagine someone who killed two people in the course of robbing them. He felt he had to and, like the person who cut down the trees, does not regret what he did, but regrets that (as he sees it) it was necessary to kill them. Would it show respect (or love) for humanity if he sought to "replace" the people he killed by producing more people? Suppose that he tries to rebut the claim that he does not respect humanity by saying, "Look, it's true that I killed two people, but I'm making a point of replacing those two by doing my part to produce two new people. In fact, my girlfriend is pregnant right now!" We would regard this as a sick joke. Of course one reason we don't take his remark seriously is that we believe that he killed unjustifiably and do not think that someone who killed unjustifiably and does not regret having done so can be correctly said to respect humanity. But the other reason we would regard his remark as a sick joke is that respect for humanity entails regarding people as not replaceable. The loss of one is not compensated for – not even a tiny bit – by producing a new one. A different example will bring this out more sharply.[21]

Imagine this time not a murderer, but a doctor who has made a few mistakes. Even though to err is human, and even though she has made very few mistakes and most of the time has acquitted herself very well indeed, she feels terrible about the three times she "lost" a patient. (Perhaps she judged that what turned out to be a malignant tumor was not malignant, and didn't bother with tests that might have spared the patient his untimely death; perhaps she prescribed a medicine carelessly or wrote out surgery orders misleadingly. I am assuming that no malice was involved, and nothing as reprehensible as, say, performing surgery while intoxicated.) She feels much better, though, when she resolves to (try to) produce three children to replace the people whose untimely deaths were due largely to an error on her part.

There is something wrong here. My suggestion is that what is wrong is the notion, implicit in her thinking, that the value of humanity is like the value of tulips. If I forget to water your potted tulips when you are away and, as a result, they die, I am culpable, and buying new tulip bulbs for you and planting them (with care) may not entirely make up for my negligence. Still, it is a very appropriate gesture. Producing new people to make up for ones who no longer exist thanks (in part) to my negligence is not an appropriate gesture. The reason it is not an appropriate gesture is that people are not replaceable.[22]

The foregoing underscores the point that different values may call for different responses. This is indicated by our attitudes toward the loss of items we value: trees *qua* trees we view as somewhat (indeed, considerably) replaceable; persons *qua* persons we do not. One of the primary ways of expressing the value that we attach to trees is to plant them. The value of humanity calls for various attitudes and courses of conduct; producing more of it is, at best, way at the bottom of the list of the courses of action it calls for.

I have been stressing the inappropriateness of regarding humanity as something to be produced (and, more generally, as a goal), but it might be argued that my remarks are unfair to consequentialists. Perhaps there is some more plausible way in which humanity could be treated as a goal, as something to be promoted. It might be suggested that we view humanity as a goal if we seek to bring about a state of affairs in which everyone respects humanity, and that seeking to bring about that state of affairs is a proper expression of respect for the value of humanity. But that won't do. It conflates humanity with respect for humanity. If my aim is to bring about a state of affairs in which everyone respects humanity (or in which respect for humanity is in some other sense "maximized"), that goal cannot be equated with humanity. So let's try a different approach. Is there some other way in which humanity could be understood as a goal? Is there some other state of affairs such that bringing it about could constitute producing or promoting humanity, and such that a proper response to the value of humanity could be, as consequentialists would have it, to bring about that state of affairs?

Grating though this exercise of translating into talk of producing or bringing about a state of affairs is to Kantian ears, there might be a way this could go. Here is one reason for thinking there is. "Humanity," in Kant's ethics, does not, strictly speaking, mean "persons." It refers to a quality that persons have. So it might be argued that one could appropriately express respect for humanity by seeking to increase or promote it. While one way to increase or promote humanity would be to produce more humans, and hence (unless those produced are all severely mentally impaired) more humanity, arguably this would not be the only way. Recognizing that humanity is not something that we value "in bulk," as an aggregate, as if it were detachable from the individuals to whom it "belongs," we might suppose it possible to promote humanity by bringing it about that each individual person has more of it. Thus understood, promoting humanity could be said to be the proper response to the value of humanity. This looks promising. But there are still problems.

First, "humanity" is not conceived, on the Kantian picture, as something of which we have more or less; except for the odd cases (people who have an impairment that inclines us to say that they *sort of* have the power to set ends, or have it much of the time but not always), either we have it or we do not. It is not as if the more virtuous you are, the more humanity you have. (Likewise, when Kantians speak of "rational beings," "rational" contrasts not with "irrational" but with "arational." Your most irrational acquaintance – assuming, again, no serious mental impairment, and assuming that she or he is an adult human – is nonetheless a rational being.)

Suppose, however, that we were to construe "humanity" more broadly, so that we could say that while all rational beings have humanity – the power to set any end whatsoever – this capacity is more fully realized in some than in others. To seek to maximize humanity could then be understood as trying to bring it about that the capacity is as fully realized as possible in as many people as possible. What could we do to bring this about? Arguably we could identify impediments to setting ends for oneself and, to the extent possible, remove them. We could, for instance, oppose aspects of schooling that (at least in some, especially girls) foster docility, subservience, excessive eagerness to please others and to remake oneself in their image. Such qualities tend to hinder individuals from becoming adults who can think for themselves, see themselves as worthy individuals and set their own goals.[23] We might also be able to locate some material impediments to fully realizing our capacities as rational agents. If people are less able to set ends for themselves if they suffer from lead poisoning, a prohibition on the sale and use of lead paint and a requirement that old houses with lead paint be fully repainted if children live in them might be in order. This would foster the development of "humanity" in children by removing one obstacle. Similar things can be said about other obstacles, for example, malnutrition, poverty, social inequality.

Such social change is nothing to sneer at. And it is reasonable to classify the removal of obstacles to the proper development of humanity as a way of promoting humanity, provided we choose to revise slightly Kant's notion of "humanity" so that we can speak of people having more or less of it. In Kant's ethics it would count as a way of promoting others' happiness, since to promote others' happiness is to help them to pursue and attain their ends (and one way of doing that – indeed a very good way – is to work collectively to improve the social environment and to remove, as far as possible, impediments to their pursuit of their ends).

Even if we accept as sufficiently Kantian the understanding of "humanity" as something that people can have to a greater or lesser degree, thus paving the way for a construal of "promoting humanity" as the removal of obstacles to the proper development (and exercise) of humanity, it would be un-Kantian to suppose that this – promoting humanity – is all there is to a proper appreciation of (and response to) the value of humanity, or even that it constitutes the core of it. A proper response to the value of humanity has two constituents: love and respect. Promoting humanity might well express love for humanity, but it does not aptly express respect. To see this, we need to explore in some detail the relation, in Kant's ethics, between love and respect.

> The principle of **mutual love** admonishes men constantly to *come closer* to one another; that of the **respect** they owe one another, to keep themselves *at a distance* from one another; and should one of these great moral forces fail, "then nothingness (immorality), with gaping throat, would drink up the whole kingdom of (moral) beings like a drop of water" (if I may use Haller's words, but in a different connection). (*MM* 449)

Obscure though this intriguing passage from Kant's *Doctrine of Virtue* is, part of it is quite clear. Both love and respect are crucial to morality, and while love bids us to come closer to each other, respect tempers this. Why? Why the need for tempering?

Love needs to be checked by a proper sense of boundaries.[24] To spell out the idea of boundaries a bit: each individual bears a relation to him or herself that is different from the relation borne to any other person. This may seem trivially true; one might claim that each interpersonal relationship is unique. The relation I bear to my son is different from the relation I bear to either of my sisters; the relation I bear to one sister is different from the one I bear to my other sister, and so on. And so, it might be thought, the relation I bear to myself will likewise be different from the relation I bear to everyone else. But the point here is somewhat different: it is that the relation that each person bears to him- or herself is different from all interpersonal relationships.

This is borne out in various ways, the most important of which is this: I am responsible for my own actions in a way that I am not responsible for anyone else's. (True, I am responsible to a fairly large extent for my dog's actions, but that is because my dog is not the sort of creature who can be responsible for her own actions and because I "own" my pet, and am supposed to have it under my control.) Another way it is borne out is that I have an obligation not to harm others which is somewhat stiffer than any obligation I have not to harm myself. More generally, I have certain obligations to others – e.g. obligations not to harm them – which are stiffer than the analogous obligations I have to myself; and I have obligations regarding myself which I do not have regarding others, such as to "do something with my life" (or, to give it a more Kantian cast, to develop my talents). We have names for people who think that they have (almost) as much business shaping others' lives as shaping their own; we call such a person a "busybody" and say of him, "Why doesn't he get a life?"

It is important not to exaggerate the boundaries here. It is not as if I have no business ever trying to shape another's life; our relations to others, while different from that to ourselves, are not uniform. It certainly is a parent's business to try to shape his or her children's lives, at least before the children reach adulthood, and it is sometimes appropriate to pry into the affairs of close relatives, offer unsolicited advice, badger a good friend into getting professional help for a drug addiction, etc. Clearly, meddling in the affairs of a sibling or a close friend has a different character from meddling in the business of a mere acquaintance (and indeed may not even count as meddling).

Nonetheless, even in these cases the question of boundaries should arise. It may be permissible for me to cajole a friend into getting psychiatric help, *but it is not obviously so*; and some reflection is in order so that I at least do it in a way that expresses respect for her. Respect entails that I not barge in, not treat her life as if it were mine.

How does the foregoing discussion of the need for love to be tempered or checked – or, thought of in a slightly less Kantian way, informed – by respect relate to the question of whether the proper response to (the value of) humanity is to promote it? The point is simply that the proper response involves a recognition of the separateness of persons, of the need to respect

others as autonomous individuals, individuals with their own
ends and, put more colloquially, their own way of doing things.
As noted earlier, this is built right into the Kantian stipulation
that in seeking to promote their happiness, we think of their
happiness primarily as they do; in trying to promote their happiness, we try to help them promote their ends. But it is worth
nothing that even in doing this – even when we take care to
avoid being heavy-handed, to avoid telling them that really their
happiness consists not in *these* ends, but in *those* – we need
also to bear in mind that zealous do-gooding can invade the
other person's space. Hence our response to the value of humanity should not be solely to bring something about. We need also
to show respect for it in other ways: by refraining from intrud-
ing.

Critics of Kantian ethics sometimes allege that a Kantian agent
would be unduly concerned about her own purity, her own goodness, in a word, about keeping her hands clean. If one values free
speech, for instance, one's response (the critics claim) should be
to try to promote it as much as possible. Refraining from limiting
others' freedom to express their ideas is fine, the critics maintain,
just as long as doing so promotes free speech better than limiting
their freedom would. Likewise for any other value. If one values
honesty, the consequentialist claims, one should seek to promote
honesty. If instead one's focus is on being honest, one is being
unduly concerned about one's own character, and insufficiently
concerned to promote honesty. Promoting honesty may require
being dishonest, but, the consequentialist claims, someone who
takes honesty seriously will be willing to act dishonestly for the
greater good of honesty (see Pettit 1991: 233).[25]

I have argued that there is no reason to think that there is just
one proper response to a value. It could, as I observed, nonetheless be the case that the value of humanity calls for a consequentialist response: that of trying to promote it. I have tried to offer a
sympathetic construal of what this might mean, and have indicated that it indeed does constitute part of an appropriate
response to the value of humanity. That response falls under the
Kantian heading of "love": helping others to promote their (permissible) ends. But the other constituent is respect. Respect
entails recognizing that others' lives – and others' characters –

are theirs, not ours. It entails appreciating and honoring humanity, not just promoting it. And it entails refraining from trying to
promote humanity in others if doing so is not consistent with
respect.

The consequentialist might retort that the reason for refraining
is that if I do not respect them as agents, I cannot really promote
their humanity. Respecting them as agents is important because it
is crucial to their sense of themselves as end-setters. Thus, my
goal should be to promote their humanity, and it is *to that end* that
I should respect them as agents. My reply is that there is no reason
to think that respecting them as agents – refraining from interfering in various ways – is more likely to promote their humanity
than not respecting them as agents is. Being heavy-handed, pater-
nalistic, and manipulative may actually help solidify their sense
of themselves as agents. If someone tries to take over my life, that
tends to make me grab the reins more firmly. So if the goal is to
promote humanity, it is by no means clear that respecting others
is the best means to that goal. No doubt it often will be, but there
will presumably be numerous circumstances in which (and individuals for which) it will not be.

There is an aspect to respect that has not yet been brought out in
my reply to the consequentialist rejoinder. I am to respect humanity not just in others, but also in myself, and the proper expression
of respect for humanity in myself is quite different from the
proper expression of respect for humanity in others. Respect for
humanity in myself entails striving to improve myself, both
improving myself morally and developing my talents. This asymmetry is interesting to reflect on. To a consequentialist it must
seem very odd and, once again, rather self-absorbed or narcissistic
to focus on developing my own talents. If the development of
talents (and moral self-improvement) is a great good, shouldn't
I, morally, be concerned to develop talents in general? Why
should I have any particular concern to develop my own? Think
of the matter this way. Suppose I don't bother to develop my own
talents and instead strive to get others to develop theirs. When
asked why I am so much more concerned that others develop their
talents than that I develop mine, I explain that altogether more
talent is developed this way. Now I might be wrong in my calculation, but suppose I am right. Isn't there something odd – morally

askew – about my view of what matters most? Clearly there is, and
this again reflects the fact that the proper response to the values
that play key roles in Kant's ethics should not be simply to
promote them.

3   Kantian Ethics and Virtue Ethics

My approach in this portion of my essay will again be one of
juxtaposition, but since "virtue ethics" is a rather slippery term,
referring to a wide range of views, and since (partly because of
this) it is really not clear to me that virtue ethics and Kantian
ethics are at odds with one another, I will be spending a good deal
of time sorting out where the disagreements lie.

Virtue ethicists seem to be united primarily by a belief that
modern moral philosophy has taken a wrong turn. We would
do better, they suggest, to look to ancient (or as some would
have it, medieval) ethics, and specifically, those approaches to
ethics that focus on virtue and character. Aristotle's is most
frequently championed as the model to look towards, so much
so that one writer begins a review essay by asking what virtue
ethics is and answering, "what Aristotle did" (Putnam 1988:
379). Without assuming that a view cannot count as virtue-
ethical unless Aristotle held it, I shall make frequent reference
to Aristotle and use his theory as a guide to what virtue ethics
holds.

In addition to the question regarding who, or what, serve(s) as
the model or inspiration for virtue ethicists, there is the related
question of the (intended) target of their criticisms. How much
of modern moral philosophy? And how far back in time does
"modern" reach? The idea seems to be moral philosophy as it
has generally been practiced from the eighteenth century to the
present, excluding contemporary virtue ethics and some related
approaches in contemporary ethics and presumably excluding
most continental philosophy after Kant as well as a number of
Anglo-American philosophers of the late nineteenth century
and the early twentieth century. Philippa Foot (1978: 1)
claims that the opinion that "a study of the topic [virtues

and vices] would form no part of the fundamental work of ethics...was apparently shared by philosophers such as Hume, Kant, Mill, G. E. Moore, W. D. Ross, and H. A. Prichard, from whom contemporary moral philosophy has mostly been derived."[26] Kantian ethics is often singled out as the paradigm of what virtue ethicists oppose, and this will of course be my primary focus.[27]

I have some quarrels with the historical claims often made by virtue ethicists. Some of what they oppose is much more recent and more minor a trend than they suggest. Here I have in mind especially the aim of finding a decision procedure or an algorithm for determining what is morally right to do (Hursthouse 1995; Pincoffs 1986). Other aspects of what they oppose actually go back much earlier than the eighteenth century, as Jerome Schnee-wind (1990) has argued. If we are looking for an example of an ethics that emphasizes right and wrong acts – and in particular, penalties for wrong acts – Catholicism, he suggests, provides a perfect example:

> From the earliest days of the practice of confession in the sixth century through the great flowering of casuistry in the sixteenth and seventeenth centuries, Catholic moralists were preoccupied with specific acts which might or might not be sins, and with the appropriate penalties for them if they were. If ever there was an ethics of acts and quandries [sic], it was here.[28]

But my main quarrel is with the virtue ethicists' understanding of Kantian ethics. Much of what most virtue ethicists want is actually part of Kant's ethics, and when it isn't, the differences are more subtle than is usually thought. In showing this I hope to clear away some misunderstandings of Kant's ethics. And in instances where it lacks some valuable elements of a virtue approach, many contemporary Kantians (myself included) see many of the virtue ethicists' criticisms as helpful suggestions that Kantians can utilize as they press forward with the Kantian project. They may not be intended as friendly amendments or constructive criticism, but they can be utilized as if they were.

Three Points of Differentiation

What are the hallmarks of virtue ethics? What are contemporary virtue ethicists trying to revive? A safe, though incomplete, answer is "An emphasis on character and virtue." Virtue ethicists emphasize that persons – or as they sometimes say, *character* – rather than actions should be the primary focus of ethics. Ethics should be much more concerned with what sort of person is good or virtuous than with what makes right actions right and wrong actions wrong. Secondly, virtue ethicists favor aretaic terms ("good," "bad," "virtuous," "vicious") over deontic terms ("right," "wrong," "duty," "obligation"). Whether this is a mere terminological difference or whether it signals the replacement of one set of ethical concepts by a different set is something we shall take up later. A third point of differentiation concerns motivation. According to many, perhaps most, virtue ethicists, it is no part of the motivation of the virtuous agent that she *morally ought* to adopt this course of action or be that sort of person. She does not, in other words, act *from duty*. Rather, she is motivated as she is because she has the desires or ends that virtuous people have. The virtuous person has virtuous desires, and insofar as virtue ethicists recognize the notion of a right action, a right action is one that issues from virtuous desires.

Let us take these points of differentiation one at a time and ask to what extent they show Kant's ethics to be at odds with virtue ethics.

Actions versus character

Kant's ethics has often been regarded as having as its main concern actions, rather than character. I shall try to show that this view is mistaken. Nonetheless, there are more subtle differences between Kant's ethics and virtue ethics in this area. While both place considerable importance on character and virtue, the nature of the interest that they have in character is somewhat different, and their understanding of character and virtue differ. To that shortly. First let us consider why Kant's ethics has often been regarded as having a focus on actions rather than character.

A quick explanation is that the work in which Kant says the most about character and virtue, the *Doctrine of Virtue*, is not nearly as well known as the *Groundwork*;[29] and it is fairly easy (though inaccurate) to glean from the *Groundwork* that Kant is much more concerned about rightness of action than about good character. A longer answer requires looking at the *Groundwork* to see why its readers might gather from it that Kant is more concerned with actions than with character. In particular, we need to look at the Categorical Imperative. (I follow the convention of using capital letters to distinguish the general principle, the Categorical Imperative, from more specific principles, categorical imperatives, that are based on it.)

The Categorical Imperative has various formulations, but the one on which Kant seems to rely primarily is the following (usually referred to as "The Formula of Universal Law"): "Act only on that maxim through which you can at the same time will that it should become a universal law" (*G* 421). The Categorical Imperative is often assumed to provide – or at least, to aim to provide – a test for determining which actions are, and which actions are not, morally permissible. Given the prominence of the Categorical Imperative in Kant's ethics, it is also frequently supposed that the whole point of Kant's ethics is to supply a test of the rightness of actions. (This is probably due in part to the expectation, particularly common at a time when utilitarianism was more dominant in moral philosophy than it now is, that the business of an ethical theory is to tell us what makes right acts right.) Kant's ethics is then criticized for failing to provide an adequate test. More recently it has been criticized by virtue ethicists of the anti-theory variety for *trying* to provide such a test.

Although there is much about the Categorical Imperative that is not clear (see section 4, below), this much is: insofar as it is a test of anything, it tests our *maxims*, not our *actions*. Very basically, maxims are the principles on which we act.[30] Kant says that a maxim is "a subjective principle of action" (*G* 421n.). A maxim is subjective in the sense that it is the principle of action of a particular agent at a particular time. So in testing one's maxim, one has to ask first what principle or policy she was acting on at that time.[31] Her maxim will reflect what she was doing and why, and will generally be tied to the particular circumstances. Exactly how much goes into the maxim is a tricky question that we'll return to later. For now the key point is that what the Categorical Imperative tests is not what we do, but the principle on which we act, and thus the reasons we take to be sufficient reasons to act. This is but one of many indications that the focus in Kant's ethics is not on "outer actions" but on agents. It does not aim to supply a test of the rightness of actions, and so this basis for thinking that the primary focus of Kant's ethics is actions collapses.

Perhaps another reason why Kant is thought to be especially concerned with actions, more than with agents, is his discussion of acting from duty. Teachers of Kant's ethics have tended to present his discussion of the moral worth of actions out of context, not recognizing that the role it plays in the *Groundwork* is to develop the idea of the Categorical Imperative via the concept of a perfectly good will.[32] Ignoring the context, one easily gets the impression that Kant is primarily concerned to provide a test for the moral worth of actions. The test is, "Was the action done from duty?" Because Kant seems, on this reading, so intent on providing a test of moral worth, readers figure that it is of paramount importance, on his view, that we assess actions to see whether they were done from duty, and thus whether they have moral worth. (Those who believe that Kant's aim in the first chapter of the *Groundwork* is to provide a test for the moral worth of actions are then puzzled to find him saying that it is in fact quite hard to tell whether an action really was done from duty. If so, they wonder, how do we have a useful test for measuring the moral worth of actions?) In fact, as I have argued at length elsewhere (Baron 1995), acting from duty has to be thought of primarily not in terms of individual, isolated actions, but in terms of conduct, viewed across a (considerable) stretch of time. What is assessed is not the moral worth of our actions, but what Kant sometimes calls "the purity of our hearts" – clearly an assessment of the agent.

Part of the blame for the mistaken view that Kant is primarily concerned with the rightness of actions has to be placed on the question itself. It is a little silly to ask whether a theory is more concerned with action or with character, as if theorists have to favor one over the other. One would expect any reasonably rich ethical theory to be concerned with both, and not to separate them sharply. Kant's ethics is particularly concerned with how to lead one's life: what to aim at, how to conduct oneself, what disposi- tions to cultivate, what impulses to discourage. It is concerned with conduct, but not with isolated actions, not, that is, with individual actions considered in isolation from the agent's char- acter and, in particular, from the agent's maxims. A concern with conduct is just what one would expect of any ethical theory or approach that places an emphasis on character – assuming, that is, that it aims to be of some use to the agent in shaping her own life and guiding her conduct. If it aims to help us not just to understand ethical concepts, and not just to evaluate others (as if we were the gatekeepers of heaven, and had to decide which people to admit) but to live well (morally speaking), it is bound to look at character not in terms of "Who is best?" but in terms of how we ought to conduct ourselves.[33]

It is worth nothing that in addition to being concerned with maxims rather than directly with actions, the Categorical Impera- tive is likely to lead the agent who makes use of it to reflect on her character, what she is about, what reasons she takes to be deci- sive, what reasons she treats as minor, and so on, rather than directly on the rightness or wrongness of individual actions. Indeed, the Categorical Imperative will often require the agent to engage in some soul-searching, for she has first to determine what her maxim is. It might be thought that any true description of the agent's action counts as her maxim. But this is not the case. As Onora O'Neill explains, "an agent's maxim in a given act must incorporate just those descriptions of the agent, the act and the situation upon which the doing of the act depends" (1989: 84). Not surprisingly, then, a maxim can be elusive. It may not be at all obvious to the agent what policy or principle underlies her action. "Just what am I doing?," "What am I up to here?," "Am I helping Joe or trying to control him?," "Why am I doing this?," are the sorts of question she will have to ask. The questions force her to think about whether something which "externally" might seem innocuous enough is perhaps an instance of snubbing someone, or of seeking self-aggrandizement at the cost of humiliating another; or whether what on the surface looks like a good deed is really an exercise in manipulating someone, or striving to make him feel dependent on or indebted to her. So if virtue ethicists are looking for a theory or approach which places emphasis on inner aspects of character, Kantian ethics would be a good candidate.

At the same time, however, there are reasons why many virtue ethicists are not likely to be very happy with Kant's ethics. For although character and virtue are of much greater importance to Kant than individual actions, the way he understands character and virtue is somewhat different from the approach taken by virtue ethicists. Some might claim that it is so different that it is a mistake to think that he shares with virtue ethicists a strong interest in character and virtue. To get a flavor of the difference between the way Kant speaks of virtue and character and the way virtue ethicists do, let us briefly rehearse some of Kant's claims.

Virtue, for Kant, is "the strength of man's maxims in fulfilling his duty" or "self-constraint in accordance with a principle of inner freedom" (*MM* 394). It is instructive to see what, on Kant's view, distinguishes good people from evil people. Not surprisingly, it is their maxims, but there is more to the story than just that. "The distinction between a good man and one who is evil cannot lie in the difference between the incentives which they adopt into their maxim (not in the content of the maxim)." Instead, it "must depend upon *subordination* (the form of the maxim), *i.e. which of the two incentives he makes the condition of the other*" (*R* 36/31). The good and the evil alike adopt into their maxims the moral law as well as other incentives (which Kant, rather misleadingly, lumps together under the heading of "the law of self-love").[34] The difference between them is that the good person subordinates the other incentive to the moral law, while the evil person does just the opposite.[35]

Kant explains evil via an interesting version of the story of the Fall. In his telling of it, it recounts the fall from impurity (described in the second sentence below) to full-blown wickedness.

The moral law became known to mankind, as it must to any being not pure but tempted by desires, in the form of a *prohibition* (Genesis II, 16–17). Now instead of straightway following this law as an adequate incentive (the only incentive which is unconditionally good and regarding which there is no further doubt), man looked about for other incentives (Genesis III, 6), such as can be good only conditionally (namely, so far as they involve no infringement of the law). He then made it his maxim – if one thinks of his action as consciously springing from freedom – to follow the law of duty, not as duty, but, if need be, with regard to other aims. Thereupon he began to call in question the severity of the commandment which excludes the influence of all other incentives; then by sophistry he reduced obedience to the law to the merely conditional character of a means (subject to the principle of self-love); and finally he adopted into his maxim of conduct the ascendancy of the sensuous impulse over the incentive which springs from the law – and thus occurred sin (Genesis III, 6). (*R* 42/37)

The Fall took humans from impurity – seeking other incentives besides duty for acting as they should – to wickedness, wherein duty is subordinated to inclination.

Clearly both this way of talking and the claims made sound quite different from those of contemporary virtue ethicists. Let's see if we can pinpoint their disagreements concerning virtue and character.

One difference that comes immediately to mind *is* a deep difference, if it in fact obtains. Kant's conception of virtue, it is often held, presupposes an independent ethical notion, namely of duty or the moral law, and this very much shapes the picture of virtue. If virtue is understood simply as what characterizes the virtuous person, with no prior ethical notions that indicate what the virtuous person aims at, or tries to be or realize, or lives by, or in accordance with which she guides her life, this does seem to be different from Kant's conception.

But we need to be cautious about highlighting this as a point of disagreement between virtue ethicists and Kant. First, it is not strictly correct to say that Kant's conception of virtue and the virtuous person presupposes an independent ethical notion. The virtuous person is in essence the person of good will, and duty is explicated via the notion of a good will, as is the Categorical Imperative.[36] It seems more accurate to say that the concepts of duty and of virtue and character are mutually dependent than to claim that the latter depend on the former, while the former is independent of the latter. If we did have to pick one concept on which all other concepts in Kant's ethics are based, the good will

would be the winner. (Interestingly, this would qualify Kant's
ethics as "agent-based," to use Michael Slote's terminology.)

Second, it is by no means characteristic of virtue ethicists to
deny a (semi-)independent ethical notion that bears on what it is
to be virtuous. As Michael Slote observes, Aristotle's picture of
the virtuous person involves the idea that the person is keyed into
such facts as what is noble (as it varies from circumstance to
circumstance). What is noble is not entirely derivative from the
nature of the virtuous person. What Slote calls "agent-based"
virtue ethics would differ from Aristotle's view, since agent-
based views "treat the moral or ethical status of actions as entirely
derivative from independent and fundamental ethical/aretaic
facts (or claims) about the motives, dispositions, or inner life of
the individuals who perform them" (1997: 240). And many contemporary virtue ethicists follow Aristotle here rather than favoring an agent-based ethic.

A difference that comes closer to capturing a disagreement
between Kantians and virtue ethicists concerns the nature of
character and the nature of the virtuous person. Many virtue
ethicists have as their model of the virtuous person someone
whose dispositions and temperament are ideal: someone for
whom acting virtuously is second nature, and whose desires,
tastes, likes and dislikes, interests, and manner just naturally are
those of a virtuous person.[37] The virtuous person, so conceived,
has character only in the sense of "character" that in Kant's
estimation, is not very interesting.

For Kantians, being virtuous is not just a matter of having the
right knack, knowing the right thing to say, being able to smooth
out an awkward situation at a dinner party, knowing how to
respond to a friend when he tells you that he just learned that
his teenage son is addicted to heroin, knowing how to help others,
being able to withstand great personal sorrow and to face tremendous danger.[38] It is not a matter of just getting things right – being
able to hit the Aristotelian mean – thanks to correct appetites and
emotional responses, well-entrenched habits, and a good appreciation of what is called for. It involves both more and less: more
conflict, typically, between one's desires and what one sees one
should do; less "automatic" a response, at least some of the time;
and more reflection.

Character, for Kant, is a question not "of what nature makes of man, but of what man *makes of himself*" (*A* 292). "What nature makes of him belongs to temperament (where the subject is for the most part passive); only by what man makes of himself can we recognize that he has character" (*A* 292). The distinction is an important one. "Temperament has a *fancy price*; one can have a good time with such a man, he is a pleasant companion. But character has an intrinsic *worth* and is exalted beyond any price" (*A* 292). Arguably, many virtue ethicists mean by "character" what Kant means by "temperament." They conceive of the virtuous person as the person who is a pleasant companion and, more broadly, who has the right sorts of desires, the right reactions to things, whose nature, in short, is good – (almost) as good as a human's nature can be.

I think it is safe to say that many virtue ethicists subscribe to this view of virtue, a view that contrasts sharply with Kant's. But it should be noted that it is not at all clear that Aristotle subscribes to it. Acting virtuously is not simply an automatic response, arising from the agent's disposition. It is not just a habit (or a set of habits), a way of being, "second nature." Because of the large role of habituation in Aristotle's account of how one comes to be virtuous, it is easy to underestimate the role of thought in Aristotelian virtue. Habituation itself is not mindless; as Richard Sorabji has pointed out, "habituation involves assessing the situation and seeing what is called for" (Sorabji 1980: 216). Moreover, habituation isn't all there is to virtue. So for those who accept Ruth Anna Putnam's characterization of virtue ethics as "what Aristotle did," this may well not be a satisfactory way of distinguishing virtue ethicists from Kantians (Putnam 1988: 379).

We can, however, isolate one facet of the difference just discussed and exploit it to understand a key disagreement between Kant and Aristotle, a point on which (virtually) all virtue ethicists disagree with Kant. Aristotle holds that part of acting virtuously is that one does not feel inner conflict – one doesn't wish that one were doing something else, or that one didn't have to pay the money one owes – whereas this seems not to be a requirement for virtue on Kant's view. Relatedly, the virtuous person is someone who is, as L. A. Kosman has put it, "properly affected" (Kosman 1980). It is part of being virtuous that one feels as one should, not only that one acts, aims, thinks, and reflects as one should. Although, as noted earlier, it is a mistake to suppose that Kant is concerned only with action, not character, there is some truth to a different (and less common) claim, namely that Kant is concerned with matters of agency to the exclusion of matters of passivity. If we juxtapose action not to character but to passion (thus contrasting *praxis* to *pathos*), we can say that Kant places rather little importance on how one is affected – on *pathos* – and Aristotle attaches great significance to it. To be sure, it is important on Kant's view that we cultivate certain affects and discourage others. But he attaches far less value than Aristotle does to states towards which persons are passive, to being affected in this way rather than that. By contrast, how one feels – *pathos* – is as central to Aristotelian virtue as how one acts. Virtue

> is concerned with feelings and actions, and these admit of excess, deficiency and an intermediate condition. We can be afraid, e.g., or be confident, or have appetites, or get angry, or feel pity, in general have pleasure or pain, both too much and too little, and in both ways not well; but [having these feelings] at the right times, about the right things, towards the right people, for the right end, and in the right way, is the intermediate and best condition, and this is proper to virtue. Similarly, actions also admit of excess, deficiency and the intermediate condition. (*Nicomachean Ethics* 1106b)

These are issues on which Kant is, arguably, quite vulnerable to criticism. At least initially, the virtue ethicists' view is far more attractive than Kant's. So – and here I move away from simply pinpointing the disagreements between virtue ethicists and Kantians, and attempt to evaluate the views – this is a matter on which the virtue ethicists seem (at least at first) to be decidedly in the lead.

Aristotle, as noted, holds that part of acting virtuously is that one does not feel inner conflict, whereas on Kant's view one can be acting virtuously (and can be virtuous) even if one has strong opposing desires. Someone who has tremendous strength in resisting temptations to act contrary to duty and resists these temptations because she is deeply committed to acting morally would, it seems, count as virtuous on Kant's view. Yet most of us would be inclined to say, depending on the nature of the temptations, that the very fact that she feels such temptations (and feels them so strongly) shows her not to be very virtuous. Imagine someone who resists her intense desire to torture small animals. The fact that she intensely desires to do this calls into question the claim that she is virtuous. But on Kant's view it would seem that she could count as virtuous, indeed as no less virtuous than someone who has the same maxims but no desires to torture anyone or anything. Or take another example. Imagine someone who resists the temptation to embezzle, and compare her to someone who never felt any temptation to embezzle. Both might count as virtuous on Kant's view (depending on further details, which we can imagine to be the same for each person), yet it does seem that the fact that someone is tempted to embezzle is relevant to an assessment of virtue. This does not look good for Kant. Let's consider how one might go about defending him.

One line of defense would question the intuition that there is something objectionable about what seems to be Kant's view. Regarding the examples I gave, it might be said that the reason that we do not view people with untoward desires as virtuous is that we worry that they will one day act on them. Even though they have so far controlled their unfortunate desires, they might yet act on them, and our worry that they will is the reason we are unwilling to call them virtuous. I do not think that this is all that there is to our reluctance to call such people virtuous. Even if we felt certain that they would never act on these desires, I think we would still hold that they are lacking in virtue. (Of course, this depends somewhat on the content of the desires. The very fact that one feels certain temptations or impulses or desires tends to make us think that, as we would likely put it, there is something wrong with the person – not as much if the temptation is to accept a bribe or to embezzle or cheat on one's income taxes, but very definitely if the desire is to rape, torture, or murder.)

Here is a slightly different line of defense: it might be claimed that we don't regard such a person as virtuous as long as we think that she may treat these desires as *reasons* to act accordingly. In other words, our worry (once again) isn't *merely* that she may act on the desires; for (and now the reason is different) even if she doesn't do that, she *still* is lacking in virtue if she takes her desires seriously, i.e. as reasons to act accordingly. This line of defense is, I think, more plausible. (And it is more Kantian to suggest that by themselves – before the agent takes them seriously, thinks of them as reasons, albeit defeasible reasons, to act accordingly – desires and impulses lack moral significance than it is to claim that they lack moral significance unless the agent acts on them.) But although it is more plausible, I don't think it suffices. This is particularly clear if we imagine the more horrendous untoward desires – say, desires to rape and murder. Of course it is better that a person with these desires doesn't act on them and doesn't feel genuinely tempted, in the sense of taking them as reasons to rape and murder. But even if we suppose him merely to *have* these desires, who among us would be willing to regard him as virtuous?[39]

A different and more promising line of response would question the accuracy, or completeness, of the above depiction of Kant's view. There are a number of considerations that serve to soften Kant's view, and I will argue that once we see it for what it is, it becomes evident that it is different from but not clearly inferior to the view of most virtue ethicists.

At the end of the *Doctrine of Virtue*, Kant writes that "the rules for practicing virtue ... aim at a frame of mind that is both *valiant* and *cheerful* in fulfilling its duties." What "is not done with pleasure but merely as compulsory service has no inner worth for one who attends to his duty in this way and such service is not loved by him; instead, he shirks as much as possible occasions for practicing virtue" (*MM* 484).[40] This passage goes some distance towards showing that Kant's view isn't as "extreme" as is usually thought. But it doesn't clinch the matter. There is an unclarity in the quotation. Do I act with pleasure if I wish that the action weren't morally required, but given that it is, accept it as my duty and, enthusiastic about doing what is right, act without a grimace and even with cheer? If so, this still is different from Aristotle's picture of the virtuous person – i.e. the temperate person – because Aristotle's temperate person feels no regrets, no wish that the moral chips lay elsewhere. The continent person, whom Aristotle regards as less than fully virtuous, could be cheerful in the way just described; his desires pull him in the opposite direction, but he resists, and there is no reason to suppose that he couldn't take pleasure – personal pride – in resisting. The temperate person, by contrast, has no conflicting desires. Although Kant's words could be interpreted along the lines of Aristotelian temperance rather than continence, it seems more in keeping with the rest of Kant's ethical writings to interpret him in the way I suggested. (I'm thinking especially of the first section of the *Groundwork*, where Kant stresses that the moral worth of an action is most evident when duty and inclination are in conflict.)[41] And so while this passage helps somewhat, it does not fully address the complaint that conflict between desires and duty is not regarded by Kant as a sign of lack of virtue. It does indicate that the virtuous person cannot be someone who wholeheartedly hates doing what virtue calls for; her sentiments have to be at least somewhat on the side of virtue. But the passage leaves open the possibility that she takes pleasure in acting virtuously under that description without taking pleasure in the particular action she performs, described without reference to its being virtuous.

A stronger reason for doubting that someone with murderous desires could count as virtuous on Kant's view comes from this consideration: desires to torture, rape, or murder are incompatible with respect for persons. More generally, even though Kant, unlike Aristotle, doesn't place a concern for proper feeling at the heart of his account of virtue, some untoward desires are incompatible with having the ends and corresponding attitudes that are obligatory on Kant's ethics. This consideration provides a potent reply to the most serious worries under discussion: the desires we find most deeply objectionable would not be among the Kantian virtuous agent's desires. This does not, however, cover all the untoward desires. Some untoward desires *are* compatible with Kantian obligatory ends; they are, however, unlikely in a Kantian virtuous person, in part for the Aristotelian reason that habituation gradually alters one's feelings. Or so we can surmise from something Kant says not about untoward desires, but about an absence of fellow-feeling. "The saying 'you ought to *love* your neighbor as yourself' does not mean that you ought immediately (first) to love him and (afterwards) by means of this love do good to him. It means, rather, *do good* to your fellow man, and your beneficence will produce love of man in you" (*MM* 402).[42] (He suggests elsewhere that we should help this process along: "The inclination... to find others lovable is one that we ought to possess. If we seek for it, we shall surely discover something lovable in them, just as an unlovable man finds in others, because he looks for them, the qualities which make them unlovable. We ought to wish our neighbour well, but we ought also to endeavour to find him lovable" (*LE* 199).)

But none of this is intended to deny that on Kant's view conflict between inclinations and duty is expected to persist in virtuous people (even if it is likely to be less pronounced in the more virtuous). Is this a flaw in Kantian ethics? I don't think so. Indeed the supposition that it is – the ideal of perfect alignment between inclination (and more generally, one's affective states) and duty (or more broadly, one's moral views) – is at the root of the moral saints problem. If we think that the most virtuous person will have no inclinations or affective responses that clash with duty, no wonder if we suspect that this person would not be fascinating, good company, a person of depth and complexity.

There are disinclinations to do one's duty which simply do not call the person's virtue into question: preferring to stay in bed rather than get up yet again to tend to a fretful baby; preferring to do almost anything other than clean up the clothes, surroundings, and person of the 3-year-old who has just regurgitated. More interestingly, there are disinclinations to do one's duty that reflect well on the person, better than would inclination to do her duty in that situation. The instances I have in mind are a subset of those in which fairness requires one thing, but one's affections for another disincline one to act fairly. One would like to be able to "pull strings" for a loved one, but recognizing that it would be wrong to do so, refrains. A similar situation would be one in which the needs of strangers make a moral claim on one, a claim that supersedes that of a loved one. Imagine an accident in which one's child, whimpering and shaking with fear, needs only comfort and reassurance, while others have been injured and need medical attention. One would like to be able to attend fully to one's child right away but knows that it would be wrong to neglect those in far greater need. (Let's assume that there are no others on the scene who could help those in urgent need of medical attention.) I doubt that we would think better of the person whose feelings were fully in line with his duty. It seems, then, that the person who has no conflicts between his feelings and what he judges to be right or good – Aristotle's temperate man – may actually be less admirable, less virtuous, in our eyes, than the person with some disharmony.

My view is that when we examine Kant's view in some detail and think about various sorts of conflicts between affect and duty, it is no longer at all clear that his view is inferior to the Aristotelian view (a view endorsed by most contemporary virtue ethicists). That the virtuous person feels no conflict between affect and duty (or virtue) is by no means evident. There certainly are desires the having of which would belie any claim that the person is virtuous, e.g. desires to murder or torture. But these would not be the desires of a Kantian virtuous person; they are inconsistent with obligatory ends and with specific duties, such as the duty to cultivate in ourselves feelings of compassion. There are other desires which are not as directly ruled out, but which tend to disappear the more one performs virtuous acts. Habituation takes care of them. The conflicts between affect and virtue that remain are not an embarrassment for Kant, and indeed some such conflicts are actually part of being virtuous.

We might put the matter this way. There are affective responses that are incompatible with virtue; there are others whose complete absence is incompatible with virtue. It is a duty to cultivate the latter and to seek to extinguish, transform, or at least weaken the former. As noted earlier, Kant does speak of such duties. He speaks of duties not to be envious, duties not to take malicious joy in others' misfortunes, duties of gratitude, and the duty to cultivate in ourselves feelings of compassion (*MM* 457–60). His list may not include enough; we further the Kantian project by adding to the list. There are, moreover, debates to take up concerning which affective responses are incompatible with virtue or with specific virtues. I'll mention just one, which I discuss elsewhere (Baron 1995: ch. 6). Less attracted to Stoicism than Kant was, I would take issue with the approval that he shows for the sage who, when he could not help his friend, said "What is it to me?" and turned coldly away. (See *MM* 457; also *LE* 199–200.) The sage's stance, in my view, is not consistent with caring deeply for another and thus is not compatible with genuine friendship.

And someone incapable of genuine friendship surely would not count as virtuous.

Virtue ethicists tend to pay more attention to affective flaws than do Kant and many Kantians. But although Kant's official remarks on virtue – his definitions, his main characterizations – make no mention of what sorts of desires the virtuous person has, or of what thoughts pop into her head upon hearing such news as that an acquaintance has died, or that a colleague has received a prestigious fellowship, I do not think it correct to claim that he regards such matters as irrelevant to virtue. What is true is that he says less about these matters than many contemporary Kantians (including me) would like. But he has a lot to say regarding attitudes and impulses that we should cultivate in ourselves, and those which constitute or are components of vice. Contemporary Kantians can utilize the work of virtue ethicists to enrich Kant's account of virtue. We do well to add to the Kantian account both what is suggested by his remarks on, among other topics, gratitude, sympathetic joy and sadness, envy, ingratitude, malice, arrogance, and wanton faultfinding, *and* ideas gleaned from virtue ethicists and others regarding what sorts of tendencies we should seek to alter or weaken in ourselves, and what we should foster and cultivate.

I began this section by enumerating three points of differentiation between virtue ethics and Kantian ethics. The first is that virtue ethicists emphasize character rather than action, whereas Kant does not. The second alleged difference is that virtue ethicists, unlike Kantians, avoid deontic terms, favoring aretaic terms; the third is that whereas Kant places a great deal of importance on acting from duty – on doing what one morally ought to do *because* one morally ought to – and even holds it to be central to virtue, virtue ethicists do not. So far I have examined only the first alleged difference (though my discussion bears on the third, as well).

I disputed the claim that Kant emphasizes action rather than character, at the same time noting reasons that tell in favor of it. But there are differences between Kant's way of understanding character and virtue and that (or those) of virtue ethicists, and the remainder of this section sought to determine just what those differences are. The vital differences are that being properly

affected is far more central to good character on the virtue ethicist's picture than on Kant's and, relatedly, that on Kant's view
conflict between what one wants to do and what one sees one
morally ought to do is no sign of a lack of virtue, whereas on the
virtue ethicist's view, it is.[43] Put in Aristotelian terms: one needn't
be temperate to be virtuous, on a Kantian view; continence could
suffice. Observing that these differences seem initially to tell
against Kantian ethics, I sought to show that in fact they do not.

I turn now to another common way of differentiating virtue
ethics from Kantian ethics: by reference to aretaic and deontic
terms. It is true that Kantians do not try to avoid using deontic terms, whereas virtue ethicists do. Is this difference merely
terminological (albeit intended by virtue ethicists as something
deeper)? Or is there more to it than mere terminology?

Aretaic, not deontic: does it make a difference?

Virtue ethicists seeking to break away from what they see to be
dominant approaches in modern moral philosophy have sought
to rely on aretaic terms: "good," "bad," "virtuous," "vicious,"
rather than deontic terms: "ought" (in the sense of "morally
ought"), "right," "wrong," "duty," "obligation." In this brief section I want to consider to what extent this break from modern
tradition is just a matter of style, and to what extent it signals a
deep and meaningful difference.

There is no need here to question whether deontic terms dominate in Kant's ethics; that is not at issue. Our concern, rather, is to
determine what is at stake if, as virtue ethicists would like, we
dispense as far as possible with deontic terms, treating them as at
best secondary to aretaic terms. (I shall gloss over some puzzles I
have concerning the exact nature of their proposal and the apparent background assumption that it is necessary for an ethical
theory to designate which terms, deontic or aretaic, are primary.)
Why would virtue ethicists like to dispense as much as possible
with deontic terms?

Put very generally, the answer is that deontic terms are thought
to give entirely the wrong shape to an ethical theory, to put the
focus on the wrong sorts of things, and to narrow the scope of
ethics quite drastically.

Deontic terms, it is often supposed, limit the scope of ethics to a narrow range of concerns. One can have a duty, it is claimed, only to perform certain actions, not to have a certain sort of character or acquire certain virtues or replace certain attitudes one has with other attitudes, and not to notice certain things or be moved by certain sorts of considerations.[44] An ethic of duty, it is then argued, will omit all of these very important ethical concerns and focus only on action. Similar claims are also made for other deontic terms: "obligatory," "forbidden," "wrong," and "right" (and for "right" in the sense of "having a right").

Sometimes the point is put by saying that duty is a legalistic notion. This is implied by J. O. Urmson's assertions in his influential "Saints and heroes" that it is "part of the notion of a duty that we have a right to demand compliance from others," and, indeed, that we have "no choice but to apply pressure on each other to conform" to duty (Urmson 1969: 70–1). "Sam has a duty to perform X" is thought to entail that others have a moral right to coerce Sam to perform X or to punish him for failure to perform X. Duty is to be exacted like a debt, and failure is to be censured (p. 70). But this comes from the utilitarian tradition, not from Kantian ethics, and more specifically from a utilitarian notion that morality is best thought of as a "moral code." This view is well-entrenched in that tradition (though by no means ubiquitous),[45] and is notably absent from Kant's work. John Stuart Mill wrote in *Utilitarianism*: "It is a part of the notion of duty in every one of its forms that a person may rightfully be compelled to fulfill it. Duty is a thing which may be *exacted* from a person, as one exacts a debt. Unless we think that it may be exacted from him, we do not call it his duty" (Mill 1979: 47). For those who think of duty as a quasi-legal notion, an ethical theory framed in terms of duty would quite reasonably seem impoverished. And while one way to address the problem would be to tack on a category of supererogatory acts, it would seem more to the point to remove the deontic concepts from center stage.

Our everyday use of "duty," and in particular, "duties," may also lead many to suppose that an ethical theory cast mainly in deontic terms is bound to be sorely lacking. One aspect of the everyday use of "duty" is that duty is seen as imposed on us from without, in the name of society or some particular institution. It is our duty, in this sense of "duty," to do our part, e.g. to serve in the armed forces. Duties are also seen as closely tied to role expectations, and these role expectations are sometimes morally dubious.

This hints at some of the misgivings that many people have regarding any talk of duties. Some years ago, a colleague remarked, when I told him that I was writing a paper that defended acting from duty, "Talk of duty always makes me nervous. It reminds me of the Vietnam war and the draft." Duties often are duties in virtue of some institution or some social expectation that is itself questionable on moral grounds. To say "I must do this; it is my duty" may thus seem to be mindlessly accepting a social role, mindlessly accepting the political status quo. "I must do this; it is my duty" may sound as if it eschews reflection, staunchly refuses to take up a stance of questioning the "shoulds" and "musts."

Thinking in terms of duty may thus seem to foster rigidity and moral complacency. And the moral complacency may be fostered in a couple of ways. One is the way indicated: it may seem to involve an unquestioning acceptance that one must do this, because it is (one has always been told) one's duty. The other has to do with the supposition that as long as one does one's duty, one has done all that morally can be expected of one. Characters who suppose this often make an appearance in literature, and in our daily lives. In her story, "The geranium," Flannery O'Conner describes the loneliness of a man whose daughter has, out of a sense of duty, persuaded him to live with her and her family.

[S]ometimes when the daughter and Old Dudley were alone in the apartment, she would sit down and talk to him. First she had to think of something to say. Usually it gave out before what she considered was the proper time to get up and do something else, so he would have to say something. He always tried to think of something he hadn't said before. She never listened the second time. She was seeing that her father spent his last years with his own family and not in a decayed boarding house full of old women whose heads jiggled. She was doing her duty. She had brothers and sisters who were not. (O'Conner 1979: 6)

Even when duty is not seen to be associated with morally questionable institutions or social expectations, there may be a worry that the person who is very attuned to duty, whose thoughts about herself and her conduct are dominated by thoughts of duty, will be insensitive. She'll be focusing on the superficial, and her concern with duty will take the place of concern for what, ethically, really matters.

Interesting though all these issues are, and relevant though they might be to some deontological approaches, it should be clear from the foregoing that they have no connection to Kant's ethics. Duty on Kant's view encompasses duties to cultivate certain feelings in ourselves, to adopt certain ends, and the like; it is by no means limited to "external acts" like paying one's bills. Duty in Kant's ethics is not imposed on one from without; it is self-legislated. One's duty is what one would do if one were fully rational. Institutional duties, duties that one has in virtue of one's social or familial role, etc. may or may not be one's duty in the Kantian sense. Kantian duty has no very close connection to the superficial or to the political or social status quo or to "what is proper" and doesn't exclude the sorts of attending and sensitivity that seem to be occluded in "The geranium" by thoughts of duty. Duty on Kant's conception does not entail a right to coerce; indeed one point of the distinction between juridical and ethical duties is to make plain that only a subset of duties, and not the ones that are the stuff of ethics (as opposed to law), entail a right to coerce.[46] And it is in a juridical context that blame and punishment have their proper place.

Suppose we are scrupulously careful to avoid pinning on to Kantian duty implications that obtain only for rather different understandings of "duty." Do there remain any reasons for wanting to break away from a duty-centered ethic in favor of one that centers on aretaic notions? Yes. Before I explain and assess the main reason, though, I want to mention a version of the proposal put forth by Elizabeth Anscombe to break away from a duty-centered ethic. That proposal would yield a virtue ethic quite different from Kant's, but one which many, if not most, virtue ethicists would balk at.

In her groundbreaking "Modern moral philosophy," Anscombe proposed:

It would be a great improvment [*sic*] if, instead of "morally wrong,"
one always named a genus such as "untruthful," "unchaste,"
"unjust." We should no longer ask whether doing something was
"wrong," passing directly from some description of an action to
this notion; we should ask whether, e.g., it was unjust. (Anscombe
1958: 8–9)

Although Anscombe, like many other virtue ethicists, particularly
tries to avoid reliance on deontic terms such as "wrong," her
proposal here is not merely to replace deontic terms with aretaic
terms, but to avoid using broad ethical terms. She favors speaking
in terms of particular virtues and vices. Her point, I take it, applies
to "vicious" (an aretaic term) as well as to "wrong" (a deontic
term). Although Philippa Foot appears to take up Anscombe's
proposal at one point,[47] most virtue ethicists do not advocate
giving up the use of broad or generic ethical terms. And they
have good reason not to. Unless they hold that the virtues are
unified – e.g. that nothing could be both charitable and unjust, or
both courageous and cruel – it will often be important to look at
the *overall ethical character* of the action or proposed course of
conduct. After all, an act might be compassionate, yet dishonest.
Rather than viewing it with respect to just one dimension, for
example, whether it expresses the virtue of compassion, or the
virtue of honesty, we may want to appraise it by reference to a
broader concept that takes into account various dimensions. On
this point most virtue ethicists are, I think, in agreement with
Kantians. While they feel that the virtues have been neglected in
much of recent moral philosophy, they do not argue that we
should only speak in terms of specific virtues and vices and
never use more generic terms such as "virtuous" and "vicious"
and perhaps "admirable" and "reprehensible."

It is tempting to think that if we set aside Anscombe's view,
since it is not characteristic of virtue ethics, and focus simply on
the proposal to replace deontic terms with aretaic terms, there just
isn't anything substantive to the proposal. It would, it seems, be
merely a terminological change, and the supposition that it
involved anything deeper than that seems to be based on associating with "duty" some or all of the baggage discussed above. And
I do think that the resistance, even aversion, that many have to

attaching value to acting from duty is due in no small part to the
notion that to act from duty is to act mindlessly, as if in obedience
to an authority whom one must not question, whose reasons one
doesn't even ask to hear, much less try to understand. There is, it
seems to me, nothing in the concept of virtue that forces a contrast
between acting from duty in the Kantian sense and acting from a
sense of what it is virtuous to do.[48] The Kantian idea of acting
from duty can easily be translated into aretaic terms: the idea is to
act from a concern to do (a commitment to doing) what it is
virtuous to do. And one indeed finds in writings couched in
aretaic terms views that, but for the terminology, sound remark-
ably like Kant's. Lord Shaftesbury, for example, writes:

> If a Creature be generous, kind, constant, compassionate; yet if he
> cannot reflect on what he himself does, or sees others do, so as to
> take notice of what is *worthy* or *honest*; and make that Notice or
> Conception of *Worth* and *Honesty* to be an Object of his Affection;
> he has not the Character of being *virtuous*. (Cooper 1964: 13)

A person who enjoys – even loves – helping others (and who does
help, even at great cost to her well-being) does not exhibit virtue if
she does not reflect on her conduct and care about its moral
character. For her conduct to count as virtuous, it has to matter
to her that she acts virtuously.

But given the way many virtue ethicists understand "virtue,"
there is a difference that separates them from Kant. *Duty involves
constraint.* It is not, as it is in the passage cited from Shaftesbury,
just that one *wants* to do what is right, wants to do one's duty; one
feels and recognizes oneself to be under a constraint. It is not a
matter of "affection" but of commitment. One acts from duty not
by virtue of doing what is right because one wants to do what is
right; rather, one does what is right because rightness makes a
claim on one. One recognizes that one should.

Now this element of constraint is not inconsistent with virtue,
but it is not central to it as it is to duty. So replacing deontic terms
with aretaic terms allows the theorist to expunge (if she so wishes)
the element of constraint that is at the heart of duty, imperatives,
and the term "ought." This, it seems to me, is what the choice of

aretaic terms over deontic terms yields: it allows one to avoid the element of constraint.

Even here, however, the difference is not as significant as it might initially seem to be. And this is simply because while it *allows* one to reject the element of constraint, it doesn't require it, and many virtue ethicists do not, I believe, reject it. Consider three possibilities.

1 The virtuous agent just does what is virtuous, without any sense of constraint about it. This is not Aristotle's view (though it is sometimes thought to be). It is the view of the virtuous agent as someone who does what is virtuous effortlessly, naturally, without having to give any thought to the matter. This is simply her way of doing things. If asked, "Why do you do that?" she'd be at a loss; "that is just what I do."

2 The virtuous agent acts virtuously with an understanding that what she is doing is virtuous, and she does so out of a recognition of the importance of so acting. She sees it as making a claim on her; it's not all the same whether she acts virtuously or not, and acting viciously isn't a genuine option. I take this to be Aristotle's view, and it seems to me to involve constraint as Kantian duty does, with one difference: the Aristotelian virtuous agent is less likely to feel the "pinch" of constraint, since her desires are in accord with virtue. She sees that virtue makes a claim on her – and in that sense recognizes the constraint – but doesn't feel the pinch that is a common feature of the Kantian virtuous agent's experience.

3 She sees virtue to make a claim on her but only because she wants to be virtuous, or cares about virtue; it is conditional on her caring about it.

It seems to me that most virtue ethicists envision the virtuous agent along the lines of either (2) or (3). Insofar as they follow (2), I do not see that avoiding deontic terms in favor of aretaic terms will make any substantive difference, since (2) doesn't reject the element of constraint. With (3) – which I develop with Philippa Foot's work in mind – things are different. Likewise with (1), but I take that view to be too crude to merit further consideration. The reason things are different in the sort of virtue ethics that Foot describes emerges in her picture of the truly moral person. Such a person is not moved by the thought that he morally ought to do this or that, where the "moral ought" is unconditional (i.e. not contingent on one's having some particular ends). Rather, truly moral persons are people who are "joining together with like-minded people to fight against injustice and oppression, or to try to relieve suffering," doing so "because, caring about such things, they are ready to volunteer in the cause" (Foot 1978: 170). Foot resists the move that she knows Kantians will want to make: Kantians will want to add that someone who did not care about these things *should* care about them. She resists, in short, the element of constraint. The virtuous person is a "volunteer," not someone who recognizes the needs of others (or anything else) to make a moral claim on him, a claim that is not conditional on the ends that he himself has, and that some people lack.

I have tried in this section to find some basis for the virtue ethicist's rejection of deontic terms (in particular, those prominent in Kantian ethics). I have tried, that is, to find reasons other than those that graft on to Kantian ethics associations with "duty" which, coming from the utilitarian tradition or colloquial speech (or from religious traditions), are simply not a part of Kantian duty. Unless one favors the approach Anscombe suggested – of talking only in terms of specific virtues – the sole basis for favoring aretaic terms is that it allows one to avoid, should one wish, the element of constraint (or as Kant says, "necessitation"). What is to be said for – and against – this will emerge as we examine the third of our three points of differentiation: the rejection, by virtue ethicists, of the Kantian notion that part of virtue, part of being a good moral agent, is that one acts from duty.

Acting from duty

This, to my mind, is the most intriguing of the three points of differentiation, and the one that most directly captures the disagreement between Kantians and (many) virtue ethicists. The first two reflect genuine differences only, I think, because they reflect *this* difference.

The disagreement is this. According to many virtue ethicists, it is no part of the motivation of the virtuous agent that she morally ought to adopt this course of action or be that sort of person. Acting from duty is not a mark of excellence. The mark of the virtuous person is that she has virtuous desires and other virtuous qualities and acts accordingly. This picture is particularly prominent in Foot's description.

Without a doubt, the view just sketched is not Kant's. The virtuous person, on Kant's view, is governed by a conception of duty. She is committed to acting morally and this commitment informs and shapes her conduct. And the commitment is not to be understood as a *desire* to act morally. But while there is no question but that Kant does not hold the view of the virtuous agent indicated in the paragraph above, there is nonetheless scope for considering just how opposed the Kantian and the virtue ethicist are on these matters. This is so for two reasons. First, virtue ethicists – and other critics of Kant's ethics – often betray a distorted view of Kant's conception of moral motivation, one which makes the difference between the Kantian and the virtue ethicist seem greater than it really is. Second, insofar as virtue ethicists often appeal to Aristotle's conception of virtue and virtuous conduct, it is noteworthy that Aristotle's account of virtue contains elements analogous to the key features of Kant's account of moral motivation.[49]

Some of what needs to be said under this heading has been anticipated in my discussion of the differences between Kantians and virtue ethicists on character, and in my attempt to figure out what the preference for aretaic terms signals. To minimize repetition I'll focus on understanding and responding to the objections raised by virtue ethicists to placing value on acting from duty. A good starting-point is the following observation, frequently offered in classroom discussions of the first section of Kant's *Groundwork*: we think more highly of the person who has fellow-feeling, loving concern, a desire to help others, and other virtuous desires, but no sense of duty than someone who has a sense of duty but lacks fellow-feeling, etc. The observation is prompted by Kant's glowing remarks concerning the person who, owing to sorrows of his own, lacks sympathy for others, but nonetheless helps others from duty (*G* 398).[50]

The point is well taken as a general observation, but I don't think that it goes very far as a criticism of the Kantian emphasis on acting from duty. First, Kant's choice of example should not be taken to imply that the person who lacks sympathy for others is in any way superior to someone who has sympathy for others; it is just that we can best discern that the person acts from duty if he lacks any other motivation for performing the action in question. If Kant had instead offered an example of someone who wanted to help and also saw that he ought to, it wouldn't be apparent that in helping, he acted from duty. Since he is trying in this discussion to make it plain that we can act from duty alone, it is crucial to put before his readers examples in which that is apparent.[51]

More importantly, the contrast drawn in the criticism is not the correct one to draw. The relevant contrast shouldn't be between (1) someone who lacks fellow-feeling, love for particular others, the desire to help others, etc. but who has and acts from a sense of duty and (2) someone who has the right desires and affections but lacks a sense of duty. Rather, it should be between (1') someone who has the right desires and affections and has and acts from a sense of duty and (2). As we have seen, Kantians don't regard as unimportant the desires and affections people have. It is true that Kant accords less value to them than many of us would like, and contemporary Kantians often seek to build upon what he does say to fill in that gap. But there is nothing anti-Kantian about regarding as part of character – part of what one makes of oneself – how we feel towards others. Kant himself recognizes as vices such feelings as malice and ingratitude. The proper contrast, then, places these two questions before us: is there something wanting in a person who lacks a sense of duty? And is there any reason to think that it is better if a person does not have a sense of duty? (There might also be a milder version of the last question: is there reason to regard a sense of duty as getting in the way, as perhaps just a necessary evil, something that we'd like to see exert only a very minimal influence on the individual?)

One basis for thinking that acting from duty is somehow unde-sirable is the assumption that to act from duty alone is to act with the sole purpose of doing one's duty. On this picture of acting from duty, the agent doesn't care, in, say, preventing the toddler from falling off the precipice, whether the toddler lives or dies, but only about doing her duty. It is important to see that this is not the Kantian picture. When you act from duty, your purpose is generally not "to do my duty." Indeed, your purpose is the same as it would be if you acted from inclination. If you act from duty in saving the toddler, your aim is to save the toddler. Kant is quite explicit about this (although translators fuel confusion when, as they sometimes do, they render *aus Pflicht* as "for the sake of duty" rather than "from duty").[52] It is not the purpose but the maxim that distinguishes the act done from duty from the act done from inclination.[53] So, acting from duty in no way precludes having as one's end to help another. In this way it doesn't displace concern for others.

But perhaps it displaces concern for others in some other way. Kant places value not merely on acting from duty, but on acting from duty alone. This surely shows that acting from duty is displacing other incentives, doesn't it?

No. It would if Kant meant by "acting from duty" that the agent is prompted at the moment of action (or the moment of deciding to act) by the thought of duty ("This is what I morally ought to do"). This is a very natural way of reading the phrase, but if we examine the various passages in which Kant discusses acting from duty, it becomes apparent that this cannot be his meaning. He says, for example,

> There is no difference... as regards conformity of conduct to the moral law, between a man of good morals (*bene moratus*) and a morally good man (*moraliter bonus*) – at least there ought to be no difference, save that the conduct of the one has not always, perhaps has never, the law as its sole and supreme incentive while the conduct of the other has it *always*. Of the former it can be said: He obeys the law according to the *letter* (that is, his conduct conforms to what the law commands); but of the second: He obeys the law according to the *spirit* (the spirit of the moral law consisting in this, that the law is sufficient in itself as an incentive). (*R* 30/25–6)

Now if we read the first sentence without thinking about it, it does indeed sound as if Kant is saying that the good man is someone whose every action is prompted by the thought of duty. (The good man is someone whose conduct always has the law "as its sole and supreme incentive.") But that cannot be his meaning, for it is impossible that one's every action be so prompted, simply because one cannot perform only morally required acts.[54] Yet it is only morally required acts that can be prompted by the thought of duty. I cannot from duty do something which it is permissible but not obligatory to do.

The second sentence in the quotation discloses what acting from duty is all about: in acting from duty, I treat the fact that something is morally required as a sufficient reason to act accordingly. When Kant speaks of duty being the sole incentive, his point is that it is to be *sufficient*. We are not to regard the fact that something is morally required as just one consideration, to be weighed against competing considerations, or even to be sweetened or rendered more compelling by the thought that so acting will please God or impress our neighbors. We are not to look for additional reasons to act as we should. That it is morally required is reason enough. To mix the incentives – to opt to do something because it is morally required and also because one will enjoy it – undermines the force of the thought "it is morally required." It is as if it is just one consideration among many, when it is supposed to decide the matter. The law is "sufficient in itself as an incentive" and the person who acts from duty recognizes that. She governs her conduct by a commitment to doing what is right; this commitment shapes her choices, and indeed shapes what sorts of things she notices and thinks about.

The Kantian virtuous agent, then, will often be drawn to the actions she performs by thoughts other than that these actions are actions that she morally ought to perform. That she acts from duty does not in any way rule this out. If she has any hesitation about performing them, the thought that they are morally required will be sufficient to move her to act accordingly. Of course the picture is more complicated than this because the imperfect duties do not translate into duties to help others at every opportunity or to perfect oneself in every way possible, and to strive to do so at every moment. The relation between duty as an incentive and acts that come under the heading of an imperfect duty will be different from the relation between duty as an incentive and acts that are required by perfect duty. But I shall not pursue that here.[55] The key point is that acting from duty doesn't preclude affection for others, a desire to help, and so on. (Even acting from duty as a primary motive – as the incentive that prompts one to act – doesn't preclude them; it does, however, preclude acting *from* such motives or desires.) The virtuous person is committed to acting from duty and subordinates inclination to duty; but other features will as a rule be what attract her to the action. She, like the person who helps just because he wants to, may want to help; the difference is that she sees the needs of others to make a claim on her while he does not. Related to this is another difference: she sees helping others under the rubric of morality; he does not.

Let's take a look now at the person who helps only because he wants to, and compare him to the person who does (at least usually) want to help but sees it as making a moral claim on her, and sees helping under the rubric of morality. What is lacking, on a Kantian view, in the former person? What, according to those virtue ethicists (and others) who object to the Kantian emphasis on acting from duty, is amiss in the latter person?

The Kantian objection is pretty apparent from my description: the former person doesn't see the needs of others as making a claim on him, and is not tuned in to (or does not care about) possible moral problems that attend helping others.[56] The objection is twofold. (1) Helping others is something he does simply because he enjoys it; and while it is good that he enjoys it, if he views it as if it were just some enjoyable activity, he fails to recognize its importance. He is, interestingly, someone who Aristotle would say has "natural virtue" but not "full virtue."[57] He lacks *ortho logos* (right reason). (2) Even good desires need moral guidance. My kindhearted action may be unfair to others or may send a patronizing message to the recipient. The goodness of the desire is no guarantee that the action is right; it may be misguided, myopic, fine from the standpoint of one virtue (say, benevolence) but morally problematic in other ways.

The second problem, like the first, can be understood in either Aristotelian or Kantian terms. In Aristotle's terminology, what is needed is practical wisdom. "Just as a heavy body moving around unable to see suffers a heavy fall because it has no sight, so it is with [natural] virtue" (*Nicomachean Ethics* 1144b). In Kant's

terms, what is needed is a good will. Recall the opening para-
graphs in the first chapter of the *Groundwork* where, having said
that it is impossible to conceive of anything which can be taken as
good without qualification except a good will, he explains that
such qualities as moderation in affections and self-control cannot
be regarded as unconditionally good because "without the principles of a good will they may become exceedingly bad." To put
the point more simply: it's not enough to know that what we are
contemplating doing is kind, or generous, or helpful, or that it will
cheer someone up, since an action can be any (or even all) of those
things and yet still be wrong. Moral conduct requires that
the agent not merely be kind and compassionate but also be
aware of the possibility that kind acts are not necessarily right,
and be attuned to signs that what she is thinking of doing or on the
verge of doing is in fact not right.

There are two responses open to the critic of Kantian ethics.
One claims that if an act is kind it is right – otherwise it is not
kind. This position is open to someone who believes that the
virtues are unified: that a person or an act cannot be kind while
in some other respect ethically defective. Since few contemporary
virtue ethicists maintain the thesis of the unity of the virtues, a
different response is more common: the Kantian agent, they suggest, has one thought too many.

Exactly what the objection is is not entirely clear; and elsewhere I try to puzzle it out. What is clear is that the Kantian
agent's motivation in, say, helping a friend, is thought to be
marred by an inappropriate thought, and the inappropriate
thought is something like "And helping now is permissible."[58]
The objection is due to Bernard Williams, who, imagining a situation in which a man has to choose between rescuing his wife or
rescuing a stranger, rescues his wife, believing it to be justifiable
to do so. Williams observes that "it might have been hoped by
some (for instance, by his wife) that his motivating thought, fully
spelled out, would be the thought that it was his wife, not that it
was his wife and that in situations of this kind it is permissible to
save one's wife" (1981: 18).[59] Kantians are quick to respond that
of course the agent need not be thinking at that very moment
that helping now is permissible. The agent's conduct is informed
by a sense of when helping is and when it is not permissible, not

magically, of course, but thanks to her occasional reflection on such things. But those who press the criticism are not satisfied with this response. There is something tainted, it seems, by the "extra" thought, even if the agent isn't thinking it at some inappropriate moment. The criticism seems to be that such people are distant, cool, their feelings somewhat attenuated, as if carefully sifted or put through a filter with the result that they are processed, unnatural. Such people seem to lack spontaneity as well as warmth. Or so it is suggested.

I have trouble making sense of the view that "and it is right" or "and it is what I should do" is one thought too many if it does not mean simply that there are times when such a thought is inappropriate. If it does mean this, fine; it is easy to see how the thought could get in the way of (or reflect a lack of) love and affection. If that is the meaning, however, it would not pose problems for Kantian ethics. If this is not the meaning, there seems to be just one other way to understand the claim, namely, as saying that love should be unmediated by moral considerations. This is not, however, something that I think many of us are tempted to endorse. We are grateful to the brother of Theodore Kaczynski for thinking that love for his brother, or his relationship with his brother, or his brother's well-being (such as it was) was not more important than going to the FBI with evidence that his brother was the Unabomber, whose mail bombs had already caused numerous deaths and injuries. We are glad that his love was not unmediated. And this is not a case where we are simply glad because of the results. We admire him for his courage and we do not judge him cold and unloving.[60] It might be replied that happily, most of us do not have as a close relative a serial killer, and therefore our love can and should be unmediated. I disagree, not because you never can know – your brother or sister may be a murderer too – but because these particularly dramatic moral considerations are not the only ones that merit our attention and that love for someone may tempt us to overlook. We need to be ready to assess the moral claim that the competing considerations make on us, and I think that we can do so without it weakening or cheapening our love.

I have tried, in examining three points of differentiation between virtue ethics and Kantian ethics, to show both that virtue

ethics and Kantian ethics are more similar than is usually thought
and that where they do differ, the core difference is that the Kantian agent recognizes herself to be subject to the moral "ought" – a
constraint, though one that arises from self-legislation. There are
other virtue-ethical objections to Kant's ethics that are being
addressed to some extent by Kantians; contemporary Kantians
are building on his positive remarks about the need to cultivate
certain impulses, and the general negative tone regarding emotion
that we find in Kant's ethics is not prominent in the work of
contemporary Kantians. Nonetheless, there remains a disagreement between Kantians and many virtue ethicists concerning
"one thought too many," a disagreement which again has to do
with constraint.

But there are some other objections to Kantian ethics which
deserve mention here, and which are often (though not always or
only) voiced by virtue ethicists. I turn to them now. These objections concern the Categorical Imperative.

4   Further Objections to Kantian Ethics

I have not said a great deal about the Categorical Imperative
despite its centrality to Kant's ethics. The reason I have not is
that our understanding of it is in a state of flux. I shall explain
some of the puzzles and problems in a moment. First I'll do
something easier: address some objections to Kantian ethics that
concern the Categorical Imperative but do not concern the details
of it. Then I'll turn to the tougher questions.

The Categorical Imperative is widely seen as antithetical to
virtue ethics. Why is this? One reason is that it seems to some
to be disturbingly reductionist. "As if all of ethics can be handled
by one big rule that tells us what to do!" critics protest. "As if we
could expect that some mechanical test would tell us how to live!
The search for algorithms, the zeal for decision procedures,
knows no bounds. Soon someone will be marketing a computer
program that tells us how to be virtuous." Clearly these are not
utilitarian critics; those who launch this criticism generally take
as their target utilitarianism and Kantian ethics in one broad

sweep. Julius Moravscik objects to the heavy stress that both of these theories lay on "big rules" (1981: 206). The objection mistakes the role that the Categorical Imperative is supposed to play in our lives. It supposes that it is intended to serve as an algorithm or a decision procedure by which we decide what to do, what to aim at, and how to live. The mistake is understandable, because exactly what the role is in fact is not clear. But although its precise role is not clear, it is at least possible to rule out some possibilities.

First, as is clear from Kant's applications of the Categorical Imperative, it is *not* expected to tell us what to do (if the idea is that it dictates to anyone, regardless of that person's interests, etc., how to live, what to care about, and so on). We have our own plans, our own interests and thoughts about what we'd like to do; the Categorical Imperative provides us with a way to evaluate them morally and determine whether they are permissible. It doesn't provide us with the content of our plans. The agent already has his plans but wonders if what he is setting out to do – and this includes his reasons for action, not just the action itself – is permissible. As Barbara Herman has pointed out, this also means that he has some idea already of what sorts of things are morally problematic.[61] If he didn't, it wouldn't occur to him to wonder whether it is permissible. The objection, in short, supposes the Categorical Imperative to be bearing a larger weight than it in fact is given in Kant's ethics.

Second, to the extent that the Categorical Imperative does supply a test by which we can evaluate our maxims – and, indirectly, our proposed courses of conduct – it certainly does not provide a mechanical test. It is not, and does not purport to be, "fool"-proof (or, more to the point, rogue-proof). As noted earlier, it engages us in reflection that requires considerable self-scrutiny, for it requires us to figure out, as well as we can, what our maxim is: what we are really doing and why. Moreover, it requires judgment, or as Kant puts it, "a power of judgement sharpened by experience" (*G* 389).

A related reason why the Categorical Imperative is often viewed as anathema by virtue ethicists (as well as by some others) is that it seems to eliminate attention to detail, to ignore the particularities of the situation. The claim presumably is not that it abstracts from some particulars,[62] but that it abstracts from all of them, or from some that it should not abstract from. Relevant particulars are treated as irrelevant. Suspicion that this is the case may be due to an assumption that what the Categorical Imperative tests is simply action-types, e.g. lying, or suicide, rather than lying in a particular set of circumstances for a particular reason or killing oneself in a particular set of circumstances for a particular reason. Although the assumption is abetted by some things Kant says,[63] it is pretty clearly false. Consider his (in)famous examples in the *Groundwork*. The person contemplating suicide "feels sick of life as the result of a series of misfortunes that has mounted to the point of despair" (*G* 421–2). It is killing oneself "from self-love" when continuing to live "threatens more evil than it promises pleasure" that Kant claims the Categorical Imperative shows to be impermissible. So the particulars matter, though there is no doubt room for arguing that still more detail should be taken into account. That the details matter is made further evident by Kant's inclusion of "Casuistical questions" at the end of his discussion of various duties in the *Doctrine of Virtue*. He asks and leaves unanswered the following questions, among others:

> Is it permitted to anticipate by killing oneself the unjust death sentence of one's ruler – even if the ruler permits this (as did Nero with Seneca)?... A man who had been bitten by a mad dog already felt hydrophobia coming on. He explained, in a letter he left, that, since as far as he knew the disease was incurable, he was taking his life lest he harm others as well in his madness (the onset of which he already felt). Did he do wrong? (*MM* 423–4)

But perhaps critics will claim that this is not the sort of detail they are looking for. What they want is detail that recognizes differences among persons and subtle differences in their situations, not just such stark differences as that one person is very sick of life and no longer enjoying it, thanks to a lot of very bad luck, while another has an incurable disease and will soon, thanks to impending insanity, pose a danger to others. Thus, Lorraine Code complains that on Kant's view moral deliberation is to be guided

"wholly by universal rules" that preclude sensitivity to context
and to differences among the relevant persons. Referring to an
illustration she developed from Anthony Trollope's novel, *The
Warden*, she objects:

> The presumption that Bold's relationship to the Warden, and his
> consequent *knowledge* of the Warden's character and circum-
> stances, creates in favor of appealing to *who* the Warden is, is
> erased in a deliberation guided wholly by "universal" rules.
> There is no space to argue that this case is different because of
> who *this* man is, in his specificity and particularity. Hence the
> Kantian impartiality principle does not generate an instrument
> finely enough tuned to translate principle into morally sensitive
> practice. If wealth in the clergy is a mark of corruption, then it must
> always be so, without exception. (Code 1991: 75)

Contrary to what Code suggests, impartiality does not require
that we view people of a certain description as necessarily all
bearing the features that most people of that description bear. It
does not require that one stubbornly hold as if it were an exceptionless law of nature something which is nothing more than a
generalization. If we see that a certain person is honest, the fact
that he bears a mark that suggested that he would not be honest
does not somehow force (or even urge) us to conclude that he
really is not honest. Impartiality only asks that we be fair, that we
not make an exception to a moral principle unless the making of
an exception is itself grounded in a moral principle. As Warner
Wick puts it,

> If something is right for me, or is demanded of me as my duty, it
> must be right for or demanded of everyone unless there is a reason
> why my case is peculiar. Even so, the reason for my being an
> exception must be based on general grounds, covering anyone
> answering to a certain description, and not just me. (1983: xvii)

None of this requires ignoring exceptions, ignoring who this person is in his specificity and particularity; it just asks that exceptions be justified.

A similar and more plausible worry is that persons are viewed, on Kantian ethics, simply as rational beings and not as the particular persons that they are. Robin Dillon has suggested that the very emphasis on respect for persons in Kant's ethics carries with it a disrespect, a disrespect for the particular person. The problem is that persons are to be respected for something that we all share, and thus we are respected only as highly abstract persons. But many of us, she suggests, would take real respect for us to be respect for us *not* as generic persons, but as the particular individuals that we are. She claims that,

> although the Kantian formula of persons as ends in themselves is claimed to regard persons as irreplaceable, there is a sense in which Kantian respect does in fact view persons as intersubstitutable, for it is blind to everything about an individual except her rational nature, leaving each of us indistinguishable from every other. Thus, in Kantian-respecting someone, there is a real sense in which we are not paying attention to *her*, for it makes no difference to how we respect her that she is who she is and not some other individual. (Dillon 1992: 121)

This is an interesting criticism but not a serious one. It is true that on Kantian ethics a person is worthy of respect in virtue of being rational (as opposed to arational), but it is not true that it makes no difference to how we respect her that she is the particular person she is. In respecting someone as a rational being we respect her as a being who sets ends for herself. Respecting a particular person requires taking her ends seriously and thus attending to what her particular ends are.

Finally, it is sometimes thought that in Kantian ethics, moral reasoning is supposed to ignore everything empirical. This mistake is easily explained: the foundations of morality, on Kant's view, are not supposed to include anything empirical, and so the Categorical Imperative is not based on, and does not include, anything empirical. But this does not entail that when we think about whether something we are considering doing is permissible, and more generally, when we reflect morally or reflect about morality, we are not to take into consideration facts about how the world actually is.[64] Empirical considerations enter in at two levels: in determining how to carry out the duty (e.g. how to promote others' happiness) and in at least some instances, in figuring out what our duties are. That Kant has been faulted for relying, in his derivation of a duty to help others, on the fact that humans are often in need of the assistance of others, is an indication that many readers have assumed that empirical facts were ruled out of court at the level of derivation of duties. The Categorical Imperative itself is free of empirical facts, but empirical facts enter in when we apply it (see *G* 389).

So much for worries about or objections to the Categorical Imperative that are fairly easy to address. There are more serious problems with the Categorical Imperative (or with our understanding of it), and it is to these that I now turn.

The hardest and most intriguing problems concern the first formulation of the Categorical Imperative, the formulation on which Kant most relies: "Act only on that maxim through which you can at the same time will that it should become a universal law" (*G* 421). This is sometimes thought to mean "Act only on that maxim that you would be happy to see become a universal law." The idea, however, is actually one of *consistency*. It is not a question of what you would like or favor. As Onora O'Neill emphasizes, moral acceptability rests not on what is wanted but on what it is possible or consistent for us to will as a universal law (1989: 81).[65] Who, it will be wondered, does "us" refer to? A good guess would be "rational beings," but in fact the domain is narrower than that. It is rational beings who are, as humans are, not self-sufficient. Or one might put it more positively: beings who are both rational and capable of forming (and in need of) some sort of community.

The first major challenge is to identify the sort of inconsistency or contradiction that is supposed to be uncovered when we attempt to universalize an unacceptable maxim. This is a matter of ongoing debate. The most plausible account, in my view, is Christine Korsgaard's, according to which the contradiction is a "practical" one (Korsgaard 1996a, ch. 3). On this understanding of the Categorical Imperative, the question to ask is, Can you consistently have and act on your maxim and will that it be a universal law – a maxim that everyone in similar circumstances has and acts on?[66] Only if you can is your maxim permissible.

There are two ways that a maxim can fail the test. (Or, to put it differently, the test bifurcates into two tests: the contradiction-in-conception test and the contradiction-in-the-will test.) The first is the one suggested by my wording: the maxim fails if there is an inconsistency between (a) having and acting on my maxim, and (b) willing it to be a universal law. This happens if the maxim's being a universal law thwarts action on that maxim (or thwarts its efficacy). Consider, for instance, making a false promise in order to secure something I don't think I can otherwise secure, e.g. money that I am in need of. My maxim, Kant says, is, "Whenever I believe myself short of money, I will borrow money and promise to pay it back, though I know that this will never be done" (*G* 422). Testing my maxim, I ask,

> "How would things stand if my maxim became a universal law?" I then see straight away that this maxim can never rank as a universal law of nature and be self-consistent, but must necessarily contradict itself. For the universality of a law that every one believing himself to be in need can make any promise he pleases with the intention not to keep it would make promising, and the very purpose of promising, itself impossible, since no one would believe he was being promised anything, but would laugh at utterances of this kind as empty shams. (*G* 422)

I could not get what I aimed to get by making a false promise if this were the usual way of going about things.

This is the first way that a maxim can fail, and it fails in this way just in case it is a violation of a perfect duty. Kant calls such a contradiction a "contradiction in conception." The second way involves a contradiction, too; Kant calls it a "contradiction in the will." It is located not between the maxim and its universalized counterpart, but instead between something one must will as a rational agent – something one cannot (on pain of irrationality) not will, if one is a rational agent – and one's maxim. Or so Kant puts it in the *Groundwork*. In the *Metaphysics of Morals* he makes it plain that the particular type of rational beings we are matters (at least with respect to the duty of beneficence). We are rational beings who have needs that we cannot meet without the aid of others. "The maxim of common interest, of beneficence towards those in need, is a univeral duty of men, just because they are to be considered fellow men, that is rational beings with needs, united by nature in one dwelling place so that they can help one another" (*MM* 453). The inconsistency that arises when one tries to will a universalized maxim of non-beneficence arises from two facts: as rational beings, we must will the indispensable means to our ends; and as beings who are not self-sufficient, the indispensable means often are, or entail, the aid of others. As Onora O'Neill puts it, "In trying to universalize a maxim of nonbeneficence I find myself committed simultaneously to willing that I not be helped when I need it and that I be helped when I need it" (O'Neill 1989: 99). A similar explanation underlies the duty to develop our talents.

Why, some ask, could a rational agent not forswear help from others, opting to pursue only those ends which do not require others' aid? This problem can, I think, be addressed, though it is beyond the scope of this essay to develop a solution. One key is the fact that on Kant's view we have what he calls "true needs," needs which we cannot, as rational agents, give up; another key is the powerful role of the notion of community in Kant's ethics. (See Herman 1993, ch. 3.)

Other problems concern "false positives" and "false negatives": instances where a contradiction appears yet the maxim seems clearly to be permissible, and instances where no contradiction is detected, yet the maxim seems clearly to be unacceptable.[67] It is peculiarly difficult to determine where an inconsistency arises in many instances of murder and assault. The problem arises in cases where the maxim is one of killing to get revenge, or killing someone one hates simply to eliminate the person. It is easier to handle cases where one murders for some further goal, e.g. to gain an inheritance or to eliminate one's more successful rival and thereby gain the job one badly wants. As Korsgaard explains, "the use of violent...means for achieving ends cannot be universalized because that would leave us insecure in the possession of these goods, and without that security these goods are no good to us at all" (1996a: 99).[68] By contrast, if one's goal is to eliminate someone or to get revenge (and if the goal does not include enjoying life free of the hated and soon to be eliminated person), no contradiction arises when one tries to universalize the maxim.

This is a problem of false negatives: maxims seem to pass the test when they should not. No contradiction is detected; yet the maxim, surely, is immoral. The problem of false positives, by contrast, is that maxims which should pass seem to fail the test. A contradiction emerges when we try to universalize, and yet it seems that it shouldn't. We see false positives in maxims that involve timing and coordination in a way that takes advantage of the fact that not very many other people do whatever it is that one proposes to do. Consider a maxim of playing tennis on Sundays at 10 a.m. in order to play at a time when the courts are not crowded.[69] Presumably there is nothing impermissible about this. Yet it seems to fail the test, if the Categorical Imperative is understood as Korsgaard proposes (and as I tentatively endorsed). The contradiction that is involved in universalizing an immoral maxim, Korsgaard explained, is that "the agent would be unable to act on the maxim in a world in which it were universalized so as to achieve his own purpose – that is, the purpose that is specified in the maxim" (1996a: 92). But that is precisely what happens in the presumably innocuous maxim of playing tennis Sundays at 10 a.m.

There are various ways to try to address the problems of false positives and false negatives. Consider false positives first. We might plausibly argue that the maxims are improperly specified. If we follow the suggestion from Onora O'Neill that I noted earlier, a maxim is to capture those features of the act and the circumstances on which the agent's choice to act depends. There is nothing, we assume, sacred to the agent about Sundays at 10 a.m.; what she is really proposing to do is to play tennis at a time when most other people do not, in order to play when the courts are not crowded. So, replace "Sundays at 10 a.m." with "at a time when most other people do not." This avoids a false positive: there is no contradiction or anything resembling a contradiction that arises if we all endeavor to play tennis when most others do not. The agent's maxim is not undercut, or rendered pointless, if everyone else acts on the same maxim. And importantly, this seems more truly to be the agent's maxim, for it captures what she is doing and why without including any details that are incidental. What she cares about is playing when the courts won't be crowded (and at a time that is reasonably convenient for her and her partner), not playing at precisely 10 a.m. on Sundays.

But maybe we were just lucky this time. Too often, as Herman stresses, false negatives and false positives are avoided, by Kant scholars seeking to defend the Categorical Imperative, only by restating what the maxim is – restating so as to yield the result they want. It is important that in the case just discussed we had a better reason than that – well, to be honest, let's say, an additional reason – for saying that the maxim should be restated. But maybe it was just luck. After all, we can imagine someone who really does want to play tennis precisely at 10 a.m. on Sundays. Maybe he thinks that is his lucky time; maybe he just has a "good feeling" about playing tennis at that time. His preference for playing at that time may well be silly, but it is hard to see that a maxim of playing tennis at 10 a.m. on Sundays because that is when one most enjoys playing tennis (or in order to have as wonderful a time as possible) is immoral, and yet as noted above, a practical contradiction arises when one tries to universalize it. Now it might be replied that once again we need only to "revise" the maxim: his maxim is to play tennis when he most likes to play tennis, and unless the world is such that everyone has the same favorite time, universalizing this maxim should not run into trouble. But this seems to be a case of something that Herman warns against: tinkering with the maxim to get the result we want. When we find ourselves doing this, we have to wonder, she suggests, if some larger change in our understanding of the Categorical Imperative is in order. More on this shortly.

What needs to be said about false negatives – maxims such as killing for revenge, where no contradiction emerges – is rather different. It is noteworthy that a contradiction does arise if instead of subjecting such maxims to the contradiction-in-conception test, we subject them to the contradiction-in-the-will test. This test asks (again, on the practical interpretation model) whether one can will one's maxim as universal law consistently (not just with willing one's maxim but also) with willing the ends which, as a (non-selfsufficient) rational agent, one must will. As a rational agent one wills anything that is necessary to being a rational agent, and one such necessity is staying alive.[70] One cannot, consistently with willing to stay alive, will a universal maxim of killing to get rid of people one dislikes, or killing to get revenge. So a contradiction emerges, and that would seem to show that the maxim is impermissible. But is it? Not quite. There is a problem: this test (contradiction-in-the-will) is supposed to show violations of *imperfect* duty, not of *perfect* duty. That is, failing this test shows a violation of imperfect duty, but not a violation of perfect duty. Yet surely a maxim of murdering to get rid of people one dislikes, or murdering to get revenge, is in violation of a perfect duty. It's not as if we may sometimes murder people we dislike as long as we don't make a practice of it.

This very problem points us in a promising direction, however. Recall that Kant's classification of duties was not developed at all fully until the *Metaphysics of Morals*, and yet the *Groundwork*, written a decade earlier, is the work in which he spells out the contradiction-in-conception and the contradiction-in-the-will tests. This, together with the curious fact that maxims of murder can be shown to be impermissible on a contradiction-of-the-will test while in some instances passing the contradiction-in-conception test, suggests that Kant did not work out the implications of his complex division of duties for a proper understanding of how the Categorical Imperative is to generate contradictions (Korsgaard 1996a: ch. 3). Perhaps the solution to the problems with the first formulation of the Categorical Imperative is to rework it in a way that reflects and does justice to the division of duties developed in *MM*.[71]

Other approaches to the problems involve trying out a different understanding of what sort of contradiction is supposed to occur or, more drastically, giving up on the notion that immoral maxims, when universalized, involve a contradiction. Some Kantians rely instead on the formula of humanity: "Act in such a way that you always treat humanity, whether in your own person or in the person of any other, never simply as a means, but always at the same time as an end" (*G* 429).[72] Others modify the first formulation so as to make use of the notion of universalizing, yet drop the idea that a contradiction is to be found if the maxim is unacceptable.[73]

Those who give up on the first formulation of the Categorical Imperative or revise it drastically avoid a problem implicit in much of the discussion above: it is hard to know what counts as the maxim that is to be tested. Now in one way this seems to me not to be a grave problem. If one favors an ethical theory that stresses self-scrutiny, the fact that we need to reflect on just what it is that we are doing, rather than apply a simple, straightforward, fairly mindless test, is no mark against the Categorical Imperative. And as I have suggested, it seems that the maxim to be tested does indeed need to reflect our reasons for action, and include those details on which our choice to so act depends. But problems do remain: if the self-knowledge required for us to determine what our maxim is is beyond our reach, the test will not be useful. Moreover, there may be more than one true description of what it is that we are doing and why. How do we know which description is (more) correct? A number of Kant scholars are striving for an understanding of "maxim" that will avoid these problems.

A novel approach, which avoids these problems (along with the problems of false positives and false negatives) is Barbara Herman's. She suggests that we need to rethink the very idea that the role of the CI procedure is to provide a method for the moral assessment of agents' actual maxims (1993: 143). Instead, the CI tests "generic maxims," maxims of the form "To do x type action for y type reason." Actual maxims, she says, are not the input of the CI procedure and duties are not its output. What is rejected by the CI procedure is a *generic* maxim. What is rejected – a kind of action for a kind of reason – sets a deliberative principle in the form of a presumption (for example, a presumption against deceit); the presumption can be rebutted by justifications of a different sort (1993: 147–8). So what gets tested is a generic maxim, and the output is a deliberative principle (a presumption that certain kinds of conduct are forbidden, for instance).

Onlookers may wonder why Kantians don't just give up on the Categorical Imperative. Why, given the enduring problems Kant scholars have grappled with, continue to tinker with the Categorical Imperative, playing around with different types of contradiction, different understandings of what a maxim is, different roles that the Categorical Imperative might play? Various things might be said about philosophers' attachments to a particular approach or theory. Setting aside such general (psychological) explanations, I think the appeal lies in the ideal it puts forth: a community of free and equal persons. Whatever the exact details of the Categorical Imperative, at its core is the idea that it should be possible for all of us to live as equals, and at the same time to pursue our own projects. (Contrast this to a picture of people and their projects according to which some people have exciting, self-fulfilling projects, and others are their servants.) As rational beings, we set and pursue our ends, but we are capable of revising them, and we need to be ready to do so if our pursuit of some end is contingent on other people playing a subordinate role to us. The Kantian ideal is a community in which agency is respected: both fostered and honored. And it is a community in which equality is taken very seriously.[74]

Notes

1 See Korsgaard (1996b) for a suggestive endnote regarding categorization of ethical theories.
2 The view that I endorse is not that a theory isn't very useful unless it tells us exactly what to do; I understand "action-guiding" more loosely. But the theory should at least point us in the right direction.
3 I should note that it would also be possible for two consequentialists to disagree about the speaker's visit. On what grounds might a consequentialist argue in support of the visit? She could argue that inviting him to campus would promote free speech by countering the suspicion that supporters of free speech support it only when the views to be advanced are views with which they agree. The fact that they support free speech in this instance would suggest that they are really in favor of free speech and are not merely supporting it in instances where the speech that would otherwise be suppressed expresses views that they share. It is important to understand that this consequentialist argument in support of the speaker's visit supports it not because doing so expresses or honors the value of free speech, but on tactical grounds: free speech will gain more support in the long run, the argument has it, if the supporters of free speech do not oppose a campus visit by a speaker who opposes free speech.
4 The contrast between goals and side-constraints is important to philosophers who, rejecting consequentialism, emphasize rights. Ronald Dworkin develops the contrast in terms of two different types of arguments that are deployed to justify a political decision, arguments of policy and arguments of principle. A policy, he explains, is "that kind

of standard that sets out a goal to be reached, generally an improvement in some economic, political, or social feature of the community." By "principle" he means "a standard that is to be observed, not because it will advance or secure an economic, political, or social situation deemed desirable, but because it is a requirement of justice or fairness or some other dimension of morality" (1977: 22). In the example I developed, those who defended the speaker's visit gave, in Dworkin's terminology, an argument of principle. Those who opposed it offered an argument of policy.

5 Smart (1967) distinguishes between extreme and restricted consequentialism. As he draws it, the distinction is the same as the distinction between act and rule utilitarianism. (Smart later indicates (Smart and Williams 1973: 10) a preference for the terms "act" and "rule.") It is important not to confuse restricted consequentialism with *restrictive* consequentialism. Philip Pettit (1991) distinguishes restrictive utilitarianism from extreme utilitarianism in a way that treats the two not as mutually exclusive, but rather sees restrictive utilitarianism as a type of extreme utilitarianism. Rules do not have the lofty status in restrictive utilitarianism that they have in restricted utilitarianism. What makes it restrictive is simply the recognition that agents may best promote happiness if, as Pettit puts it, "they restrict the tendency to calculate, abjuring the right to consider all relevant consequences." In other words, the restrictive utilitarian recognizes that happiness may be best promoted not by calculating what will best promote it, but by following rules of thumb or, "within suitable contexts," putting oneself "more or less blindly on automatic pilot" (1991: 236–7).

6 And indeed he is thought by many to be the first rule-utilitarian.

7 The notion that there are side-constraints that we should rigidly adhere to even when doing so means omitting to perform a utility-maximizing act is prominent in David Hume's discussion of justice. Though not a utilitarian, strictly speaking, Hume helped utilitarianism along, especially rule-utilitarianism. Justice, according to Hume, is a virtue precisely because it promotes utility; yet in some circumstances an individual act of justice will promote less utility than will an act of injustice.

> A single act of justice is frequently contrary to *public interest*; and were it to stand alone, without being follow'd by other acts, may, in itself, be very prejudicial to society. When a man of merit, of a beneficent disposition, restores a great fortune to a miser, or a seditious bigot, he has acted justly and laudably, but the public is a real sufferer . . . But however single acts of justice may be contrary, either to public or private interest, 'tis certain, that the whole plan

or scheme is highly conducive, or indeed absolutely requisite, both to the support of society, and the well-being of every individual... Tho' in one instance the public be a sufferer, this momentary ill is amply compensated by the steady prosecution of the rule, and by the peace and order, which it establishes in society. (Hume 1978: 497)

8 Having devoted some space to rule-consequentialism, I should note that it is not held in high esteem by most consequentialists. See, e.g. Smart (1967). I have discussed it in order to locate more precisely the disagreements between Kantians and consequentialists.

9 In citing Kant's works, I use the abbreviations and translations given below. All references except *Lectures on Ethics* are to *Kants gesammelte Schriften* (*KGS*), *herausgegeben von der Deutschen* (formerly *Königlichen Preussischen*) *Akademie der Wissenschaften*, 29 volumes (Berlin: Walter de Gruyter (and predecessors), 1902). Where the translations used do not provide the page number of the German text, I also provide the page number of the translation. *Lectures on Ethics*, it should be noted, is a compilation of notes from Kant's students (carefully checked against other students' notes). Page references are to the English translation. Occasionally I have altered the translations, but I always alert the reader that I am doing so. Most alterations concern the translation of *Mensch* as "man." Since *Mensch* in German is gender-neutral while "man" in English is not, I have in some instances altered the translations of *Mensch* so as to make clear that there is no reason to assume that only men are intended.

A   *Anthropologie in pragmatischer Hinsicht* (*KGS*, vol. 7).
     Anthropology from a Pragmatic Point of View, trans. Mary J. Gregor, The Hague: Nijhoff, 1974.
G   *Grundlegung zur Metaphysik der Sitten* (*KGS*, vol. 4).
     Groundwork of the Metaphysics of Morals trans. H. J. Paton, New York: Harper & Row, 1964.
LE *Eine Vorlesung über Ethik*, ed. Paul Menzer, Berlin: Rolf Heise, 1924.
     Lectures on Ethics, trans. Louis Infield, Indianapolis, Ind.: Hackett, 1981.
MM *Die Metaphysik der Sitten* (*KGS*, vol. 6).
     The Metaphysics of Morals, trans. Mary J. Gregor, Cambridge: Cambridge University Press, 1991.
PrR *Kritik der praktischen Vernunft* (*KGS*, vol. 5).
     Critique of Practical Reason, trans. Lewis White Beck, Indianapolis, Ind.: Bobbs-Merrill, 1956.

R   *Die Religion innerhalb der Grenzen der blossen Vermunft* (*KGS*, vol. 6).
     Religion within the Limits of Reason Alone, trans. Theodore M. Greene and Hoyt H. Hudson, New York: Harper & Row, 1960.
WE   "Was Ist Erklärung?" (*KGS*, vol. 8).
     "An answer to the question: What is enlightenment?", in *Perpetual Peace and Other Essays on Politics, History, and Morals*, trans. Ted Humphrey, Indianapolis, Ind.: Hackett, 1983.

10 I should note that many Kantians accept both the idea of respecting humanity as an end in itself and the construal of humanity as the power to set ends for ourselves but do not accept the conception of freedom implicit in the above quote. There is, moreover, considerable disagreement as to how Kant's theory of freedom is to be understood. See Allison 1990 and Wood 1984 for differing views on Kant on freedom. For a very helpful discussion of humanity see Hill 1992, ch. 2.

11 Occasionally one encounters the mistaken view that there is no concern at all in Kant's ethics to seek to bring about certain goods. That this is mistaken is evident from (among other things) the duties to promote others' happiness and to develop one's talents, discussed below.

12 For extensive discussion of both responsibility and friendship in the context of Kant's ethics, see Korsgaard 1996a, ch. 7.

13 Why we have a duty only to promote others' happiness, not our own, is somewhat more mysterious. Kant's view is not entirely clear, and insofar as it is clear, many contemporary Kantians, myself included, find it unconvincing. Kant says that we have no duty to promote our own happiness because we seek it anyway, and we only have a duty to those things which we have some temptation to neglect. Yet at *G* 399 he recognizes the temptation to neglect one's own happiness, and indicates that a person so tempted might nonetheless further his happiness from duty. The duty he says, is indirect; it is a duty to assure one's own happiness because "discontent with one's state, in a press of cares and amidst unsatisfied wants, might easily become a great *temptation to the transgression of duty*" (*G* 399). Cf. *MM* 387–8, where he says that while this might seem to ground a duty to promote one's own happiness, in fact the end in this case "is not the subject's happiness but his morality." He adds that "to seek prosperity for its own sake is not directly a duty, but indirectly it can well be a duty, that of warding off poverty insofar as this is a great temptation to vice. But then it is not my happiness but the preservation of my moral integrity that is my end and also my duty."

14 Kant classifies the first three under the heading of duties of love to others. They are "vices of hatred for others" (*MM* 458). Contempt and arrogance violate the "duties of respect for others" (465). (In both quotes I substitute "others" for "other men.") But though these vices are classified under a different heading, they clearly are at the same time qualities the rooting out (or moderating) of which would constitute self-improvement. This is one of many instances in which the duty to promote others' happiness and the duty to perfect oneself converge.

15 The wealthy, however, would do well not to have too strong a sense of entitlement to their riches. His staunch defense of property rights notwithstanding, Kant suggests that for the wealthy, helping the needy should not be strictly a matter of charity; it may be required by justice.

> Having the means to practice such beneficence as depends on the goods of fortune is, for the most part, a result of certain men being favored through the injustice of the government, which introduces an inequality of wealth that makes others need their beneficence. Under such circumstances, does a rich man's help to the needy, on which he so readily prides himself as something meritorious, really deserve to be called beneficence at all? (*MM* 454)

16 For those who would like more detail, ch. 3 of my *Kantian Ethics Almost Without Apology* might be helpful. I argue there that some imperfect duties admit of more latitude, in Kant's scheme, than do others. The duty to perfect ourselves morally involves the least latitude.

17 A passage that suggests that it *is* his view is *MM* 390.

18 The direction that I am taking is not the one that Wolf takes. She emphasizes that on her view it is not a defect of a moral theory if the sort of person who would be morally ideal on that theory is someone whom we regard as less than perfect. Instead, she thinks that this is simply the way things are: the perfectly moral person may not be the sort of person we want to spend a lot of time with. And "a person may be *perfectly wonderful* without being *perfectly moral*" (1982: 436). So on her view, "the flaws of a perfect master of a moral theory need not reflect flaws in the intramoral content of the theory itself" (p. 435). The flaws in the perfect master are not moral flaws, though they are flaws from another standpoint (one which is in no way inferior to the moral point of view, according to Wolf). Just what that other standpoint is is not entirely clear, but what is clear is that "we must be willing to raise normative questions from a perspective that is unat-

tached to a commitment to any particular well-ordered system of values" (p. 439). The flaws in the moral saint point not to the limitations of particular moral theories, as she sees it, but to the limitations of morality itself.

19 For a discussion of both pitfalls, see Louden 1992. For a discussion of maximizing in connection with the "moral saints" problem, see Adams 1984.

20 Here I should acknowledge that Kant wouldn't speak of respect for trees. Only rational beings merit respect; non-rational beings have "only a relative value as means" (*G* 429). I think one can, without inconsistency, disagree with this while still holding that rational beings have a distinctive status. What we should say about non-human animals is tricky, and not something that I take up here. I am inclined to think, though, that what makes persons rational beings is something that some non-humans have to some degree. It is by no means clear that non-human animals lack altogether the capacity to set ends for themselves (though the range of ends surely is smaller than the range open to humans). To the extent that they do, this seems to warrant according them some respect. For Kant's views on the proper treatment of animals, see *MM* 442–3.

21 Depending on the trees, the reason for erecting the apartment building, the location, etc., we might not think that cutting the trees was justified, but I'm supposing that most of us are ready to believe that it was. It is noteworthy that if we doubt this, the fact that he replaces them tends to allay the doubt (or at least diminish our disapproval of him).

22 Though persons are not replaceable *qua* persons, persons *qua* consumers, workers, warriors, baby producers, etc., are, and so it would not be a sick joke if, say, after a war that wiped out a significant proportion of the population, the surviving community judged that it would be good if the birth rate increased. To that end they might seek to make it more feasible for couples or individual women to have several children, perhaps offering inexpensive or free (and good) childcare or a subsidy to help defray expenses, lengthy parental leaves, and the like. The idea would not be, though, that the deaths of those lost were made up for by producing babies; the loss of those people is in no way diminished by the birth of a great many babies. The decision is simply a forward-looking one, one aimed to help the society continue, not one which looks back and seeks to partially rectify a wrong.

23 The motto of the enlightenment, according to Kant, is "Have courage to use your own understanding!" Immaturity is tempting. "It is so easy to be immature. If I have a book to serve as my understanding, a

pastor to serve as my conscience, a physician to determine my diet for me, and so on, I need not exert myself at all. I need not think, if only I can pay." And others encourage us to remain immature: "The guardians who have so benevolently taken over the supervision of men have carefully seen to it that the far greatest part of them (including the entire fair sex) regard taking the step to maturity as very dangerous, not to mention difficult" (WE 35–6).

24 I discuss this in greater detail in Baron 1997.

25 One consequentialist who takes a different view is Peter Railton (1984). See also William Wilcox's reply (1987), as well as Railton 1988.

26 Surely Hume did not share this view, and whether Mill and Kant did is debatable. See e.g. Mill 1978: 74.

27 Thus Gregory Trianosky writes, "What unifies recent work on the virtues is its opposition to various central elements of a view which I will call *neo-Kantianism*" (1990: 335). He acknowledges that it "is not necessarily Kant's own view" but he seems not to recognize how far some of the tenets he lists – particularly those whose rejection is most central to virtue ethics – are from being Kant's view. The first two tenets are "(1) The most important question in morality is, 'what is it right or obligatory to do?' and (2) Basic moral judgments are judgments about the rightness of actions" (p. 335).

28 Schneewind 1990: 45. Christianity, he claims, brought with it an approach to ethics that was at odds with the virtue approach. Thomas Reid remarked on this opposition: "Morals have been methodized in different ways. The Ancients commonly arranged them under the four cardinal virtues of prudence, temperance, fortitude, and justice. Christian writers, I think more properly, under the three heads of the duty we owe to God, to ourselves, and to our neighbor" (cited in Schneewind 1990: 44).

29 *Religion within the Limits of Reason Alone* and *Anthropology from a Pragmatic Point of View* also contain considerable discussion of character and are also far less often read, discussed and taught than is the *Groundwork*.

30 For a detailed discussion of maxims, see Potter 1994.

31 I am borrowing here from O'Neill 1989: 83.

32 For more on its role in the *Groundwork*, see Korsgaard 1996a, ch. 2.

33 Of course sometimes we do need to evaluate each other. If we are going to have a penal system, one which is based at least in part on desert, we need to have a way of evaluating whether the accused person is guilty and if so, what sort of sentence is appropriate. But importantly – and something that is nicely brought out in the very structure of Kant's *Metaphysics of Morals* – the project of deciding

whether someone is deserving of punishment is entirely different from the tasks of moral philosophy (except, perhaps, when the tasks are those of rearing children). Our concern in moral philosophy is not to evaluate other people *qua* people, decide whether they deserve good or ill, decide which person is best and which is second best, and so on; our focus should be forward-looking and should be on how to conduct ourselves, how to flourish as human rational beings, and how to alter social and political conditions so as to facilitate the flourishing of all persons.

34 Misleadingly, because it may suggest something that is pretty clearly false (but often believed), namely that Kant is a psychological hedonist with respect to all incentives other than that of duty. Korsgaard (1996b) offers an explanation of Kant's use of "self-love" in contexts such as this one. See also Reath 1989.

35 It should be noted that maxims, on Kant's view, are freely adopted. It is important to Kant that what distinguishes the good person from the bad person is not temperament or some aspect thereof (which is not chosen) but maxims (which are).

36 This is evident in *Groundwork* 397. For an excellent discussion, see Korsgaard 1996a, ch. 2.

37 "Naturally" in the sense of "second nature." The idea is not that the virtuous person is congenitally predisposed to be virtuous, and in that sense virtuous by nature, but rather that for the virtuous person, being virtuous is never a struggle.

38 As will soon become evident, I don't mean to suggest that this is Aristotle's view; it is a view that virtue ethicists often endorse and which is (wrongly, I think) often attributed to Aristotle.

39 Similar points could be made regarding what a person finds sexually arousing. If I learned of someone whom I liked and thought well of that he was sexually aroused, watching films, by scenes of rape and murder, I'd revise my opinion of him – though certainly not as much as I would if I learned that he made a point of going to such films because he enjoyed the rape and murder scenes so much, and of course not as much as I would if I learned that he actually desired to rape and murder.

40 See also *R* 24n/19n.

41 It is sometimes claimed that Kant's view is not merely that the moral worth is more apparent when there is such conflict, but that an action only has moral worth when duty and inclination conflict. I argue against that claim in Baron 1995: ch. 5.

42 But what about the desire to torture small animals? This, it might be argued, is perfectly compatible with respect for persons and thus

might well be a desire of the Kantian virtuous person. Kant's response would be that such a desire "is opposed to man's duty to himself." Indeed, he holds that even a "propensity to wanton destruction of what is *beautiful* in inanimate nature…is opposed to man's duty to himself; for it weakens or uproots that feeling in man which, though not of itself moral, is still a disposition of sensibility that greatly promotes morality or at least prepares the way for it: the disposition, namely, to love something (e.g. beautiful crystal formations, the indescribable beauty of plants) even apart from any intention to use it" (*MM* 443). Although Kant is speaking here of a propensity, not a mere desire, it is clear that a desire to torture animals, and the attitudes it reflects, would be at odds with qualities in us that are important for morality, including a concern not to inflict unnecessary suffering.

43 Virtue ethicists would not put it quite this way, however, since they avoid speaking in terms of "morally ought." In their terms, it is part of being virtuous that one's inclinations are not at odds with one's sense of what it is virtuous to do.

44 Lawrence Blum attributes this view to Kantians through a slightly different line of reasoning. "Morality takes the form of obligations …Only that which we can bring about through the medium of our will is something which we can be obliged to do. And we cannot be obliged to have certain feelings; as Sidgwick says, 'it cannot be a strict duty to feel an emotion, so far as it is not directly within the power of the will to produce it at any given time.' Thus feelings lie outside the scope of moral obligation." Blum takes it to be part of the Kantian view that "our feelings and emotions cannot reflect on us morally" (1980: 170–1.) The central error here is inferring from the claim that it cannot be a duty here and now to have a certain feeling that our feelings and emotions cannot, on a Kantian view, reflect on us morally (and that they lie outside the scope of moral obligation). We can be obligated to cultivate in ourselves certain feelings and not to foster others, and we can, Kant explicitly recognizes, shape the feelings we have by placing ourselves in certain sorts of situations (*MM* 457). Thus they do not lie outside the scope of moral obligation. Furthermore, they reflect on us in that they undermine (or support) the claim that we have adopted certain obligatory ends.

45 It is not entailed by the principle of utility and is not something that utilitarians must hold. Indeed, a number of utilitarians assert that the rightness of censuring persons is itself determined by the utility of doing so and deny that the fact that *x* is a duty entails that it is right to censure those who violate *x*. Others, Urmson among them, regard the

claim that *x* is a duty itself to be determined (at least in part) by the utility of generally regarding it as a duty; and they hold that the fact that it is a duty entails that it is right to censure failure to comply.

46 The distinction between juridical and ethical duties is presented in *MM*. For a helpful discussion of Kant's classification of duties, see Hill 1992: ch. 8, and Gregor 1963.

47 The suggestive remarks at the end of Foot 1979 are in the spirit of Anscombe's proposal, though Foot does not specifically endorse the idea that we should avoid using broad ethical terms. The discussion of the virtuous person at the end of Foot 1978 is also in keeping with Anscombe's suggestion without speaking to it.

48 For a comparison of acting from duty and acting from virtue and an account of what it is to act from virtue, see Audi 1995.

49 See in particular Korsgaard 1996b and other essays in the same volume.

50 In saying "glowing" I am being more generous to Kant's critics than I should be. Kant is not presenting the person who lacks fellow-feeling as a model human being. He says parenthetically of the man in whom "nature had implanted little sympathy" that he would "not be the worst product of nature" (*G* 398). This is not high praise.

51 For more on this, see Baron 1995: ch. 5.

52 It fuels confusion, since "for the sake of duty" suggests that duty serves as a goal. See, e.g., Paton's translation of *Groundwork* at 397 and 398; he sometimes translates it correctly as "from duty," sometimes as "from the motive of duty," and sometimes as "for the sake of duty." See also Greene and Hudson's translation of *Religion* at 29–30/25.

53 "An action done from duty has its moral worth, *not in the purpose* to be attained by it, but in the maxim in accordance with which it is decided upon" (*G* 399).

54 It might be replied, "True, but does Kant know this? Maybe he thinks that one always can." That would be an odd suggestion, but in case one has any doubts, the fantastic virtue passage at *MM* 409 should lay them to rest.

55 I do so in Baron 1995, ch. 5.

56 The first problem is suggested by some remarks in *Lectures on Ethics*:

Consider the man who is benevolent from love, who loves his neighbour from inclination ... Such a man will be charitable, by inclination, to all and sundry; and then, if someone takes advantage of his kind heart, in sheer disgust he will decide from then onwards to give up doing good to others. (*LE* 193)

57 Aristotle 1985: 169–70 (*Nicomachean Ethics* 1144b). Or rather, Aristotle would if he counted this particularly quality – concern for others' well-being and eagerness to help them – as a virtue at all. See Korsgaard 1996b.

58 That the Kantian agent has one thought too many was suggested by Bernard Williams (1981) and has been picked up by other critics of Kantian ethics, among them Annas (1984). I try to figure out just what the criticism is in Baron 1996. See also Powers 1993.

59 As others have observed, some, e.g. his wife, would probably feel happier if the husband's thought were not that it was his wife, but that it was *she*.

60 It is interesting that in *A Father's Story*, Lionel Dahmer is at some pains to assure his readers that his love for his son did not lead him to try to shield Jeffrey from arrest and imprisonment for his various offenses and indeed that when Jeffrey was to be granted an early release from the prison where he was serving a one-year sentence for sexual molestation, he sought to block the early release.

61 Herman 1993, ch. 4. Herman also observes that "we do not imagine normal moral agents bringing maxims of grossly immoral acts to the CI procedure routinely, only to discover (to their surprise?) that these acts are forbidden" (1993: 76). I should note that in other articles in the same collection Herman calls into question the standard assumption that the role of the Categorical Imperative is to test the agent's actual maxim for moral acceptability. See below.

62 As Onora O'Neill points out, abstraction in itself is something both innocuous and unavoidable. "We abstract whenever we make claims or decisions or follow policies or react to persons on a basis that is indifferent as to the satisfaction or non-satisfaction of some predicate in a given case" (1991: 3). The objection, then, has to be not to abstraction *per se* but to abstraction from some relevant quality.

63 I am thinking especially of *G* 389.

64 Kant contributes to the confusion about the permissibility of taking empirical considerations into account because, as Pogge points out, he tends to contrast only two levels, "(a) pure morality, establishing the moral law that is valid for all rational beings" and "(c) the application of morality to particular situations, with the aid of (rational and) empirical anthropology." He neglects the intermediate level, "(b) the application of pure morality to a world of human beings for purposes of developing *human* morality, with the aid of rational anthropology" (Pogge 1989: 178).

65 It is of utmost importance to Kant that the principle contains "no reference to what everybody or anybody wants, nor to anything that lies beyond the agent's own capacity to will." If it did, it would be "heteronomous." The Categorical Imperative, by contrast, is "part of a moral theory for agents who, in Kant's sense of the term, act *autonomously*" (O'Neill 1989: 81).

66 See Korsgaard 1996a, ch. 3 for discussion of three different accounts of what the contradiction consists in and development and defense of her "practical contradiction" account.

67 To obviate confusion, I should note that my use of "false positives" and "false negatives" is the reverse of Herman's.

68 If, however, what one wants is to win a race – or perhaps an Olympic gold medal – one's maxim of murdering a more successful rival to secure this end might survive the CI test. After all, remaining alive to enjoy the glory need not be part of one's end; one's end is simply to be the winner.

69 The example comes from a lecture by T. M. Scanlon to the 1983 National Endowment of the Humanities Institute on Kantian Ethics (Baltimore) and is discussed by Herman (1993, ch. 7).

70 This raises interesting questions regarding the moral (im)permissibility of self-sacrifice, but I shall not take them up here.

71 Of course Kant distinguished between imperfect and perfect duties in the *Groundwork*, but his distinction was largely unexplained, and even treated as "arbitrary." ["It should be noted that I reserve my division of duties entirely for a future *Metaphysics of Morals* and that my present division is therefore put forward as arbitrary (merely for the purpose of arranging my examples)" (*G* 422n).] Moreover, the category of "duties of virtue," which includes both perfect and imperfect duties, is introduced only in *MM*. As Korsgaard points out, given the central role played by obligatory ends in duties of virtue, there is reason to think that the contradiction in the will test might be needed to identify those perfect duties (e.g. the duty not to kill oneself) that are duties of virtue (1996a, ch. 3).

72 For discussions of the relation between the different formulations of the Categorical Imperative (formulations which Kant claimed are equivalent) see O'Neill 1989, ch. 7; Korsgaard 1996a, ch. 5; and Pogge 1989.

73 In Lecture II of the lectures he delivered to the 1983 NEH Institute on Kantian Ethics, T. M. Scanlon suggested that the Categorical Imperative "asks us to imagine that we are in a position to adopt 'second order maxims,' i.e. maxims concerning the acceptability or unacceptability of maxims, on behalf of all rational agents. (This is the

position of *legislating* members of a kingdom of ends.)" (Scanlon 1983: 18).

74 I completed the first draft of this essay while holding a fellowship at the University of Melbourne. I would like to thank the philosophy faculty and staff for providing an ideal work environment. I am also very grateful to Philip Pettit, Michael Slote, and especially Christine Swanton for helpful comments on earlier drafts.

References

Adams, Robert Merrihew (1984) "Saints," *Journal of Philosophy* 81: 392–401.

Allison, Henry (1990) *Kant's Theory of Freedom*, Cambridge: Cambridge University Press.

Annas, Julia (1984) "Personal love and Kantian ethics in *Effi Briest*," *Philosophy and Literature* 8: 15–31.

Anscombe, Elizabeth (1958) "Modern moral philosophy," *Philosophy* 33: 1–19.

Aristotle (1985) *Nicomachean Ethics*, trans. Terence Irwin, Indianapolis, Ind.: Hackett.

Audi, Robert (1995) "Acting from virtue," *Mind* 104: 449–71.

Baron, Marcia (1995) *Kantian Ethics Almost Without Apology*, Ithaca, NY: Cornell University Press.

—— (1996) "Impartialism and its critics," paper presented at the Second Annual Utah Philosophy Colloquium: Partiality and Impartiality, Salt Lake City, May.

—— (1997) "Kantian ethics and claims of detachment," in Robin Schott (ed.) *Feminist Interpretations of Kant*, University Park, Pa.: Pennsylvania State University Press.

Blum, Lawrence (1980) *Friendship, Altruism, and Morality*, Boston, Mass.: Routledge & Kegan Paul.

Code, Lorraine (1991) *What Can She Know? Feminist Theory and the Construction of Knowledge*, Ithaca, NY: Cornell University Press.

Cooper, Anthony Ashley, Earl of Shaftesbury [1699; repr. 1732] (1964) "An inquiry concerning virtue or merit," in *British Moralists*, ed. L. A. Selby-Bigge, Oxford: Oxford University Press [1897], reprinted in one volume with a new introduction by Bernard H. Baumrin, Indianapolis, Ind.: Bobbs-Merrill.

Dahmer, Lionel (1994) *A Father's Story*, New York: William Morrow.

Dillon, Robin S. (1992) "Respect and care: toward moral integration," *Canadian Journal of Philosophy* 22: 105–32.

Dworkin, Ronald (1977) *Taking Rights Seriously*, Cambridge, Mass.: Harvard University Press.

Foot, Philippa (1978) *Virtues and Vices*, Oxford: Blackwell Publishers.

—— (1979) "William Frankena's Carus Lectures," *Monist* 62: 305–12.

Gregor, Mary J. (1963) *Laws of Freedom: a Study of Kant's Method of Applying the Categorical Imperative in the "Metaphysik der Sitten"*, Oxford: Blackwell Publishers.

Herman, Barbara (1993) *The Practice of Moral Judgment*, Cambridge, Mass.: Harvard University Press.

Hill, Thomas (1992) *Dignity and Practical Reason in Kant's Moral Theory*, Ithaca, NY: Cornell University Press.

Hume, David [1739] (1978) *A Treatise of Human Nature*, ed. L. A. Selby-Bigge, 2nd edn with text revised and variant readings by P. H. Nidditch, Oxford: Clarendon Press.

Hursthouse, Rosalind (1995) "Applying virtue ethics," in Rosalind Hursthouse, Gavin Lawrence, and Warren Quinn (eds) *Virtues and Reasons: Philippa Foot and Moral Theory: Essays in Honor of Philippa Foot*, Oxford: Clarendon Press.

Kant, Immanuel [1775–80] (1981). *Lectures on Ethics*, compiled from the lecture notes of Theodor Friedrich Brauer, Gottlieb Kutzner, and Chr. Mrongovius by Paul Menzer in 1924, trans. Louis Infield, Indianapolis, Ind.: Hackett.

—— [1784] (1983) "What is Enlightenment?", in *Perpetual Peace and Other Essays on Politics, History, and Morals*, trans. Ted Humphrey, Indianapolis, Ind.: Hackett.

—— [1785] (1964) *Groundwork of the Metaphysics of Morals*, trans. H. J. Paton, New York: Harper & Row.

—— [1788] (1956) *Critique of Practical Reason*, trans. Lewis White Beck, Indianapolis, Ind.: Bobbs-Merrill.

—— [1793] (1960) *Religion within the Limits of Reason Alone*, trans. Theodore M. Greene and Hoyt H. Hudson, New York: Harper & Row.

—— [1797] (1991) *The Metaphysics of Morals*, trans. Mary J. Gregor, Cambridge: Cambridge University Press.

—— [1798] (1974) *Anthropology from a Pragmatic Point of View*, trans. Mary J. Gregor, The Hague: Nijhoff.

Korsgaard, Christine (1995) "Rawls and Kant: on the primacy of the practical," *Proceedings of the Eighth International Kant Congress*, vol. I, part 3, ed. Hoke Robinson, Milwaukee, Wis.: Marquette University Press.

Korsgaard, Christine (1996a) *Creating the Kingdom of Ends*, Cambridge: Cambridge University Press.

——(1996b) "From duty and for the sake of the noble: Kant and Aristotle on morally good action," in Jennifer Whiting and Stephen Engstrom (eds) *Aristotle, Kant and the Stoics: Rethinking Happiness and Duty*, Cambridge: Cambridge University Press.

Kosman, L. A. (1980) "Being properly affected: virtues and feelings in Aristotle's *Ethics*," in Amélie Rorty (ed.) *Essays on Aristotle's Ethics*, Berkeley and Los Angeles, Calif.: University of California Press.

Louden, Robert B. (1992) *Morality and Moral Theory: a Reappraisal and Reaffirmation*, New York and Oxford: Oxford University Press.

Mill, John Stuart [1859] (1978) *On Liberty*, Indianapolis, Ind.: Hackett.

——[1861] (1979) *Utilitarianism*, Indianapolis, Ind.: Hackett.

Moravscik, J. M. E. (1981) "On what we aim at and how we live," in David Depew (ed.) *The Greeks and the Good Life*, Indianapolis, Ind.: Hackett.

O'Conner, Flannery (1977) "The geranium," in *The Complete Stories of Flannery O'Conner*, New York: Farrar, Strauss, and Giroux.

O'Neill, Onora (1989) *Constructions of Reason: Explorations of Kant's Practical Philosophy*, Cambridge: Cambridge University Press.

——(1991) "Kant's ethics and Kantian ethics," paper presented to the North American Kant Society at the Central Division meeting of the American Philosophical Association, Chicago, April.

——(1996) *Towards Justice and Virtue*, Cambridge: Cambridge University Press.

Pettit, Philip (1991) "Consequentialism," in Peter Singer (ed.) *A Companion to Ethics*, Oxford: Blackwell Publishers.

Pincoffs, Edmund L. (1986) *Quandaries and Virtues: Against Reductivism in Ethics*, Lawrence, Kan.: University of Kansas Press.

Pogge, Thomas (1989) "The Categorical Imperative," in Otfried Höffe (ed.) *"Grundlegung zur Metaphysik der Sitten": Ein Kooperativer Kommentar*, Frankfurt: Vittorio Klosterman.

Potter, Nelson (1994) "Maxims in Kant's moral philosophy," *Philosophia* 23: 59–90.

Powers, Madison (1993) "Contractualist impartiality and personal commitments," *American Philosophical Quarterly* 30: 63–71.

Putnam, Ruth Anna (1988) "Reciprocity and virtue ethics," *Ethics* 98: 379–89.

Railton, Peter (1984) "Alienation, consequentialism and the demands of morality," *Philosophy and Public Affairs* 13: 134–71.

——(1988) "How thinking about character and utilitarianism might lead to rethinking the character of utilitarianism," *Midwest Studies in Philosophy* 13: 398–416.

Reath, Andrews (1989) "Hedonism, heteronomy, and Kant's Principle of Happiness," *Pacific Philosophical Quarterly* 70: 42–72.

Ross, W. D. (1930) *The Right and the Good*, London: Oxford University Press.

Scanlon, T. M.(1983) "Kant's *Groundwork*: from freedom to moral community," three lectures presented to the National Endowment of the Humanities Institute on Kantian Ethics, Baltimore, Md.

Schneewind, Jerome (1990) "The misfortunes of virtue," *Ethics* 101: 42–63.

Slote, Michael (1997) "Agent-based virtue ethics," in Roger Crisp and Michael Slote (eds) *Oxford Readings in Virtue Ethics*, Oxford: Oxford University Press.

Smart, J. J. C. (1967) "Extreme and restricted utilitarianism," in Philippa Foot (ed.) *Theories of Ethics*, London: Oxford University Press.

Smart, J. J. C. and Williams, Bernard (1973) *Utilitarianism: For and Against*, Cambridge: Cambridge University Press.

Sorabji, Richard (1980) "Aristotle on the role of intellect in virtue," in Amélie Rorty (ed.) *Essays on Aristotle's Ethics*, Berkeley and Los Angeles, Calif.: University of California Press.

Swanton, Christine (1995) "Profiles of the virtues," *Pacific Philosophical Quarterly* 76: 47–72.

Trianosky, Gregory (1990) "What is virtue ethics all about?," *American Philosophical Quarterly* 27: 335–44.

Urmson, J. O. (1969) "Saints and heroes," in Joel Feinberg (ed.) *Moral Concepts*, London: Oxford University Press.

Wick, Warner (1983) "Kant's moral philosophy," intro. to *Ethical Philosophy: the Complete Texts of "Grounding of the Metaphysics of Morals" and "Metaphysical Elements of Virtue,"* trans. James W. Ellington, Indianapolis, Ind.: Hackett.

Wilcox, William (1987) "Egoists, consequentialists, and their friends," *Philosophy and Public Affairs* 16: 73–84.

Williams, Bernard (1981) *Moral Luck: Philosophical Papers 1973–1980*, Cambridge: Cambridge University Press.

Wolf, Susan (1982) "Moral saints," *Journal of Philosophy* 79: 419–39.

——(1992) "Morality and partiality," *Philosophical Perspectives* 6: 243–59.

Wood, Allen (1984) "Kant's compatibilism," in *Self and Nature in Kant's Philosophy*, Ithaca, NY: Cornell University Press.

——(1995) "Humanity as end in itself, "*Proceedings of the Eighth International Kant Congress*, vol. I, part 1, ed. Hoke Robinson, Milwaukee, Wis.: Marquette University Press.

2

The Consequentialist Perspective

Philip Pettit

Consequentialism or teleology has been demonized among a range of recent ethical thinkers; it has become the object of a stylized contempt among deontologists and Kantians, contractualists and virtue theorists. I think this is a great pity. The demonizing of the approach reflects a failure to appreciate fully the constraints to which moral reasoning is answerable. And it often leads, so I believe, to a trivialization of the moral point of view.

This essay is an attempt to provide a fair overview of consequentialism and its alternatives and to show why, by my lights, the consequentialist perspective is both attractive and compelling. The discussion is organized in five sections. First, I present a number of assumptions in moral psychology that ought to be agreed among consequentialists and non-consequentialists alike; it is important to begin with these, because consequentialism is often mistakenly criticized for not recognizing one or other of them. Second, I identify the question to which consequentialism and its rivals offer different answers; this is the question as to what makes a right option right: I call it, the question of rightness. Third, I outline the different sorts of approaches, consequentialist and non-consequentialist, that may be taken to the question of rightness. And then in the fourth section, I present the case for the consequentialist answer: for the answer, roughly, that the right option in any choice is that which produces the goods, that which promotes expected, neutral value. In the fifth and last section I consider the tenability of that answer in face of standard objections to consequentialism, arguing that it represents a challenging but still intuitive understanding of ethical demands.

1   A Moral Psychology for Consequentialists and Non-consequentialists

Consequentialism does not just attract criticism among its opponents; it arouses downright hostility.[1] Why is this? The main reason, I think, is that opponents see consequentialism as culpably and fundamentally misrepresenting the moral psychology of agents: the commonplace psychology of human beings, so far as it bears on moral matters. Consequentialists, so their critics allege, carry on in the criticism and prescription of choice as if human agents were of a different character from that which is revealed in our everyday experience of ourselves and which is charted in this commonplace psychology. Consequentialists carry on, so it is said, as if human agents were cast in an alien, unfamilar mould or were made of alien, unfamiliar material. Anxious to develop a systematic moral perspective they ignore the basic facts of our moral psychology; they fail to keep touch with the realities of motivation and deliberation, affection and reason, that are salient to ordinary subjects.

The opponents of consequentialism, as we would expect from this line of criticism, consciously take their starting-point from a picture of how things stand in the realm of commonplace psychology. Drawing on a variety of traditional sources – often literary as well as philosophical sources – they sketch a picture of the human being in action and they argue that that picture gives the lie to the model of the human agent that is allegedly presupposed in consequentialist thought. The agent of the consequentialists, they suggest, is a theoretical fiction and consequentialism is incapable of intellectually surviving exposure to the real thing.

Widespread though it is, I do not think that this line of criticism is on the right track. Let us endorse all the moral-psychological claims that opponents of consequentialism wish to put in place. If the criticism pressed by opponents is correct, then this fidelity to moral-psychological facts ought to undermine the consequentialist or teleological perspective. It ought to remove the question to which consequentialism offers an answer; or it ought to make clear that the correct answer to that question is not the consequentialist one. But neither of these things happens. Or so at any rate I wish to argue.

In this section I identify three broad psychological assumptions that non-consequentialists emphasize and that, by my lights, we should all endorse (see Scheffler 1988). They represent an image of human beings which it is hard to envisage anyone failing to satisfy; certainly it is hard to envisage anyone failing to satisfy it with benefit. Since the principles will be embraced by the majority of non-consequentialists, I shall not bother to say much in their defense. In each case I will try to explain the assumption, highlighting its inevitability and attraction, and I will show how it has been taken to be inconsistent with a teleological perspective in ethics.

Non-atomism: People's Projects Often Essentially Involve Particular Individuals

The first assumption is that the deliberative considerations that motivate people – the considerations that give people intrinsic (though perhaps defeasible) reason to act – often involve other individuals essentially; they are considerations that obtain and motivate agents only in the presence of those other individuals. The springs of human action are not solipsistic or atomistic. They involve other people immediately.

Suppose that I go to some trouble to help a friend, Mary, who is in financial difficulty, and that I do this for reasons of friendship. There are two possible pictures of how my deliberation goes in such a case, one atomistic, the other not. The first picture of my reasoning is this. I am concerned with the general value of having friends and of helping those who happen to be my friends – this gives me intrinsic reason to act – and, seeing that Mary is a friend, I judge that I can best promote that value by now helping her: she falls, as luck would have it, on the trajectory of my general friend-helping project. Under this picture, Mary does not figure essentially in the consideration that gives me intrinsic reason to act: her part is not to motivate me, as it were, but only to provide me with the occasion for satisfying the independent motivation to help anyone who happens to be a friend.

This picture is distinctively atomistic. I am supposed to be resourced with all the motivation I need by the consideration of values that do not require the existence of any particular individual, let alone Mary: I am fully resourced by the consideration of the good of having friends and of helping those who happen to be my friends. If another individual breaks in on my consciousness, then, it is only by way of offering me an opening for the pursuit of projects that do not essentially involve the other. The project may be that of helping whoever are my friends but equally it may be that of enjoying company, achieving sexual satisfaction, or having a certain degree of status or power.

The non-atomistic claim denies, surely plausibly, that people's reasonings are generally like this. It adopts a different picture of my reasoning in regard to Mary, holding that if people pursue the good of their friends, that is normally because they care for those particular individuals, and not because of the independent appeal of the general value of having and helping friends. The reasoning involved is not of the form: helping needy friends is good; Mary is a needy friend; so I should help her. Rather it takes the form: my friend, Mary, is in need; so I should help her. The consideration that moves me essentially involves Mary, as it may essentially involve friendship; it contrasts in this way with the thought that helping needy friends is good. Mary does not just happen to provide the opportunity for satisfying my friend-helping project. Mary provides the opportunity, as only Mary can, for satisfying a project that essentially engages her.

Under the first picture of my reasoning, the consideration that intrinsically moves me is there also to move the counterfactual self which confronts, not Mary, but some other indiscernible individual, or even an illusion. My counterfactual self is moved, as I am moved, by the value of having and helping friends. Under the second picture, the common motivation fails. The consideration that intrinsically moves me is that my friend, Mary, is in need and this is not a consideration that can move the counterfactual self envisaged. It is a consideration that presupposes the impact of that other person, Mary, on my mind. The thought that binds me to Mary, the thought that moves me to action on her behalf, could not exist – could not logically exist – if she did not exist and have an impact on me. It is not a thought that I can share with the counterfactual self which inhabits a Mary-less world.

The non-atomistic claim is clearly true to the everyday phenomenology of motivation. People do not generally pursue friendship or company or even sex in such a way that others are well described as offering them contingent occasions for the satisfaction of the projects involved. People enter one another's minds and lives in the more intimate manner described. If anyone thinks that things are otherwise – or thinks anything that supposes that things are otherwise – then that is likely to be the result of adopting a false picture of the mind: a picture under which the contents of our thoughts, and therefore the considerations that ultimately move us, cannot presuppose the reality of entities outside our skin (McDowell and Pettit 1986; Pettit 1993a).

Some critics of teleology suggest that according to consequentialists moral agents cannot be non-atomistically involved in the manner projected in this first principle. According to their characterization of the approach, consequentialists can only endorse a concern for more or less abstract states of affairs – say, the state of affairs in which human happiness is maximized – and if they support a care for individuals, that is only so far as the promotion of the desired state of affairs requires that certain individuals fare well; the promotion of happiness requires that some individuals be happy. The non-consequentialist agent can care about this individual, and can care in particular about his or her happiness. The consequentialist agent, so it is said, can only care about the abstract value of happiness – or whatever value is thought relevant – and will direct attention to this individual only so far as he or she falls on the trajectory of the happiness-promoting project (see Foot 1985; Kymlicka 1988).

Were consequentialism to reject the propriety of individual-centred concerns, then it would be a highly revisionary and, to my eye, a very unattractive moral theory. It would deny the legitimacy of ways of feeling and acting that are surely inevitable in some measure and that figure in the finest commitments to which human experience and literature testifies. Love, loyalty, and fidelity may not be the sum total of moral excellence but they are certainly a part of it. If I am a teleologist or consequentialist, that is only because I think of the doctrine, contrary to the suggestion of many critics, as supportive of our first principle, not inconsistent with it.

Non-moralism: People's Primitive Motivations are Often Non-moralistic in Character

In presenting the claim that people's minds and concerns can involve particular individuals essentially, I suggested that their attachments and affections can derive entirely from particularistic sources. I can care for Mary, not because caring for people is good, not because it is required by our friendship, not even because Mary is the better off for my care. Or least not just for such more or less moralistic reasons, as I shall call them. I can even care brutely, for no reason. Mary can matter to me in her own right. Maybe she doesn't matter as much as Jane or Joseph; maybe she doesn't matter so much that I would give up my life for her. Maybe, in other words, she does not matter unconditionally. But she can still matter. And she can matter independently of any moralistic cause that I may happen to espouse; she can matter to me in an unmediated way.

Not only is it possible for my motivations *vis-à-vis* a friend like Mary to be non-moralistic in this way. It is necessary that they should be so, at least in some measure, if I am really to be a friend to that person and if I am really to act out of friendship for her. Michael Stocker (1976) has argued the point persuasively. Let my motivations become moralistic, let my commitment to Mary come to derive even from a commitment to the value of friendship, and I cease to conform to the profile of a friend. I become indistinguishable from the crusader who wants to further some abstract good and who treats individuals only as loci where that good can be realized. The fact that I want to advance the good of friendship, and not some more remote cause, is neither here nor there. It still remains that my focus is resolved at the wrong level. My eye is directed, not to the good of my friend, but to a moralistic goal that only incidentally involves that friend.

But while we have already given sustenance to this non-moralism in arguing for the first non-atomistic principle, such non-moralism is plausible, in any case, on its own terms. Every human agent finds themselves with more or less brute commitments already in place, more or less brute projects and desires. While more abstract and moralistic categories may be invoked to explain or justify continuing with those commitments, as I may invoke the category of friendship to explain and justify my commitment to Mary, those categories should not be thought of as the actual motivators, or as the only legitimate motivators, of the agent. It is hard to imagine anyone being able, without an annihilation of agency, to reconstruct and remotivate their every commitment on an abstract, moralistic basis. But even if someone could do this, it should be clear that in achieving the required detachment they would cease to be an ordinary loving and lovable human subject (see too Smith 1994: 71–6 and Wolf 1982).

Consider the ways in which people get themselves involved, for example, in certain hobbies or even in certain social movements. They take such pleasure in building model aircraft, and develop such an expertise in doing so, that they can hardly imagine themselves giving it up. Or they involve themselves so intimately in the cause of preventing local pollution, or developing facilities for the neighborhood children, that this becomes a dominant feature of their persona; it becomes an essential mark, in their own mind and in that of others, of the sort of individual they are. Non-moralism amounts to the recognition that with a variety of such projects and desires, even with the projects that people are in the habit of justifying to themselves and others – everyone needs a hobby, someone has to organize against pollution – it is inevitable that people should be attached to those projects on a more particular basis than any justification is likely to highlight.

And not only is it inevitable; it may also be a very desirable feature of human psychology. The person who seeks the good of their friends, not for love of them but only for love of friendship, represents a figure too angelic or demonic to be humanly attractive, and certainly a figure too angelic or demonic actually to be a friend. And equally the person who selects and sustains a hobby or involvement only because they believe that this is in some way required or expected of them represents, if not a sort of depravity, at least a denaturing of the human being. They are something more or something less than the ordinary sorts of people whom

we cherish for their particularistic and individualizing enthu-
siasms.

Bernard Williams (Smart and Williams 1973) is well known for
marking the fact of motivational particularities, as Michael
Stocker is known for arguing that acting out of friendship is not
acting for the promotion of friendship. So far I am with them. But
Williams and Stocker also suggest that the truth of non-moralism
gives the lie to the teleological approach to ethics (see Scheffler
1982). They insinuate that the consequentialist agent can con-
done the particularistic sourcing of personal projects only so far
as the motives involved are derived from more abstract springs:
only so far as the motives are mediated by a moralistic concern to
increase overall happiness or whatever. If they are right in thinking that people are motivationally particularistic as a matter of
fact, and I believe they are, then the suggestion is that the consequentialist must look for a motivational reconstruction that
leads agents to silence particularistic promptings and put themselves under the control of purely moralistic pilots.

I see no reason to reject motivational particularism, or to be
reluctant about condoning it. More particularly, I see no inconsistency between admitting the fact of particularistic motives, and
even the desirability of preserving such motives, and embracing a
consequentialist or teleological point of view. The question that I
raise in the next section arises even though we accept the assumptions, including the assumption of non-moralism, that are docu-
mented in this. And consequentialism, as we shall see, is a
possible, and by my lights a persuasive answer, to that question.
As I understand the doctrine, then, it no more rules out non-
moralism than it does the non-atomism presented in our first
principle.

Non-actuarialism: People do not Often Make their Decisions in a Calculative Way

The third moral-psychological claim that is often stressed by
opponents of consequentialism represents human beings as non-
actuarial in character. The claim is that they are not on the whole
a rationalistic or calculative species and that it is an essential part

of realizing many of the things they cherish that they do not calculate rationalistically about what they should do. Granted that the things that count with human agents may involve other people essentially. Granted also that they may be desired in their own, non-moralistic right. Still, it could be that so far as the matters in question go, human agents typically concern themselves with them in a calculative, actuarial spirit: they itemize alternatives, draw up an inventory of possible consequences, assign appropriate probabilities to those consequences, and then try to work out which alternative does best by the values they embrace. The third non-actuarialist claim denies that human beings do carry on in this way, denies that they could ever manage to do so, at least without a sort of self-destruction, and denies that doing so would help them to realize many of their concerns.

Two points will serve to illustrate the idea. The first is that many of the virtues which people recognize and admire in one another are such that their exercise is incompatible with rationalistic calculation. The point will be obvious with a virtue like that of spontaneity but it also applies with more characteristically ethical virtues. Take generosity, for example. To be a generous person is, presumably, to be someone who within certain limits tends to want to help whenever a suitable cause presents itself, to be someone who within those limits does not first have to consider the cost before being prepared to make a commitment. But this means that to be a generous person is to be someone who is disposed not to calculate about all relevant costs and benefits when confronted with certain demands (Williams 1981).

The second point in support of the non-actuarialist claim is perhaps even more important. This is that many human relationships are built upon the common belief that each will treat the other in a manner that is incompatible with rationalistic calculation. If we count one another as friends then we will individually assume, and assume that the other assumes – and so on, perhaps, up the familiar hierarchy – that if either of us is in certain sorts of difficulty, then the other will be prepared to offer whatever help may be called upon – subject, no doubt, to certain limits – without having to calculate about the cost–benefit ratio. The sign of affection and friendship is precisely that calculation is not going to be needed in a case like this. Again, if we count one another as mutually respectful members of a well-ordered society, then we will individually assume, and assume that the other assumes, that if either proves to be an obstacle in the other's pursuit of their projects, then the other will be prepared – subject perhaps to certain limits – to respect the rights of the obstructing person without calculating about whether this is really to their advantage. As affection requires unthinking consideration, so a dispensation of respect – a civil society – requires a more or less unthinking recognition of rights. I am not truly befriended if the other must do their sums before being prepared to help me out. I am not truly respected if the other must do a check-list of the advantages and disadvantages before being prepared to refrain from interfering with me.

Bernard Williams (1981) and others have been to the fore in arguing that as we human beings are not a moralistic species, so we are not actuarial in character either. But those writers have often wanted to argue also that consequentialism or teleology is undermined by this observation. They have generally assumed that the approach recommends that in making our decisions, or at least our non-trivial decisions, we should always calculate in a certain pattern about what to do: we should take stock of all the possible consequences of our actions, consider their probability, weigh their relative attractions, and make up our minds on the basis of the costs and benefits that we find associated with each option. These critics of consequentialism follow the lead established in the nineteenth century when F. H. Bradley (1962: 107) argued, for example, that so far as it was consequentialist, utilitarian doctrine would require us all to think like casuists. "So far as my lights go, this is to make possible, to justify, and even to encourage, an incessant practical casuistry; and that, it need scarcely be added, is the death of morality."

Consequentialists have almost always resisted this charge. Thus, Henry Sidgwick (1966) in the last century, and J. J. C. Smart in this, have argued forcibly that utilitarianism does not require that agents all make their decisions by explicit reference to how the options will do by the promotion of happiness (see Smart and Williams 1973). The point they have wanted to make was nicely summed up early in the nineteenth century by the jurisprude, John Austin, in defending the utilitarian thinker.

"Though he approves of love because it accords with his principle, he is far from maintaining that the general good ought to be
the motive of the lover. It was never contended or conceived by a
sound, orthodox utilitarian, that the lover should kiss his mistress
with an eye to a common weal" (Austin 1832: 108).

Like all these others, I am happy to assume that we are indeed a
non-actuarial species and that any moral doctrine which required
the development of a sustained actuarial posture would be more
or less outlandish. I am happy to assume this, in particular,
because of believing that consequentialism does not require either
a rejection of the non-actuarialist assumption or a recommendation that human beings should begin to make their decisions in a
more actuarial way. Consequentialists may join non-consequentialists, not just in embracing non-atomism and non-moralism, but
also in endorsing the non-actuarialist principle.

2   The Question of Rightness

An Unavoidable Issue

Let us assume, then, that the moral psychology of human beings –
their psychology, so far as this bears on moral matters – is non-
atomistic, non-moralistic, and non-actuarial in character. It
allows other subjects to enter directly into people's individual
concerns. It allows the concerns that move people to motivate
them independently of moralistic mediation. And it allows and
encourages people to be spontaneous, non-calculative servants of
the ends they embrace. Let us assume not just that this is how
people are in their psychological make-up but that this is
how they should be allowed to remain under any plausible
moral theory. No alteration would really be feasible, and no
alteration promises to be desirable.

Those assumptions notwithstanding, there are many questions
that remain to be asked in moral theory. And among those questions is the issue, as I understand it, that divides consequentialists
from their opponents. This is what I call the question of rightness.
Take any particular choice where we judge that the right option

for the agent to take, or to have taken, is such and such. The question is what it is about that option, and what it is in general about any right option, that makes it the right option for the agent to take or to have taken.

Does the moral psychology sketched in the first section leave this question in place? Of course it does. No one would want to say that whatever the ordinary sort of agent does is right, so long as they are not atomistic or moralistic or actuarial in their approach to things. The demand for justification, the demand to show that what you have done or propose to do is the right course of action, is ubiquitous in human life. We pose that demand to one another as a matter of course and, internalizing the social point of view on our own persons, we pose it regularly to ourselves. And as the demand for justification is ubiquitous, so is the assumption that we cannot respond adequately to it just by arguing that in taking the course of action challenged, we are exemplifying a run-of-the-mill human psychology. If some of the things that an agent does are right and some are not, then we are naturally left with the question as to what it is that makes one option right and another wrong.

But what sort of question is the question of rightness? We need to elaborate on what it is that is being asked and on what different approaches might be taken in answering it. Otherwise we shall lack a proper sense of the terrain on which consequentialism and its rivals join battle. I discuss matters bearing on the nature of the question of rightness in this section and then in the next I look at the alternative ways in which the question may be approached.

The Need for a Participant Moral Theory

The most important thing to note about the rightness question is that if it is to mark a dividing point between consequentialist and non-consequentialist theories, then it must be understood in the same way by people on the different sides. I shall assume that what is involved in designating something as right, as surface semantics suggests, is a belief that it is right – a cognitive state of ascribing the property of rightness to it – not just a feeling or a prescription or anything of a purely non-cognitive kind; more on this in a moment. People in the different camps on the question of rightness, then, must share some common presuppositions about what is to be expected of an option that is designated as right: about what the term "right" means and, if this is taken to involve something extra, about how its reference is fixed. If consequentialists mean or refer to one thing by "right" and their opponents mean or refer to another, then there will be no issue of significance between them. There is a substantial division on the question of what makes a right option right only so far as there are shared views on the question of what "right" means and of how its reference is determined.

The assumption that judgments of rightness are beliefs, which I mentioned in passing, is attractive from my point of view, since I am committed to this representation of judgments of rightness and of various other evaluative judgments (Jackson and Pettit 1995; Pettit 1997b). But I maintain the assumption here, only for reasons of convenience. Those who reject the assumption and think of evaluations as non-cognitive need not balk at it, since they can translate my talk of the meaning and reference of "right" into other terms. All non-cognitivists have to claim that if people are involved in a substantial division on the question of what makes an option right, then they must share some common presuppositions that dictate the use of the word "right"; they must posit some shared assumptions about what is involved in calling something right, even as they deny that it involves ascribing a property designated by the word "right." People might share the view that to say something is right is to express approval, for example, or to prescribe it for anyone in the agent's situation; we shall notice some views of this sort later. The common presuppositions will serve, in the non-cognitivist perspective, not to fix the meaning and reference of "right" – the term does not pick out a property, on this view – but rather to fix its non-cognitive, expressive role: to determine what sort of approval or prescription, for example, goes with its use. Non-cognitivists will not like the way I talk here of the meaning and reference of "right," then, but they should be able to translate such cognitivist idiom into their own preferred language. Where I talk of what makes something right, they can translate what I say into talk of what makes something fit to be suitably approved or prescribed or whatever.

What are the candidate factors, then, for determining the meaning and reference of a term like "right"? Plausibly, the things that those who use the term believe in common about its actual and possible instances; the things that they take for granted, though perhaps without thinking much about them and perhaps without being able to spell them out in words. The candidates for fixing meaning and reference are, in a word, their shared working assumptions about right options: the presumptions about rightness that they put in play so far as they participate in moral discourse (Jackson and Pettit 1995). Those presumptions may fix the meaning of "right" in the way in which the commonplace linkage with unmarried males fixes the meaning of "bachelor." Or they may fix the meaning and reference of "right" in the more complex way in which the commonplaces about water combine with the way the world actually is to fix the meaning and reference of "water"; the commonplaces pick out water as the actual kind that unites instances of the drinkable, cleansing stuff that falls from the sky and the actual world identifies that kind as H_2O.[2]

Someone may retort that it is sheer dogma to believe in the need for such shared assumptions: such participant presumptions, as we might call them. I reply that the possibility of communicating information by the use of a term in a given conversation depends on your conversational partners sharing certain presuppositions about what will hold of any bearer of the term; it depends indeed, not just on there being such shared presuppositions, but also on its being recognized in common that those presuppositions are made. If I say "That is an M," then I cannot communicate anything more than that that is called an "M" unless it is presupposed in common between us – unless it is a priori so far as the conversation goes – that any M is going to have such and such properties, or at least a certain number of such and such properties. Those presuppositions, those contextually a priori principles, will be the relevant assumptions that serve for us as fixers of the meaning and reference of "M"; they will determine the content of what I communicate in saying to you that that is an M. They will be a sort of theory of M-ness that we share as participants in that conversation.

Of course there is an abstract possibility with a given term that the presuppositions which facilitate its communicative use vary wildly from one conversation to another, so that there are no presumptions that are associated robustly with the term; there are contextually a priori principles that govern its use in any situation but there are none that hold across different contexts. I think it is so unlikely that this occurs with a term like "right" that we need not dwell on this. When I debate with you as to whether what you did was right, or when you go on in another context to have a similar exchange with a third person, or when I consider with myself whether my own choice in some situation was the right one, there is no reason to think that now one set of presuppositions, now another, is serving to fix the content of what is said or thought. Perhaps in discussions between the members of a particular moral sect or circle the communicative use of the term turns on presuppositions that are specific to those people; perhaps it goes without saying between them, for example, that anything which is right must fit with the dictates of some authority. But since discussions of rightness flourish across the widest of sectarian gulfs, and not just in such in-group exchanges, variation of this kind cannot be ubiquitous. There must be some common presuppositions that serve to underpin more familiar out-group conversations. There must be some participant theory of rightness that is more or less widely shared: if you like, there must be some folk moral theory that gives us our bearings in discussions of rightness.

The Likely Shape of that Theory

The idea that the meaning and the reference of "right" is determined by certain shared presumptions, in particular by presumptions shared between consequentialists and their opponents, is not just appealing in the abstract. It is borne out by the fact that only a little reflection is required in order to find plausible candidates for the role of fixing the communicative potential of the term. The candidates may not be presumptions that are readily accessible to the reflection of ordinary participants in moral discourse. They are generally things to which such participants are committed only so far as they treat certain examples as paradigms of rightness, only so far as they recognize certain constraints in how to argue for the rightness of an option, only so far as they give certain grounds in support of claims of rightness, and only so far as they countenance certain sorts of challenges to those claims. They are things which the participants show themselves to believe rather than things which they need be readily disposed to avow. They are claims which the existing discourse-related dispositions of the participants would make compelling, did they understand them, not things that they must be currently in a position to understand (Pettit forthcoming).

Here is an illustrative list of some widely shared beliefs about rightness. They may not all figure in fixing the meaning or reference of the term "right" (more on this in the next section) but they are all certainly candidates for presumptions that help in that role.

1 If one option is right and others wrong, then the agent ought to take the right one: to say it is right in such a context is to prescribe the option or at least to approve of it.

2 If one option is right and others wrong, then the right option is better in certain respects than the alternatives.

3 The rightness-relevant respects – the values – that serve to make one option better than others include such features as being fair, being honest, relieving need, being an act of friendship or loyalty, and so on.

4 Values vary in strength, so that the value displayed by one option – for example, that it is honest – may be overridden by a different value displayed by another: say, that it will prevent a murder; thus the dishonest option may be the right one.

5 A right option that is chosen because it is right will always be unobjectionable or justifiable; no one will be able to find good reason to blame the agent for taking it.

6 A number of options in any choice may sometimes be equally unobjectionable, even when one is better than others, even when one is an act of supererogatory merit. In such a case, depending on context, the word "right" may be used loosely for any unobjectionable option in the set or more strictly for the best option.

7 There may be no right option in some hard choices; there may be no option which is unobjectionable, to go to the weak usage of "right," and no option that counts as best and deserves to be called "right" in the stronger sense.

8 A right option will prove more attractive to the agent than a wrong option to the extent that the agent sees that it is better and does not suffer a malaise of the spirit, a weakness of will, or something of that kind.

9 The virtuous person is reliably disposed to recognize right options and to choose only such options.

10 A uniquely right option will present itself as something that the agent has to do: as something that binds or obligates them.

11 If one option is right and another wrong, then there must be some difference between them besides any difference in rightness or in rightness-making respects; the options must be descriptively as well as evaluatively distinguishable. (Rightness is descriptively supervenient, as it is said.)

12 If any two choices and options correspond in all respects other than those involving particular individuals – if they correspond, for example, in everything other than the identity of the agent – then if one option is a right choice for the agent in the first case, the corresponding option is a right choice for the agent in the second. (Rightness is universalizable.)

13 There are various paradigms of right choice with which any user of the term will be familiar, even if there are few paradigms that will be common to all.

14 If an option is right, or has any evaluative property, then everyone ought to believe that it is right or that it has that property; what is right or valuable in one perspective is right or valuable in all.

15 It is a matter of the greatest importance that an option is right or wrong, for the possibility of a decent human community depends on the possibility that what each does can be justified to others

This list of working assumptions about rightness may occasion a query. How could such assumptions serve to guide the usage of "right," it may be asked, when many of them involve words that are so closely tied to it as "ought to," "better than," "unobjectionable," "virtue," and so on? How could they serve to guide the usage of "right" when it may well appear that we cannot understand many of the terms they use without in turn understanding the meaning and reference of "right" itself? The obvious answer is that if the presumptions that prove to determine the meaning and reference of "right" involve terms of this kind, then they must help at the same time to determine the meaning and reference of the other terms. We should think of "right" and those other terms as being bound together by the presumptions in such a constrained way that, at least in the presence of suitable paradigms, the presumptions simultaneously determine the meanings and references of the lot. In short, we should think of the terms as each occupying a distinctive position in a network of connections with the other terms: a position which is distinctive enough, at least in the presence of actual paradigms, to fix the meaning and reference of each (Jackson and Pettit 1995).

What will it be, then, to say or think that a certain option is right? It will be to envisage that it has that property – that unique property, as it is assumed – on which we triangulate from the different network connections. It has that property associated in such and such ways with being what ought to be done, with being better than alternatives, with being unobjectionable, with being attractive, and so on. The content of the thought that the option is right will be a content that is accessible only on a holistic basis and only on a basis that simultaneously makes related contents accessible too.

I had observed that if the rightness question is to divide consequentialists from their various opponents, then the question had better be understood in the same way on all sides. By the account just given, what all sides presuppose in asking what makes a given option right is that rightness is identified as the satisfier of a variety of conditions, including, if the network picture is right, a variety of connections with other moral properties. The challenge that is taken up in different ways by the different sides is the challenge to say which presumptive conditions or connections are the crucial ones in the determination of rightness. Which presumptions are a priori for purposes of moral discourse and, among those that are a priori which, if any, are fundamental: which are such that if we take them as axioms we can derive the rest as theorems? If you like, which presumptions serve to provide us with the ultimate criterion of rightness?

We move on to consider the different answers to that question in the next section. But there are a couple of matters which it will be useful to address before we do that. One bears on the nature of the property of rightness that we have to postulate, if we are to think in cognitivist terms. The other, which is of greater relevance to our immediate concerns, bears on the method whereby we may expect the question of rightness to be resolved.

The Nature of Rightness

Can we say anything more on the nature of the property of rightness that is picked out via the sorts of presumptions envisaged for our participant theory? It might be thought that we cannot without involving ourselves in contingent and a posteriori assumptions about the nature of the world and, in particular, about the sorts of property that it offers as targets on which we might triangulate from relevant conditions and connections. Consider an analogy. I may identify the kind of thing that an automobile throttle is on the basis of its required connections with other things in a car. I may identify it as an instrument that is directly controlled by the driver, that ensures that a greater or lesser amount of fuel is made available to the engine and that thereby controls how fast the car goes under any given conditions. But if I am to be able to derive anything more about the nature of the throttle in a particular sort of car I have to draw on empirical assumptions about how the car is constructed. It may seem, in parallel to this, that if I am to be able to derive anything more about the nature of the property that we triangulate on under the name of rightness, then I must be able to draw on empirical assumptions about how the world is constructed: say, on physicalist assumptions to the effect that the world is composed entirely out of microphysical materials and is completely controlled by microphysical laws (Pettit 1993c).

Surprisingly, however, this is not so. There is something more that we can say about the property that we triangulate on under the name of rightness – and indeed about any other properties that we may triangulate on from within the moral network – without having to draw on any empirical assumptions. One of the central presumptions for rightness and for other evaluative properties – the supervenience principle – is that if two items differ in regard to such a property, then they differ in a purely descriptive way. We endorse this presumption in ordinary discourse to the extent that we countenance the challenge to back up any evaluative discrimination – any discrimination to the effect that this is right and that is wrong, for example, this is just and that is unjust, he is virtuous and she unvirtuous – with a discrimination of a purely descriptive kind. No evaluative difference without a descriptive difference. No evaluative difference even between whole worlds without some descriptive difference in those worlds (Jackson and Pettit 1995). And that means that the property that we identify under an evaluative specification – the property that we identify as rightness, or justice, or virtue, or unobjectionability, or whatever – must be descriptively specifiable too. There must, in principle, be a descriptive mode of picking out all and only the bearers of the property; the property must have a descriptive character.

What makes a specification evaluative, it may be asked, what descriptive? I assume that an evaluative specification, but not a descriptive specification, will connect with presumptions about justification and the like. Thus it will be a priori true that any evaluatively specified property, taken as such, can play a justificatory sort of role whereas nothing of the kind will be a priori true in relation to descriptively specified properties. The claim that an evaluative property – an evaluatively specifiable property – is also descriptively specifiable is a very substantive claim, it should be noticed. An evaluative property will not be descriptively specifiable just because it can be indirectly identified, say as the property that so-and-so is thinking about, in descriptive terms. Such an indirect identification picks out the property by means of its having the distinct descriptive property that so-and-so is thinking about it. A descriptive specification proper will pick out the property without relying on such further connections (see Jackson and Pettit 1996 and Van Roojen 1996).

Assume that the participant moral theory from which we start in moral discourse, the theory which fixes the meaning or reference of moral terms, involves presumptions that refer us to connections between different moral terms. That means that each term, and in particular the term "right," picks out its referent as something that fits the function or role identified by those connections; it picks it out as a realizer of those linkages. What we have just seen is that the realizer in question in each case must be a descriptive property. What is the property of rightness, then? It is that descriptive property – though we have no prospect of giving its descriptive specification – which makes an option imperative for the agent, which makes any similar option imperative for any similar agent, which is instantiated in virtue of such and such values, which serves to make an option unobjectionable, to attract agents who are not weak of will, to connect reliably with virtue, and so on.[3]

The Method of Resolving the Question of Rightness

The question of rightness, as we presented it above, is that of deciding which presumptions are the crucial ones in the determination of rightness: which are a priori for purposes of moral discourse and among those a priori assumptions which, if any, are fundamental; which, if any, serve as axioms from which to derive the others. Understood in this way, the question of rightness is a question in metaethics and it parallels the metaethical questions that may be raised about the nature of value in general, about the nature of particular values like fairness, and about the nature of approval, justification, and the like.

But metaethics, I now want to emphasize, inevitably shades off into normative ethics; that is, it shades off into the enterprise of resolving ground-level issues about what is right in particular sorts of situations. The evidence that certain presumptions are a priori for rightness is that we cannot imagine right options that do not satisfy them. We might take the best metaethical theory of rightness as that which identifies the presumptions that best fit what by our current judgments are right options. But the fact is that our current judgments of rightness are often divergent, often inconsistent and often vague. And so it is natural to take the best metaethical theory – the best account of the fundamental a priori postulates for rightness – as that which gives us presumptions that fit the judgments of rightness that we are disposed to adopt as we look for greater convergence, greater consistency, and greater precision than our current judgments offer. But in identifying the judgments that we want to adopt in this way – in identifying the normative ethics we want to espouse – we will look among other things for judgments that fit with presumptions about rightness that are reasonably intuitive and theoretically satisfying; we will look for a normative ethics that is satisfactory, not only in matching considered intuition, but also in pairing off with an intuitive and attractive metaethics. Metaethics and normative ethics are inextricably connected with one another.

Otherwise formulated, the observation made here is that any equilibrium we are likely to achieve between our metaethical principles and the particular judgments of rightness that we defend in our normative ethics is bound, in John Rawls's (1971) phrase, to be a reflective equilibrium. It is bound to be achieved in a process of adjusting, now the general principles or presumptions, now the particular judgments. Different accounts of the nature of rightness, different accounts of the presumptions that ought to be taken as fundamental in determining rightness, will go with different accounts of the right lines to take on a variety of ground-level questions. Not only should we expect consequentialism, for example, to give us an account of what it ultimately is that makes one option right and another wrong; we should also expect it to defend particular views on what is the right thing to do in a variety of situations. No surprise, then, to find that consequentialists are associated, not just with a distinctive view of the nature of rightness, but with distinctive ethical positions on a number of ground-level questions.

While the question of rightness is a metaethical question about which presumptions should serve to fix the meaning and reference of the term "right," therefore, it is at the same time a question that bears on which sorts of options we ought to take as right in various situations; it is at the same time a question in normative ethics. Before leaving this discussion of method, one further query calls to be answered. Does the search for a reflective equilibrium hold out the prospect that we will each be led towards a different set of views and, in the process, towards a different way of triangulating on rightness: towards a different way of understanding the term "right"?

If this happened then that would mean that we could not continue to debate the rightness of different choices, for we would each mean and refer to a different property in talking of what was right: the property answering to our different, revised presumptions. But the very fact that reflectively equilibrating on a purely personal basis – that is, without concern for where others are led – would lead to such a Babel provides reason for thinking that one of the concerns in reflective equilibration should be to bring other people with you; in this sense – and it is not the only one associated with the word – the reflective equilibrium should be wide (Rawls 1995: 141; see Pettit 1994b: 218–19). Were reflective equilibration to lead us in quite different directions, then it would lead to a breach of what are surely very basic presumptions: that rightness is an intersubjective matter for us to debate in common and that issues of rightness, issues of justification, are of the greatest importance to us in organizing our lives together. Let the business of rightness diversify into different enterprises – a different one for different individuals or different coteries of individuals – and it is not clear that it remains a moral business: a business of testing and claiming justification, not just among your kindred spirits, but in society at large.

If we were forced to admit the impossibility of reflectively equilibrating in the same direction, then we would be forced to give up on the participant theory of rightness with which we currently work; we would be forced to say that the theory fails to direct us to any single property and that in this sense it is deeply in error. We may yet be forced to take this view – some would say that we are indeed forced to take it – but the important thing is that we should resist the view until the very last. It involves holding that we each mean different things by the moral words we use – we each mean things that answer to our own particular presumptions – and that moral discourse fails to achieve its main objective (see Pettit 1997b).

3 Different Answers to the Question of Rightness

Anti-theory

Before coming to the accounts which consequentialism and rival theories provide of the presumptions that fix the meaning and reference of "right," it is important to recognize that there is one approach that would undermine the debate between those doctrines. This approach argues that it is impossible to identify any favored set of presumptions as the fundamental determinants of the meaning and reference of "right" and that the only answer to the question of what makes a right option right is ultimately the fact that it is right. If there is a shared moral theory at the origin of our use of "right" and other moral words, then it is not a theory that we can ever usefully articulate or axiomatize. There are many different versions of this approach but they all serve to underpin an anti-theoretical line and so I lump them together under the label of "anti-theory" (see Gaita 1991; Louden 1992).

We can usefully distinguish three major types of anti-theory. One is the approach that is often described as intuitionism (Rawls 1971: 34–40). This holds that while we may be able to say that the right option is that which best coheres with relevant values, for example with relevant desiderata or duties – while we may be able to go that far with what I later describe as value theory – there is no possibility of spelling out what coherence involves. The problem is, allegedly, that the principles whereby we weight those values defy abstract specification; we rely on intuition to tell us, case by case, how relevant values weigh against one another and what option they determine as right.

A second anti-theoretical approach can be described as particularism or contextualism (see Dancy 1993; McNaughton 1988; Timmons 1996). This argues that there is no saying what will lead us to see an option as right in advance of particular issues and so that there is no saying what in the abstract makes a right option right. As we consider what is right in one context, the satisfaction of this or that presumption may weigh heavily in support of a particular option; as we consider what is right in another, different presumptions may assume significance and the satisfaction of the original presumption may carry no weight or may even weigh in the opposite direction. Moral argument is essentially contextual, so it is said, and depending on the context involved, any of the sorts of presumptions mentioned may be introduced as relevant and as relevant in a positive or negative way. There is no privileged set of presumptions and no set of presumptions that always play the same role in the determination of rightness. Hence there is no prospect of ever specifying, or even outlining the shape of, a criterion of rightness. The idea of a criterion of rightness is essentially illusory.

A third anti-theoretical approach represents a variety of what is often known as virtue ethics, though a variety that is distinguishable from what I later describe as a virtue theory of rightness. This approach puts great emphasis on the virtue of practical wisdom and argues that there is no way of systematizing the considerations to which judgment is sensitive – sensitive in a quasi-perceptual way – when a wise agent passes verdicts on what is right and what is wrong (see Beiner 1983; McDowell 1981). Ethical judgment is like aesthetic judgment, under this account of things. While it may be defended by reference to one or another supporting consideration, such reasons never exhaust the practical know-how encoded in the judgment; all they ever do is to pick out certain aspects of the inarticulable complex to which the wise judger will be attending.

All of these approaches derive a certain plausibility from the fact that ethical judgment is a complex, situationally sensitive business in which we are often conscious of having to take account of more than we can readily put in words. But the fact is that we challenge one another to justify our judgments of rightness and that as we press such challenges, we are never content to be told that the option under question is right because it answers to some inarticulable weighting system, or because it is supported by contextually relative considerations, or because it reveals its rightness to the judgment of a suitably virtuous agent. We want to know what singles the option out from alternatives, in particular what singles it out in respects that we recognize in choice situations generally as having justificatory relevance. The practice of ethical challenge and response strongly suggests that rightness is not as theoretically elusive a property as these approaches would make it. Or so at any rate I shall assume.

Not only are the approaches unpersuasive, however, they also fall foul of a general and important problem. If ethical judgment is to be judgment proper, then the semantic content of that judgment – including the meaning and reference of "right" – must be fixed independently of particular judgmental dispositions and context. It must be fixed, moreover, in such a salient way that by everyone's lights a person judging has to remain faithful to that independent content – faithful to an independently determined meaning and reference for "right" – in passing judgment on this or that particular case. The trouble with all of the anti-theoretical approaches is that they make it seem that the content of ethical judgment, in particular the meaning and reference of "right," is too fluid to be able to serve as the required sort of independent constraint. For all the evidence that would be available if these approaches were sound, it would not be salient that there is an independent content available to constrain ethical judgment. People involved in ethical judgment could be making up the content as they went along; they could be involved in an enterprise that does not deserve the name of "judgment."

I shall have nothing further to say in this essay on anti-theory. The anti-theoretical approach dismisses the question that divides consequentialism from its rivals, not acknowledging the validity of the challenge to articulate and perhaps axiomatize the presumptions that fix the meaning and reference of "right." In setting itself against such a theory of rightness – against such an attempt to sketch out a criterion for rightness – it sets itself *a fortiori* against a consequentialist theory. But the anti-theoretical variety of non-consequentialism is not as plausible as the more theoretical forms of opposition – not at least to my eye – and I shall give it no further attention here.

Different Theories of Rightness

What other, more theoretical, lines might we follow in responding to the question of rightness? By the account that we have given, everyone identifies rightness on the basis of certain shared, tacit presumptions about what must hold of any right option. Different theories of rightness come into view as we see different ways in which people may select from those presumptions, and may systematize the presumptions selected, in spelling out their preferred criterion of rightness: their preferred account as to what it is that makes a right option right.

Three broad varieties of theory are particularly salient. The attempt to spell out a criterion of rightness may start from central presumptions that give a certain structure to rightness: say, the presumptions that associate rightness with prescription and that hold it to be subject to constraints like universalizability and supervenience; it may amount to what Susan Hurley (1989: 10– 15) describes as a centralist theory. Or the attempt to spell out a criterion may give importance to presumptions that associate rightness with other, less centrally placed matters as well. One non-centralist theory begins from the presumptions that link rightness with the reactions of certain respondents: say, with the judgment of the impartial spectator, with the choice of the virtuous agent, or with the lack of objection on the part of fellow agents. And a second sort of non-centralist theory begins from the presumptions that hold rightness to be answerable to values, arguing that an option is right if and only if it displays relevant valuable properties; consequentialism, as I shall argue, is a version of this approach.

These different approaches represent rival ways of articulating and axiomatizing the participant presumptions – axiomatizing them in a rough and ready sense – from which we triangulate or should triangulate on the property of rightness. It is possible for any such approach to be deeply revisionary of our ordinary views, rejecting some of the things that we might have been inclined to regard as platitudinous. But equally it is possible for any approach to save, not just the presumptions that it casts as axiomatic, but other common presumptions as well. The other presumptions may be derived as theorems that share the same a priori status as the axioms – in this case they retain a place in the participant moral theory – or they may be derived, in the context of plausible empirical assumptions, as things that contingently hold true; they may not belong to the participant theory proper but they remain matters of shared opinion. While admit-

ting broadly the same standard beliefs about rightness – no surprise there – the rival approaches can each hold up a different
presumption or set of presumptions as directing us to what ultimately or fundamentally makes an option the right one for an
agent to take or to have taken.

In doing this, of course, the approaches will almost certainly
lead us in different directions on particular issues of rightness;
they will support different judgments of rightness across a variety
of situations. To the extent that they do lead us in such different
directions, they will each have to argue that they represent a more
satisfactory mode of reflectively equilibrating principle and judgment than the alternatives. The debate between the approaches
will not bear just on which offers the theoretically most attractive
axiomatization but also on which represents the practically most
compelling moral perspective. It will be a debate that belongs at
once to metaethics and to normative ethics.

Universalizability Theory

The most important example of the first, centralist approach is
universalizability theory. This says that what constitutes an
option as right is the fact that it is uniquely capable of being
prescribed – held up as what the agent ought to do – and prescribed universally; that is, it is prescribed not just for this agent
but for any relevantly similar agent in relevantly similar circumstances. Such a theory will say that the other presumptions about
rightness are sound only so far as they can be derived from this
one. And, like any such theory, it may be more or less revisionary
on the question of what can and cannot be derived.

Universalizability theory may seem to run into problems, so far
as there are too few constraints on what different people may be
prepared to prescribe universally; I may be content to prescribe
this, you that, and so on. But the theory is usually espoused in
tandem with an assumption that is designed to beef up that constraint. Immanuel Kant assumed that for any option there is a way
of identifying a fairly general principle as the unique maxim that
the option instantiates and argued, on the basis of that assumption, for his famous Categorical Imperative. This holds that that an

option is right if and only if the maxim involved can be willed as a universal law that everyone follows (Kant 1966). Suppose I steal your book and that the maxim instantiated in my action is: let anyone steal another's property at will. That maxim cannot be willed as a universal law, so Kant would have argued, because the universal prescription of the maxim would amount to undermining the very institution of property that it supposes. And so by Kant's lights the stealing of property comes out as wrong.

R. M. Hare (1981) uses a different supplementary assumption in developing his universalizability theory of rightness. He assumes that the reasons why people are led to prescribe options for themselves, or for any other particular agents, are that the options promise to satisfy their own desires or preferences. He then goes on to argue that if a person is prepared to prescribe an option universally, and not just for themselves or for some other particular agent, then that must be because they see that no matter what their own particular position – no matter, for example, whether they are someone adversely affected – the choice of that option must represent something that is satisfactory in preference-related terms: this, at any rate, provided the person is not a fanatic. It must be a sort of option that promises to do pretty well by the preferences of everyone involved, that promises to maximize overall preference-satisfaction.[4]

It is noteworthy that while Hare's universalizability theory offers a non-consequentialist account of rightness – roughly, an account that links rightness with something other than the promotion of value – it leads to a view that those options which are right happen to have a characteristically consequentialist configuration; they happen to be just the options that maximize expected preference-satisfaction. Universalizability theory gives a non-consequentialist account of the role that the rightness property has to play: the role of being universally prescribable. But in Hare's version it leads to the view that the descriptive property that occupies or realizes that role, the descriptive property held in common by those options that prove to be universally prescribable, is one of maximizing expected preference-satisfaction.

Hare is not a consequentialist on the question of rightness, then – the role question – but he is a consequentialist on the related realizer question. He does not think that what makes an option right is that it maximizes expected preference-satisfaction; rather, what makes it right is that it is universally prescribable by ordinary, non-fanatical people. It is just that right options, on his view, all turn out to be options that maximize expected preference-satisfaction. Hare breaks with consequentialism on the upstream question of what makes an option right but, in arguing that right options satisfy the consequentialist constraint, he rejoins consequentialism at a point downstream.

With any centralist theory of rightness, any centralist theory of the essential characteristics of the rightness role, it is a more or less open question as to where the theory leads – leads a priori or leads in the light of empirical assumptions – on the realizer issue. Thus an upstream non-consequentialist theory may always lead to a downstream form of consequentialism, as on Hare's approach; indeed the same is true also of consequentialist theories that privilege people's responses (see Scanlon 1982: 115). Or an upstream form of non-consequentialism may lead to a downstream approach that is also non-consequentialist. According to Kant, for example, the universalizability theory of rightness leads at a downstream point, not to a Harean utilitarianism, but a sort of personalism. This is the view that it is never right for someone to treat another person just as a means, that other people must always be treated as ends in themselves.

Contract Theory and Virtue Theory

The second sort of approach to the question of rightness starts from non-centralist presumptions, in particular presumptions that link right options with various possible responses. These responses include: the response of fellow agents in finding no objection to the options; the response of the virtuous agent in finding that the options engage his or her dispositions; perhaps even the response of the idealized desirer in wanting that the agent should perform those options in the situations on hand.

Contract theory holds, in a formulation close to Tim Scanlon's (1982) – I shall take this as an exemplar of the family of doctrines possible – that what constitutes an option as right is that no one could reasonably object to it, under a scenario where it is a matter of common knowledge that people are seeking agreement with one another about matters of rightness. Contract theory takes the presumption that links being right with being unobjectionable and maintains that it represents an axiom – the parent presumption – from which the other presumptions, or at least the other reflectively compelling presumptions, derive. The idea is that in determining what is right we need only consider what is contractually satisfactory in the relevant way: that if we start from this basis then we shall find it possible to develop, not just an economical way of thinking about matters of rightness – not just an axiomatization of the plausible presumptions – but a way of thinking that generates judgments which prove on the whole to be congenial and compelling.

As I take contract theory to be a way of axiomatizing the presumptions for rightness, and of identifying the basis on which rightness is fundamentally determined, so I understand virtue theory in a corresponding manner. I take it to be the theory that the presumption from which other presumptions derive, and the ultimate determinant of rightness, is the principle according to which virtuous people are reliably disposed to recognize right options and only to choose from among such options (see Hursthouse 1991: 225; Oakley 1996). The idea is that, contrary to ordinary inclinations, we should not think that it is the independently constituted rightness of options that make them appealing to virtuous agents. Rather what we should say is that the rightness of any option is constituted by the fact that it is the option that the virtuous person would choose; the right option just is that option which virtue requires (McDowell 1979).

In taking contract theory and virtue theory as theories of rightness, as answers to my question of rightness, I should say that I am ignoring the very different things that people sometimes have in mind when they speak of contract theory and virtue theory (Slote 1992: 89–90). Virtue theory, as it appears in the literature, is a particularly multifaceted thing. Sometimes it seems to be just the belief that virtue is essential for reliable moral behaviour; sometimes it seems to be the belief that virtue is an epistemological precondition for recognizing the demands of morality (this fits with the anti-theoretical stance described earlier); and sometimes it seems to be the belief that the virtues are the primary goods or values. And, equally, contractualism is popularly understood in a variety of ways: sometimes it means just the belief that asking what people would contract into under certain circumstances is a useful heuristic for identifying the right; sometimes it means the belief that you cannot believe that something is right – you cannot be confirmed in that belief – without having grounds for believing that the option in question would pass one or another contractual test (Pettit 1994b); sometimes it means the belief that however rightness is determined, values are determined – values in general or particular values like fairness – as those properties that have a certain contractual appeal; and so on. Moreover, both virtue theory and contract theory may be taken, not as theories of rightness as such – not as general theories of rightness – but only as theories of rightness for certain restricted domains: say, as theories of what makes certain general principles or rules right, not as theories of what makes any choice right (see Scanlon 1982).

I shall consider only contract theory and virtue theory as examples of the second approach to the question of rightness. But other theories in this family are also possible. One would privilege the idealized desirer – the impartial spectator – rather than the contracting party or the virtuous agent, arguing that what makes an option right is just that it is what the idealized desirer would want the agent to do. If I do not discuss that theory explicitly it is because approaches that favor idealized desire, whether in a cognitivist (Smith 1994) or non-cognitivist (Blackburn 1984) version, are more naturally taken as theories of value rather than as theories of rightness proper. They trace the fact that an option has a moral or action-guiding appeal – it is *pro tanto* desirable – to the fact that there is an aspect under which it engages the idealized desirer. But in doing this they are not necessarily saying that an option is constituted as right by the fact that it would appeal to an idealized desirer (Smith 1994: 71–6). They may hold only that what makes properties into values – where rightness may be a function of value – is the fact that their bearers tend to engage idealized desire. If it is true that right options are options that would appeal to idealized desirers, that truth may not have axiomatic status on these approaches; it may derive from the truth about what makes properties values.

Value Theories

The third approach to the question of rightness that I want to distinguish begins from the non-centralist presumptions that link right options and valuable properties. The value theorist that I imagine – the axiologist, as it used to be said – holds that the fundamental assumption about rightness is that a right option always does better than a wrong option in regard to acknowledged values like fairness or honesty. The right option is the option that best coheres, under the best theory of coherence, with the values that are relevant in the situation on hand (Hurley 1989).

Like the other approaches discussed, value theory is best seen as a rival axiomatization of the presumptions about rightness, not as an approach that necessarily rejects presumptions that do not figure in its preferred base; it may preserve the other presumptions either as derived a priori truths or as contingently true generalizations. Value theory can save the universalizability assumption about rightness to the extent that it maintains a universalizability assumption about value. It can save the virtue-theoretic presumption by defining virtuous people as those who are sensitive to value and disposed to recognize the best options. And it can save the contract-theoretic presumption by taking options that are saliently best in regard to certain common values as precisely options to which others cannot object. In brief, it can acknowledge a wide network of presumptive connections for rightness – acknowledge them even as a priori – while giving an axiomatic status to the association between rightness and value.

Value theory is a schema that fits a variety of quite different substantive theories and we need to identify the rival doctrines that may be put forward from this quarter. As we have seen, there are different varieties of universalizability theory, contract theory, and virtue theory. But those possible variations are as nothing compared to the different directions in which the value-theoretic approach may be taken.

There are two dimensions on which the value-theoretic approach can ramify. First of all, the values that are relevant in the determination of rightness may be restricted to neutral values such as happiness, freedom, wisdom, solidarity, friendship; if these are values, then they are values for all. Or, alternatively, the values relevant to rightness may be held to include also certain relativized values such as the value for you, whoever you are, of being sufficient in yourself, or of looking after your own children, or of advancing the interests of your country. Both of these sorts of values are universal, in the sense that in specifying them we need not rigidly refer – say, need not refer by name – to any particular individual person or place; thus they are not like the value associated, in President Chirac's words, with the higher interest of France. I shall assume that the only values countenanced in moral thought are universal in this way and henceforth shall speak just of neutral and relativized values, taking it for granted that the values involved are universal in character.

But not only may the values invoked as determinants of rightness be neutral or relativized in character. They may also be taken to determine rightness in either of at least two broadly contrasted ways. Under the standard reading, the right option in any choice will be that which best promotes the relevant value or values, however promotion is more exactly analyzed. Under an alternative, it will be that which relates to the value – say, that which instantiates it – in such a manner that the value is honored, even if it is not promoted (Pettit 1991a).

The best way of explaining the distinction between neutral and relativized values may be to consider a situation where we are told that there is a value present and that there is someone who values it. The value will be a neutral value, we can say, if and only if we can know what it is that is valued without knowing who the valuer is. It will be a relativized value, on the other hand – an agent-relative or agent-centred value (Nagel 1986; Parfit 1984) – if and only if we cannot know what it is that is valued without knowing the valuer's identity.

Suppose that you are the valuer. Under the proposed test, then, it will be a relativized value that you be self-sufficient, that you care for your children, that you do your duty, that you keep your hands clean of guilt, even that your country win lots of Olympic medals. We do not know what it is that is valued in any of these cases, and so cannot identify the valued prospect in question, without knowing who you, the valuer, are. We do not know whose self-sufficiency is to be advanced, whose children are to be cared for, whose duties are to be discharged, unless we know who you are.

According to the test outlined, however, it will be a neutral value that happiness increase, that there be a greater degree of freedom in the world, and indeed that people become self-sufficient or love their children. That people become self-sufficient or love their children are reflexive values in the sense that they involve states of affairs where agents do things that are identified essentially by reference to who they are. But such reflexive values are still such that we can identify the states of affairs in question without knowing who you, the valuer, are; we know that what is required is that everyone should be self-sufficient or should look after their children. The prospects in question count, like happiness and freedom, as things that are values for all, if they are values for anyone.

The distinction between promoting and honoring a value is most easily explained by reference to the different responses that people take to a value like that of peace. Some pacifists say that the important thing for any country is to do all it can to promote peace. Bertrand Russell was a good example of this attitude. It led him to oppose British involvement in the First World War, even to the point of getting himself imprisoned. But it led him, because of his different estimate of what peace required, to support Britain's involvement in the Second World War. His attitude was that being peace-loving, as he thought Britain should be peace-loving, meant doing all that the promotion of peace required and while that meant avoiding wars that did nothing for the cause of peace – as most wars do indeed do nothing for peace – it entailed waging wars, however reluctantly, that genuinely looked necessary for the long-run prospects of peace.

Other pacifists take a different view. Many Quakers who went to prison with Russell during the First World War were shocked at the support that he was prepared to give to the Second. They may well have thought that Britain's participation in the Second World War increased the chances of peace in a world where an unopposed Hitler would otherwise run amok; they may well have thought that Britain's participation was necessary to promote peace. But they took the view that a peace-loving country should instantiate peace, not necessarily promote it.

While instantiating peace may not mean promoting it – while it may come apart from promoting peace in the context of a Nazi state – instantiation still bears a salient relation to promotion. To instantiate a value is to behave in the way that would promote the value in a world, roughly, where others were equally compliant. It is to honor the value in an intuitive sense; it is to do your proper part – your part under an idealized scheme of general compliance – by the value. The general idea behind the non-promotional line is that with any value the thing for an agent to do is not necessarily to promote it but to behave in a way that would promote it in a suitably compliant context, even if it does not promote it in the actual, imperfect world. The thing for the agent to do is honor the value, whether or not honoring it means promoting it.

An agent may honor a value in this sense, even if it is not a value bearing primarily on how to act, as in the case of peace, even if it is not a value that calls to be instantiated. Whether the value be that of political liberty, human happiness, or my own self-sufficiency I always face the choice either of promoting or of honoring that good. I may seek to promote political freedom by using my power in government to suppress a dangerous group of fanatics. Or I may honor it by renouncing measures that themselves violate people's freedom. I may seek to promote human happiness by taking measures which, while they make this or that person unhappy, promise to do more than compensate in the case of others. Or I may seek to honor human happiness by refusing to take any measures which deny happiness to some, whatever the effects of this refusal, in particular, whatever the effects of the refusal in terms of overall happiness.[5] Finally, I may seek to promote my own self-sufficiency by doing whatever promises the best self-sufficiency returns over the course of a lifetime, even if this involves putting myself temporarily in the hands of a master and ceasing to be self-sufficient for the period in question. Or I may seek to honor my own self-sufficiency by refusing ever to compromise myself in such a manner: by insisting at every point on remaining independent of others, even where that refusal at early stages in my life will do worse for my long-run self-sufficiency than would a period of apprenticeship.[6]

To believe that the right thing for any agent to do is to honor a certain value is distinct, I should emphasize, from believing that

the right thing is always to do whatever will promote the corresponding reflexive value. Take the value of peace. To believe that
the right thing for any agent, say for any country, is to honor the
value of peace – to do its part, however that is understood, in
relation to peace – is not to think that the right thing for it to do is
to promote the reflexive value of each such country's doing its
part in relation to peace. That reflexive goal might require a
country to wage war in order to promote the goal and the honoring
theorist will not allow that possibility. This theorist says that a
country should honor peace independently of a reference to any
such reflexive goal. Honoring a value V is distinct from promoting
the reflexive goal – the neutral goal – of every agent's doing their
part in relation to V.

I have characterized honoring by reference ultimately to promotion. Honoring a value, I said, is acting in the way that would
promote it in, roughly, a compliant world. But what does it mean
to promote a value?

Some say that to promote a value is not necessarily to maximize
it but just to produce enough of it, by some contextual measure of
sufficiency: to "satisfice", not necessarily to optimize, in relation
to the value (Slote 1989). I disagree, on the grounds that when
other things are equal, there can never be reason to produce less of
a value rather than more (Pettit 1984). Some suggest that what
makes an action right is that it promotes the best actual consequences – that it maximizes actual value – not that it meets a
more probabilistic constraint (Lewis 1969). Again I disagree, this
time on the grounds that an option which maximizes actual value
may be very objectionable (Jackson 1991). Suppose that a doctor
prescribes a drug for a non-fatal skin condition and that the drug
has a 10 per cent chance of killing the patient. Imagine now that
the drug does not kill and that the complaint is cured. The decision made by the doctor maximizes actual value but there are
clearly good grounds for objecting to the doctor's procedure.

What sort of probabilistic constraint should maximizing satisfy
in order to count as promoting value? The most straightforward
suggestion is the decision-theoretic one that to promote a value,
V, is to maximize its expected realization. Suppose we don't
know if circumstance $C1$ or $C2$ is going to obtain. To maximize
expected V is to maximize the sum of two products: V times the

probability associated with *C1* and *V* times the probability associated with *C2*. This approach to promotion may be taken in different ways as the appropriate probability is cast as conditional or unconditional, and as subjective or objective, and as relevant alternatives are differently identified in any choice, but I shall abstract from such issues here (see Jackson and Pargetter 1986).

The distinction between values and the distinction between value-responses cross one another and give a matrix with four compartments.

	Neutral values	Neutral and relativized values
Promoting response	1	2
Honoring response	3	4

This matrix gives us a picture of the different directions in which the value-theoretic approach to rightness may be taken. The value theorist may say that the values which determine rightness are all neutral values or that they include also relativized values. And in either case the value theorist may say that they determine rightness in the promotional or the honoring fashion.

Consequentialism

These distinctions enable us, finally, to identify the answer to the question of rightness that I think of as the teleological or consequentialist response. The consequentialist says, first, that values determine rightness in the promotional, not the honoring way. And the consequentialist says, second, that the values which determine rightness are all neutral values, not values that have a distinctively relativized reference.

No one is likely to quarrel with my characterization of consequentialists as being concerned with the promotion of value, rather than with its honoring. Honoring a given value – say, the good of truth-telling, or respect for property, or indeed peace – would require, not that the agent do whatever best promotes the value, but rather that they perform that sort of act, assuming there is a salient category, which is such that if every agent performed it – every agent, including themselves at later times – then the good would indeed be best promoted overall. But this runs counter to the central core in the received idea of consequentialism. True, rule-consequentialists argue for something like an honoring line (Hooker 1994). They say consequentialism points us to what makes certain principles right but that what makes more specific options right is the fact that they instantiate – instantiate and intuitively honor – the principles or values in question. Such thinkers, however, are incomplete or, in J. J. C. Smart's terms (1967), restricted consequentialists. They go part of the way, and only part of the way, with consequentialists proper.

It may be readily conceded that consequentialists, under any representation, defend a promotional view of how rightness is fixed by values and that they spurn the honoring approach. But why associate consequentialism with the view that it is only neutral values that serve in this promotional way to determine rightness? The answer is that otherwise it will be possible to represent characteristically non-teleological positions as forms of consequentialism. Take someone who says that they want to promote value but that they countenance relativized values such as looking after their own future, caring for their own children, discharging the duties assigned to them, respecting the rights of those who happen to make direct claims on them, and so on. Such a person will defend characteristically non-consequentialist lines on a broad range of topics: they will insist on special commitments to oneself or one's children or they will cast such attachments as external constraints on morality (Wolf 1982); or they will defend a deontological emphasis that makes duty or obligation primary to maximizing the good; or they will maintain that certain rights – natural rights (Nozick 1974) – enjoy such primacy. Indeed it will be hard to distinguish the person from someone who says that their aim is to honor certain reflexive values: say, that of each person's looking after their own future, caring for their own children, discharging their duties, respecting the rights of those who deal directly with them, and so on. Consequentialism will only retain a distinctive profile of its own if it stipulates, not just that right options promote value, but that the values which they promote are neutral in character.

Our characterization of consequentialism opposes it, then, to two rival sorts of value theory: the sort that makes room for the honoring response and the sort that gives a place to relativized values. But this should not be surprising, for those opposed theories have a lot in common.

The person who believes in the honoring of neutral values – the person who takes rightness to be determined on such a basis – stands in contrast to someone who holds that an option may be made right by how it serves such relativized ends as their helping their own children or friends or country, their carrying out their duties, or their not offending against the rights of anyone who comes into direct contact with them. But the contrast covers up a more basic similarity. For however far the first person insists on the importance of the neutral values hailed, what they really prize is their doing their part in relation to those values, not their promoting the values. Thus they can be seen as having a concern to promote the relativized value of their doing their part in that sense. They can be seen as defending, ultimately, the same sort of relativism about values that the other sort of non-consequentialist espouses. Both approaches make some ultimate value or values relative to the person valuing; both embrace a sort of valuer-relativism (Sen 1982).

The contrast between consequentialism and these two sorts of valuer-relativist theory comes out in the different way they perform on an artificial but revealing test.[7] Imagine that a valuer is given full information on different ways the world may be as a result of agents acting differently and on how relevant values are satisfied in those different possible worlds. Suppose that they are not told who they are in those worlds; thus they do not know how they act in the worlds imagined, and they do not know how they or theirs fare. Can the valuer use the function that determines rightness, according to their view of rightness, to rank those worlds?

If the valuer adopts a consequentialist perspective, then this will be no problem. The function that determines rightness according to such a person – the promotion of neutral value –

will lead them to rank at the top that world in which neutral value is maximized. But if the valuer espouses relativized values, or if the valuer believes in honoring values, then it will be impossible for them to use their function for determining rightness to rank the worlds. The valuer must know who they are in the worlds surveyed if they are to tell how far the relativized things they cherish – their looking after their children, their keeping their promises – are realized in the different worlds. And equally they must know who they are if they are to tell how far they honor the relevant neutral values, how far they do their part and keep their hands clean, in the different worlds.

Is it an adequate account of consequentialism or teleology to say that it is that species of value theory which holds that the rightness of an option goes with its promoting the relevant neutral values? I believe so. Many consequentialists endorse further commitments. Some are utilitarians, for example, who hold that the only relevant value is happiness. Some are subjectivists who hold that the only relevant values are those which involve human sensibility. Some are "subsequentialists," as we might call them, who hold that values are relevant only so far as their promotion affects the future. I abstract, however, from such extra commitments. Under my conception of consequentialism or teleology, it amounts to nothing more than the view that rightness is determined on the basis of the promotion of neutral – neutral and, of course, universal – values; it says nothing on what the relevant values are.

Not only does consequentialism say nothing on the nature of the values by reference to which rightness is determined. It does not suppose even that there are always values available by reference to which the rightness of a certain option or subset of options is determined in a given choice (*pace* Freeman 1995). For all that the consequentialist says, it may be that there are some choices where no option is right, a possibility that is signalled in one of our illustrative presumptions. The consequentialist will have to say that where there is no right option there can be no best option, since rightness goes with bestness on this account, and that means that some story must be given – say, in terms of the incomplete ordering of our values (Anderson 1993) – to explain how there can be no best option. But the important point is that consequentialism is not forced to hold that there is always a best and a right option in any choice, though it does naturally assume that there will usually be such an option. In this as in many other ways, the doctrine is relatively non-committal.

This completes our illustrative account of different sorts of responses that may be given to the question of rightness: the undercutting, anti-theoretical response, the answer of universalizability theory, the contract-theoretic and virtue-theoretic answers, and the different answers that fall under the heading of value-theory. These latter include the consequentialist answer which privileges the promotion of neutral values and the valuer-relativist answers which favor other sorts of values or another, non-promotional sort of response. I turn in the next section to put the case for the consequentialist answer.

4   In Favor of the Consequentialist Answer to the Question of Rightness

My argument in favor of consequentialism is conducted in this section in three main steps. First, I argue that universalizability theory suffers from an indeterminacy that thinkers like Kant and Hare do not satisfactorily remedy. Second, I try to show that there is a common failure which makes contract-theoretic and virtue-theoretic approaches much less appealing than a value-theoretic line. I believe that such problems will affect any approach that follows the centralist pattern illustrated by universalizability theory or that seeks to determine rightness by reference to human responses. And then, third, I argue that those value-theoretic lines which favor the honoring of values or that countenance relativized values are all subject to a serious difficulty that consequentialism avoids. The difficulties identified in each case involve failures to satisfy compelling presumptions about rightness and they argue for a rejection of the approaches, independently of where it may be found that the approaches lead us in particular judgments of rightness.

Philip Pettit

Against Universalizability Theory

The claim that a right option in any choice is one that can be universally prescribed raises the question, as we noticed, that there seem to be few constraints on which choices can be universally prescribed, so that almost anything looks capable of being justified under this approach. Suppose I steal a book from someone on the eve of a vital examination. I may not be able to prescribe universally that anyone can take another's property at will but I will certainly be able to prescribe universally that anyone on the eve of a vital examination can steal a book from another if the other does not need the book, if the book makes the difference between passing and failing the examination, if failing the examination would represent a result of horrific dimensions, and so on.

Kant and Hare, as I mentioned, can be seen as each making a move that is designed to remedy this problem. But neither move succeeds. Kant just assumes that there is a unique maxim, or a uniquely suitable maxim, associated with any option: say, in our example, the maxim that anyone can take another's property at will. But that assumption is hard to sustain. There is no known method or algorithm whereby we can be reliably directed to the maxim on whose universal prescribability the rightness of the option depends. And there is no plausibility in the claim that we can just tell in every case what the relevant maxim is: that innate or culturally shaped intuition can do the job. Kantian philosophers have begun to investigate reasons for not being troubled by the indeterminacy problem but these are unlikely to support a continued attachment to his pure universalizability theory of rightness (see Herman 1993; Korsgaard 1996; O'Neill 1975, 1989).

Hare's response to the indeterminacy difficulty assumes that when I prescribe an option for myself I prescribe it on the grounds that it promises to serve my desires well; he goes on to argue, then, that when I impose the universal prescribability test, I have to satisfy myself that the option promises to serve well the desires of all those affected. If he is right, then the test is extremely discriminating; it picks out in each case the option that a certain sort of utilitarian would favor. But it is demonstrable, I believe, that Hare is not right about this (Pettit 1987; Pettit and Smith 1990).

Most of the actions that I prescribe for myself are prescribed on grounds that do not refer to my own desire-satisfaction, even though I must desire them if I am to do them. I prescribe a morning at the desk, away from my students, because it is important to finish a paper, not because I want to satisfy my desire to finish it: not, that is, because finishing it would remove that desire in the way eating would remove hunger. I prescribe a regular mathematics exercise with my children because it would help them at school, not because I want to satisfy my desire to help them: not, that is, because going through the exercise would relieve that desire as scratching would relieve an itch. Suppose I ask whether I can universally prescribe such an option, then. Suppose I ask whether I can prescribe the option for anyone in my position and regardless of who I am: regardless of whether I am a student neglected by my teacher's morning at the desk, for example, or regardless of whether I am a child imposed upon by their overbearing father. What to answer?

Hare's line is that I cannot universally prescribe such an option, or at least that I may not be able to do so, because reflecting on what I would desire in the position of others affected is liable to undermine my current desire and therefore my current disposition to prescribe it. As I imagine that as a student I might feel neglected, so the line goes, this will impact on my current desire to finish the paper. And as I imagine that as a child I might resent a mathematical drill with my father, this will tend to undo my current attraction to the exercise. But this is surely mistaken. For if my grounds for prescribing the morning at the desk, or the mathematical exercise, have nothing essentially to do with satisfying my desires – my desires as distinct from those of my students or children – then reflecting on how my actions will frustrate the desires of my students or children need have no particular impact on my prescriptions. As I imagine that as a student I might feel neglected, I am likely to think that that is because I would not then be recognizing the importance of finishing the paper. And as I imagine that as a child I might resent a mathematical drill with my father, I will be disposed to conclude that that is because I would not then be sensitive to the importance of having a grounding in mathematics. In neither case would the test tend to force me towards a utilitarian sort of decision. As Kant's way of making the test determinate fails to work, so I believe does Hare's.

It is no accident that universalizability theory suffers from the indeterminacy discussed. The universalizability test is intuitively compelling when it is understood, not as a test of the rightness of an option, but as a test of whether the values introduced in justification of a choice are really good justifying reasons. The test is to ask whether you would be willing to see them mandate all the counterpart choices that they would justify in other situations if they justify this choice in this situation. The test is to ask whether, given a value-based justification – given something close to a Kantian maxim – that justification can be endorsed, not just for the case on hand, but for all those cases which are alike in universal features. But if the indeterminacy problem is solved only when such a value-based justification is already in place then that suggests that values play a more basic role in the determination of rightness than universalizability itself. It suggests that, as consequentialists think, we should be looking towards value-theory in seeking a criterion of rightness.

Against Contract Theory and Virtue Theory

As I described them, both contract theory and virtue theory start out from an assumption that there is a certain epistemological position on rightness that is privileged. The person of virtue is privileged to the extent that rightness is characterized just as that property that is reliably tracked under the promptings of virtue. The contracting parties are privileged to the extent that rightness is characterized just as that property that is reliably tracked in the enterprise of trying to find those options to which no one can reasonably object among parties who seek to reach agreement with one another about such matters. The fundamental, a priori axiom of morality, according to virtue theory, is that an option is right if and only if the virtuous agent would be disposed to choose it. The fundamental, a priori axiom, according to contractual theory, is that an option is right if and only if parties to the sort of contract envisaged would be disposed to find no objection.

There are a number of reasons why it might be a priori that a property such as rightness is present if and only if certain subjects display a certain type of response; it is present, for example, if and only if virtuous agents are disposed to choose the bearer of the property – the right option – or if and only if contracting parties are disposed to find no objection to the bearer. One extreme possibility is that the reality of the property depends on the reality of the response, as under an idealist image, and another that the reality of the property ensures the reality of the response, as under an image of infallible knowledge. But the two more plausible possibilities are these:

1 It is a priori that the explanation for why the response occurs in the relevant circumstances, or the explanation for why the response that occurs in those circumstances counts as the sort of response it is – counts, say, as virtuous – is that it is non-accidentally occasioned by the property of rightness.

2 It is a priori that the explanation for why something is right, or the explanation for why the property it has counts as rightness – earns the designation "rightness" – is that it non-accidentally occasions the response in the relevant circumstances: it non-accidentally attracts the endorsement of the virtuous or the no-objection of contractors.

The first of these views takes rightness as given, and as subject to determination on a basis independent from the preferences of the virtuous agent or the contractual parties. While it would establish an a priori connection between the fact of rightness and the response favored by the contract theorist or the virtue theorist, then, it would not give support to either approach. For where those approaches aspire to give a certain priority in the explication of rightness to the response favored – the choice of the virtuous subject, the no-objection of contractors – this line would confer priority on the property of rightness itself.

The only plausible way for the virtue theorist or the contract theorist to go is the second one indicated. And this route may actually look quite attractive. It would give the virtuous or contractual response the sort of privilege sought. And it would do so in a way that appears to be paralleled in other cases.

Consider the putatively a priori principle that something is red if and only if it looks red to normal observers under normal conditions. If this is sound, as I believe it is, then that may well be because it is a priori that the explanation for why the property shared by red things should count as red – should earn the designation "red" – is that its presence causes red sensations in normal conditions (Pettit 1991b). Imagine, contrary to some views, that the property in question is a certain quite objective feature, *F*. Why should *F* get the name of "red"? Our linguistic dispositions make it a priori decidable, so at least it may be argued, that the reason has to do with *F*'s occasioning red sensations, at least in those conditions that come to be regarded as normal. The word "red" – if you like, the concept "red" – hooks up with *F* in virtue of this sensation-eliciting effect of that property. It is a priori that something is red if and only if it looks red in suitable conditions because it is a priori that a property deserves the name of "red" if and only if the bearer looks red in those conditions.

The best hope for the virtue theorist or the contract theorist is to be able to argue that as a certain property gets to deserve the name of "red" only in virtue of eliciting certain sensations, so the property that makes an option right gets to deserve the name of "rightness" only in virtue of attracting the choice of the virtuous agent or the no-objection of the contractual parties. The idea would be that as our best angle on the property that we name "red" is given by our sensations, so our best angle on the property of rightness is given either by the perspective of the virtuous agent or by the contractualist perspective. We conceive of redness, under the story told, as that property – however in physical terms it may be described – that makes things look red in normal conditions. And under these parallel stories we would conceive of rightness as that property – however in descriptive terms it may be characterized – that makes options appeal to the virtuous or which enables the options to survive contractual objection.

But the stories told are downright implausible in a way in which the corresponding story for color is not (see Pettit 1993a: 297–302). The normal perceiver in normal circumstances experiences the redness of things in a primitive, unmediated fashion: things present themselves as red, things look red, in a relatively brute and belief-insensitive way. That is why it is appealing to say that we conceive of redness as that property which has such a sensation-eliciting effect: that property which makes things look red. But the position of the virtuous person or the contracting party is quite different. The person of virtue does not just look and see that an option or kind of option is right, at least not if the literature and reportage of centuries is reliable. Nor do they generally come to identify an option as right on the basis that it is what this or that moral hero would choose. Rather they come to identify an option as right on the basis, explicit or implicit, of recognizing that it compares well with other options in regard to certain values. Certainly they refer to that basis in values as they answer the challenge to justify the choice which they make. They do not claim to see the rightness of the option neat, they claim to see it in the relative helpfulness or fairness or utility of taking that course.

The same is true of the contracting parties we are invited to imagine in the business of identifying unobjectionable options. They presumably argue with one another, and indeed with themselves, about the merits and demerits of the alternatives they consider and if one alternative appears as something to which no one can object – in particular, no one can reasonably object – then that must be because it scores well in such characteristics. It is not as if the contractors are brute yea-sayers and nay-sayers who identify certain alternatives as attracting no nays without there being anything about those alternatives that makes them independently salient: salient, say, on grounds of distributive fairness or collective utility. If we were to imagine contractors in this brute mould, and contract theorists do not suggest we should, then it is unclear why their verdicts would have any hold on our moral imagination. Why should we associate rightness with not attracting objection among a breed of contractors whose brute responses are utterly alien to the ways in which we ourselves think of options?

The common point against virtue theory and contract theory is that the respondents to whose responses they would tie the concept of rightness – tie it in the way in which the concept of

redness is tied to the responses of the normal observer of colors —
themselves think of rightness in a way that is mediated by values.
These theorists say that the right option is just what the virtuous
person or the contracting parties would embrace. But the virtuous
person and the contracting parties suggest that the right option,
rather, is the option that coheres best with the values by reference
to which they make and justify their choices as right. The line
ascribed to virtue theory or contract theory would be plausible
only if the rightness-detectors that the theories claim to find
among those of a virtuous or contractual disposition were primitive detectors of the kind we find in normal color-detection.

This line of thought knocks out what I see as the only plausible
way for virtue theory or contract theory to go. But it also serves us
more positively. Since the respondents to which the other theories would direct us think of right options themselves in a value-
related way, that gives us good grounds for thinking that we
should explore the possibility that rightness is determined just
by reference to values. It should be clear from our discussion that
if the property that makes an option right can be identified just by
reference to values, then we can explain the connection with
virtue and with being unobjectionable in the first manner distinguished above. We can say that it is a priori that the virtuous will
track the right because to be virtuous is to be sensitive to values
and to the ways in which values make options right. And we can
say that it is a priori that parties to the sort of contract envisaged
will find no reasonable objection to right options, given an agreement on values, because right options are those that best serve
values and any reasonable objection must cite a disservice to such
values.[8]

Against Non-consequentialist Value Theory

And so to value theory. I assume that the considerations
rehearsed suggest that as we should avoid anti-theory, so we
should resist universalizability theory, virtue theory, contract
theory, and indeed any theories in the same category. I assume
in other words that if we are going to be able to say in perspicuous
terms what it is that makes a given option right for an agent to take

or to have taken, then we can do so only by reference to the way in which the option serves the values that are assumed to be relevant in the choice. The answer to the question of rightness must be value-theoretic in character.

But that is yet to say little, for we know that value theory ramifies on two dimensions, depending on whether relativized values are countenanced as relevant and depending on whether any values are taken to require honoring rather than promoting. I want now to argue against the non-consequentialist way of going on those dimensions. I want to argue that only neutral values are relevant in the determination of rightness and only the promotion of those values, not the honoring of them. My aim is to show that there is a problem for any approach that gives a place to relativized values, or to the honoring response: for any approach that is valuer-relativist, in the phrase introduced in the last section.

The problem that I find with such approaches, the problem that leads me to espouse a consequentialist version of value theory, derives from the universalizability constraint on judgments of rightness. This constraint is given unique authority in the universalizability theory of rightness – mistakenly, as I suggested – but it is certainly deserving of some authority. Understood as a constraint on value-based justifications of action it is so commanding that, anti-theory notwithstanding (Dancy 1993, McNaughton 1988), I believe that every account of rightness must give it countenance (see Rabinowitz 1979).

The universalizability constraint says that if two choice-scenarios differ in regard only to particulars, then whatever option is right and justifiable in one scenario, the counterpart option must be right and justifiable in the other. If I face a choice between helping my friends or my country, and you face a choice between helping your friends and your country, and if the differences in our situations are indiscernible, then whatever is right for me, the corresponding option must be right for you. I cannot be so relatively important, nor you so unimportant, that the sort of thing that is right for me is not right for you. Nor can our friends or countries differ in importance in a way that would make for a difference in rightness. If the situations contrast only in matters of individual identity, not in any non-individual or universal respects, then there can be no difference in matters of rightness;

whatever justifies the one choice will serve also to justify the other. Any claim that it is right for individual *A* to to help *A*'s friends or to keep *A*'s promises or whatever must be universalizable into a claim that applies to any individual of the relevant kind: any individual who is similar to *A* in relevant respects.

The universalizability constraint, as I understand it, cannot be plausibly rejected. To reject it would be to argue that some individual agents or people or places or whatever are so special that while something involving them is right to do, or is right for them to do, it is not right in general for that sort of thing to be done, or for that sort of individual to do it. But to take this line is to say that there is nothing persuasive to be said in moral exchange between people who differ in their attachment to the individual in question. The one attached will say that a certain option is right for them, or is right so far as it affects their favored individual, but will have to deny that anything corresponding is true for the other person. They will have to respond to any challenger on these lines: "You and yours are inferior to me and mine; and you cannot force me to admit that because something is right for me, the corresponding thing is right for you." This would be an intolerable result. It would flout the presumptive constraint on which the contract theorist rightly insists, that for an option to be right is for it to be capable of being justified in a certain way to others.

How do valuer-relativist theories fare in relation to the universalizability constraint? In my own view, they fare so badly that we should give up on them in favor of a consequentialist approach. I will defend this claim in the course of discussing a particular example, since the points to be made generalize very readily. Consider France's decision in 1995 to test nuclear weapons. What can President Chirac say in a universalizing defense of this decision, if his line is that the 1995 tests were in the interest of his country? And does anything he can say fit well with the valuer-relativist point of view?

One thing that he might say is that any nuclear power should test its weapons, subject to provisos that are allegedly met in the French case. But while this response would have the merit of being straightforward and non-chauvinistic – it does not treat France as special – it is not consistent with valuer-relativism. The response says that whatever consideration makes it right for

France to test its nuclear weapons, that same consideration makes it right for any nuclear power – or at least any nuclear power that satisfies the provisos – to do so. It is a consideration that calls, not just for France to test its weapons, but for all nuclear powers to do so too. But the sort of thing that would call for all nuclear powers to test their weapons – the sort of thing that might lead President Chirac to encourage other powers besides France to test their weapons too – has to be a promotional cause, and in particular a cause of promoting some neutral value. This response to the universalizability challenge, so it appears, gives the game away to the teleological side; it gives up on valuer-relativism.

The consequentialist will go on from this sort of example to suggest that many apparently valuer-relativist defenses of an option as the right one for the agent to take or to have taken will give the game away in the same fashion. A father helps his children at the expense of other children. What makes it right, if it is right, for him to do that? Something, so the defendant will have to say, that makes it right for any father to favor his children: something that points us towards a value, intrinsic or instrumental, that is promoted in the promotion of that reflexive state of affairs. Whatever this is, it will have to be a neutral value. A pacifist country refrains from the use of force and does its part by the value of peace, even where peace would be better promoted by some limited force. What makes it right, if it is right, for it to behave in that way? Something, so the defendant will have to say, that makes it right for any country to refrain from using its force: something that reveals an intrinsic or instrumental value that is promoted in promoting that reflexive state of affairs. And again, whatever that is, it will have to be a neutral value.

The consequentialist's suggestion is that under the pressure of having to universalize judgments of rightness, valuer-relativists will be forced to give up on their valuer-relativism – to give up on their attachment to honoring responses or to relativized values – and to endorse the promotion of certain neutral values as the only determinant of rightness. There is nothing that the chauvinistic government or the partial father or the principled pacifist can say that will not ultimately reveal a teleological commitment to some neutral value.

But needless to say, this line of argument is not likely to end the debate between the consequentialist and the valuer-relativist. The argument depends on understanding the valuer-relativist response to the universalizability challenge in a way that is itself distinctively consequentialist. Or so at any rate it will be said.

Consider how we took the line ascribed to President Chirac, when he says that it is right for any nuclear power in France's position to test its weapons. We took him to be saying that by his lights not only should France test its weapons, so should any other similarly situated nuclear power. We took him to be espousing an evaluative base that supported the testing of weapons, not just by France, but by any similar power; that was why we could argue that the base had, therefore, to be neutralist and promotional in character. But it will be said against this that there is a completely different way of understanding what someone like President Chirac might mean in universalizing his defence of France by saying that it is right for any nuclear power to test its weapons. He might mean, not that it is right by his lights for any power to test its weapons, but rather that as it is right by his lights for France to test its weapons, so he is prepared to admit that it is right by the lights of other nuclear leaders to test the weapons that their countries possess. He might not be endorsing the universal claim that it is right for every nuclear power, or at least every power in France's position, to test its weapons. Rather he might be endorsing the claim that for every nuclear power in France's position, it is going to be right from the perspective of that power's leaders that it should test its weapons.

The defense articulated here can be readily generalized. Take any particular claim that it is right for individual A to do something that is self-referentially described as helping their children, respecting the rights of those they deal with, discharging their duties, or whatever: anything that counts in any sense as trying to advance a cause that falls particularly to them. Suppose now that we challenge A, or A's champion, as to how far they are prepared to universalize this claim of rightness. One response will certainly be the familiar one that it is right for any agent, or any agent in similar circumstances, to try to advance their cause; this suggests that the rightness of A's ø-ing is determined by something that equally determines the rightness of anyone's acting in the corresponding way and that it is determined therefore in the neutralist and promotional manner. But there is another response that is also available. This is to say that for any X, where "X" varies over A and B and other possible agents, it is right-in-X's-terms for X to try to advance their cause. It may not be right, period, for A to advance their cause but, so it is suggested, that sense of rightness is irrelevant or non-existent. The point is that it is right-in-A's-terms for A to try to advance their cause – it is A-right, as we may say – and the answer to the universalizabity challenge is that for any X it is X-right for them to try to advance their cause (cf. Dreier 1990). As it is A-right for A to help their children, to keep their promises, to do their duty, or whatever, so it is B-right for B, C-right for C, and so on, to take corresponding courses of action.

The first response to the universalizability challenge assumes that universalizability is to be understood in a neutral way, so far as it takes rightness to be a property that is common to all perspectives. The second response rejects this line, taking rightness itself, at least in certain contexts, to be a relativized property. If universalizability is taken in the neutral way, so it will be argued, it should be no surprise that taking up the challenge to universalize any judgment of rightness will mean endorsing neutral values and going over to a consequentialist point of view. But if universalizability is itself taken in a relativized way, so that X-rightness replaces rightness period, then it should equally be no surprise that the challenge can be handled without recourse to consequentialism.

At this point the argument between the consequentialist version of value theory and the alternative, valuer-relativist versions has to become an argument about the intersubjective character of rightness. The argument as to what makes an option the right option for an agent to take or to have taken has to become an argument about whether the presumptions governing rightness allow that rightness is a single property with which all are concerned in common, or a different property, at least in some contexts, for every individual: for A, A-rightness; for B, B-rightness; and so on. Is searching for the right thing to do something that points everyone in the same direction, like looking towards the stars? Or is it something that points each in a direction of their own, like looking at their toes or perhaps, in a more favorable metaphor, like looking into their heart?

I think that the evidence is overwhelmingly on the side of a neutral account of rightness and that the fact that non-consequentialist forms of value theory have to have recourse to relativizing rightness is a sign of how counterintuitive they are. If we relativize rightness then we postulate an ambiguity in ethical debate to which participants are clearly insensitive; we say that many apparent differences of ethical opinion are not really differences at all. One person says that an action is right, another that it is wrong, but in many cases there is no issue at all between them. What the first person, *A*, means is that it is right-in-*A*'s-terms; what the second person, *B*, means is that it is right-in-*B*'s-terms. What were they arguing about, then? Nothing, it seems; or at least nothing distinctively ethical. They were confused by the non-indexical feel of a term like "right" into treating it as having a common meaning and reference for them both.

This is a deeply counterintuitive position. For in ordinary ethical discussions we question the rightness of what we or others do, we invite judgments as to whether we did the right thing in this or that case, we discuss the rightness of the choices made in works of fiction, on the robust assumption that there is a common question at issue and that if we disagree, there is something substantial we are disagreeing about. Thus if Mayor Daley says that it is right for him as mayor to help out his son – what decent father, he asks, would do less? – then in disagreeing with him, and in denouncing him, we represent him as mistaken. We do not fail to engage with his opinion as we would do if what he meant was that it was right-in-his-terms to help his son and what we meant was that it was wrong-in-ours.

But not only would the relativization of rightness give the lie to how we ordinary people think of ethical discussions. It would render ethical assessment incapable of playing its distinctive justificatory role. In particular, it would make ethical evaluation indistinguishable from evaluation in terms of prudence. As I relativize to your long-term interests in speaking of what it is prudent for you to do, and to mine in wondering about what is prudent for me, so I would relativize in a parallel manner in asking about what it is right for you to do, right for me to do, and so on. As "prudent" has an indexical aspect, and directs us here to what is prudent for A, there to what is prudent for B, so "right," at least in certain contexts of usage, would be indexical too. In reference to any individual X, it would have the sense of "conducive to X's ends," or perhaps "conducive to X's moral ends."

In ordinary moral thinking, we contrast the demands of rightness with the promptings of prudence, and in general with any self-interested promptings, and treat them as having a greater authority. And if we think that our acting in prudence's name is really the right thing to do – the right thing, and not just a sign of our moral failure – then we are willing to give this a neutral justification. We are prepared to think that what justifies us in doing so – what justifies us, say, in staying on a course of study and not going on some important political demonstration – is the neutral sort of consideration that would justify anyone in our position taking that line. Someone who relativizes rightness loses the contrast between rightness and prudence and, even more strikingly, makes rightness out to be a sort of prudence that lies beyond the need or possibility of that sort of justification.

When you are called upon to justify a choice to me, it will not be intuitively sufficient for you to show me how prudent the choice was from your point of view. So it was prudent. Fine. But was it right? Was it something that you can represent to those of us who do not necessarily share your prudential interests as a justifiable action? You may explain your action to us by citing its prudential character. You may even give us a perspective from which we can excuse your doing what you did; we can recognize that in your situation perhaps we too would have been moved by the corresponding prudential consideration. But you cannot justify the action in the sense in which we asked for justification, simply by showing that you were prudent.

Relativizing rightness on the model of prudence would mean that in many areas the best that can be achieved in the way of justification is explanation and excuse. You cannot justify your course of action in terms of values that we countenance in common. All you can do is show that it served ends of your own that parallel ends that I recognize in my own case: ends like looking after your children, keeping your promises, maintaining a clean record in regard to some value. All you can do is appeal to me for understanding: appeal to me as someone who has children of my own to understand why you give such preference to your children; appeal to me as someone who has made promises myself to understand why you feel bound to keep your promises; and so on.

These considerations do not demolish the valuer-relativist ways of being a non-consequentialist but I hope that they do at least suggest that such moves would involve a revision in our ordinary ways of thinking about rightness and that we should not follow those paths without considerable reluctance. The relativization of rightness would make moral discourse and moral exchange radically incapable of unifying the different points of view of different people. It would give a philosophical basis to despair about the prospect that people might reconcile their different interests and commitments by appealing to moral argument. Such despair may yet be borne out in the development of our species but it is surely inconsistent with the hope around which moral argument continues to be built: the hope that by weaning ourselves away from more partial perspectives, and by submitting ourselves to the demands of fairness and equality and rationality and the like, we may yet manage to see things from a common, moral point of view.

Partialism versus Impartialism

Consequentialism represents a belief in impartialism: a belief that there are common values in the name of which we are each required to justify our individual courses of action to one another; and this is so even if those values are only articulated in the critical, reflective exercise of justification, not in the day-to-day practice of decision-making. The valuer-relativist alternative to consequentialism holds that impartialism is a chimera, that there is no common point of view from which we can ever hope to be able to justify ourselves to one another. It represents a belief in partialism: a belief that the business of justification runs out short of our ever finding common values; that it runs out at a point where we must each rest content, as we are content in prudential self-explanation, to cite ends that are structurally similar to, but substantively different from, the ends of others.

It may be useful to make vivid this partialist aspect of valuer-relativism (see Parfit 1984, pt 1). Imagine two mothers, *A* and *B*, who each believe that it is right – respectively *A*-right and *B*-right – to favor their children in certain contexts. Suppose now that they are in a situation where neither can favor her children without making it impossible for the other to favor hers; they are in direct competition. Under the valuer-relativist vision, neither will or should be the slightest bit inhibited by the damage done to the other's cause through her doing what is right-in-her-terms. Not only may she be motivated just to look after her own, at whatever cost to the children of the other. This, on the relativist vision, is also what it is right-in-her-terms to do; it is what is right in the only relevant sense of right that is available to her. Moral commitments, even what all will agree are sound moral commitments, can lead to a situation of civil war – better perhaps, moral war – under the vision that this brand of non-consequentialism defends. And the point applies not just in the case of special obligations, such as parents may have to their children. It arises in any case where two or more agents are required, and required in a self-relativized manner, each to try to advance a cause that falls particularly to them. The cause may be that of looking after certain dependants, doing one's duty in some regard, respecting the rights of those with whom one happens to deal directly, or just trying to maintain a clean record in regard to certain neutral values.

The partialist edge that these valuer-relativist approaches give to moral commitments comes of the fact that universalizing no longer means recognizing a commonly espoused goodness or rightness. All that it means is recognizing a common structure in the essentially different properties of rightness by which we are each required to steer and orientate. I, *A*, recognize that as it is *A*-right for me to help my children, keep my promises or whatever, so it is *B*-right for *B* to do so. But recognizing that does not mean recognizing any common value, even the value for any *X* of their doing what it is *X*-right for them to do. It only means recognizing that as I find this or that course of action *A*-right, so that other person will find a corresponding course of action – one that may directly conflict with mine – B-right. There is no common value in sight, only a common structure in our essentially different, and potentially rival, valuings.

The commitment to looking only at your own allotted part in promoting a value, or to looking only or principally at values that involve your own domain, was justified in an older way of thinking on the grounds that God could be trusted to take care of the overall consequences. That gloss is unavailable to most contemporary non-consequentialists. All they can say in defense of their point of view is that ultimately we can only expect people to care in the appropriate way about their own children, their own friends, their own country, and their own clean hands. All chains of justification end somewhere, it will be admitted, but there is nowhere where all chains end. The approach represents a surrender to the partiality of interests and perspectives that has traditionally been seen as a challenge for the enterprise of moral argument to meet: as an obstacle for it to surmount.

I said at the beginning of this essay that I thought non-consequentialism could have the effect of trivializing the moral point of view. What I had in mind is precisely this sort of surrender to diversity and divergence: this complacent acceptance that there is no higher point of view, no point of view of the kind that morality was traditionally taken to represent, from which we can reconcile our different perceptions of what we ought to do in looking after our children, respecting those we deal with, keeping our own hands clean, and so on. If this surrender is the best that non-consequentialists have to offer – and it is, if my earlier arguments are sound – then the choice that faces us in the debate we are conducting is a choice between consequentialism and complacency.

5 The Tenability of the Consequentialist Answer

The consequentialist perspective, as it has emerged so far in this essay, holds that while people are inherently involved with one another, while they are often particularistically motivated and while they have good reason to resist actuarial calculation, there is still a question as to what it is that makes one option right to take, another wrong. It holds that answering this question means looking for the fundamental determinants of rightness among the different factors associated with the property in the network of our moral ideas; that the fundamental determinants of rightness are the values on the basis of which the property is predicated of options; and that these values, if they are to satisfy the relevant version of the universalizability test, must ultimately be all neutral in character. What ultimately makes any option the right one for an agent to take or to have taken, as consequentialists say, is the fact that that option best promotes the neutral values that are relevant in the situation on hand.

The issue that we must now confront is whether this consequentialist viewpoint is one that we can happily endorse as moral agents: whether it is a perspective that fits. While the viewpoint proves superior to non-consequentialist alternatives, at least if the argument so far is sound, it may yet be a difficult position to occupy. It may be that what we are intellectually driven to endorse is a position that we cannot practically embrace; it may be that the judgments of rightness it would support fail in some significant measure to fit with various assumptions that we find it difficult to drop. That would be a very unhappy result, of course, and might even give us reason to despair altogether of folk moral notions but it is a result that remains logically possible.[9]

There are three broad types of objection that will be raised against the tenability of the teleological perspective (see Frey 1984; Scheffler 1982 and 1988; Sen and Williams 1982). One is that being a consequentialist is going to require an agent often to do things that are intuitively wrong. A second is that it is going to require an agent often to do intuitively the right things for what are intuitively the wrong reasons. And a third is that it is going to require an agent often to do things that are intuitively good but that are intuitively too demanding to require of anyone: too demanding to make a matter of obligation as distinct from supererogation.

First Objection

The complaint that consequentialism requires the agent often to take what is intuitively the wrong option is usually illustrated in lurid colours. We are invited to ask what consequentialism, allegedly, would require the sheriff to do when, faced with a riot, he can restore law and order only by releasing the untried defendant to be lynched by the mob (McCloskey 1957). The suggestion is that it would require the sheriff to give the defendant over to the mob, thereby undermining everything that he stands for. This sort of complaint is usually made against utilitarianism; it is made against the form of consequentialism which argues that ultimately what makes a property a value is the fact that it tends to increase happiness, so that ultimately what is right is just what best promotes overall happiness. But many critics suggest that the complaint carries against any form of consequentialism. The idea is that no matter what values, within plausible limits, the consequentialist agent countenances, there are going to be extreme situations where the promotion of those values will require the doing of something that is intuitively horrible.

The initial point to make against this objection is that it may not be compelling in really extreme circumstances, such as that of a sheriff who is faced with what we must regard as a choice between two great evils: the lynching of a possibly innocent party or, as it may be, widespread disorder and loss of life. Make the circumstances extreme enough and it ceases to be so intuitively obvious that one line of action is right and the other wrong. Suppose, for example, that if the untried defendant is not given to the mob then they may do something that will set off a nuclear holocaust and end life on earth. At that sort of extreme – in that sort of moral catastrophe, as some non-consequentialists will call it (Nozick 1974: 30n) – it certainly becomes unclear what exactly is the right thing to do. If God is there to look after the consequences, and the consequences extend into eternity, then perhaps it may seem that the sheriff should still refuse to release the prisoner. But if no such consolation is thought to be available, then doubts must surely begin to arise as to whether that is really the right thing for the sheriff to do.

But short of going to such extremes, it is still possible to motivate the first objection to the teleological or consequentialist perspective. The recipe for generating the objection is this:

- Find a role or office such that it is intuitively right for the occupant of that office generally to act in a certain way: to discharge the duties of their office. The role or office may be that of parent or promisor or authority or just that of an ordinary person dealing with someone who can invoke a right to be treated by them in a certain way: not to be violated, not to have their property taken, not to have their privacy invaded, or whatever.

- Having identified such a role or office, find a neutral good that any consequentialist is likely to regard as important and relevant in the exercise of the role. Such a good will always be provided by the value, intrinsic or instrumental, associated with establishing or preserving the very role in question: the good, say, of having parents discharge their duties towards their children, of having promisors keep their promises, of having people respect one another's property, and so on.

- Having identified such a role and such a value, find a situation where the promotion of that value requires the agent to break role, that is, to do what is generally the intuitively wrong thing for them to do. The consequentialist is bound to think of any such situation that what it is right for the agent to do is that role-breaking action: that action, as it will often be, which intuitively seems like the wrong thing to do.

There are two points I would like to make in response to this line of objection. The first is that it is important to recognize that there are some situations where it may indeed be right for an agent to break role and to do what may intuitively seem, or at least what may at first blush seem, like the wrong thing. There are surely situations where a parent should let down their own children in some way, where the promisor should break a promise, where someone should infringe on what is intuitively the right of another person, and so on. There will be disagreements, no doubt, about the point at which it becomes right to break role in some way. But for almost any role there is surely some point at which even the most fanatical non-consequentialist will recognize a moral catastrophe and admit that the role should be broken. We need only think of the sheriff in the scenario where a

nuclear holocaust threatens in order to feel the force of the observation.

The second and more important thing I want to notice, however, is that the recipe for generating this first objection may not
be capable of being used very frequently against the consequentialist. Suppose that the consequentialist thinks, as is surely plausible, that it is a value in itself that any child should feel great
confidence in the affection and attachment of its parents and, in
particular, that it should feel a sort of confidence that would be
undermined by the belief that the parent will look after its interests only in the event that doing so furthers some impersonal goal,
perhaps only in the event that it furthers the goal of increasing the
degree to which children in general feel this confidence in their
parents. That is not an implausible scenario. But the effect of its
obtaining would be to put a severe limit on the extent to which a
parent could be justified in breaking role on the grounds that
breaking role is going to promote the value in question. Breaking
role would have to promise to deliver a very high expectation – an
implausibly high expectation – of promoting the value in other
quarters in order to compensate for the really great damage it
would do to the promotion of the value nearer home (Jackson
1991). Imagine the parent who is led in the name of promoting
the confidence of children in their parents to neglect their own
children and to launch a moral crusade designed to increase the
realization of the value. That parent would have to be very effective, and would have to be pretty sure of being very effective
indeed, in order to be able to justify the neglect of their own
children in the name of promoting that value elsewhere.

Or, to take another example, suppose the consequentialist
thinks that it is a value in itself that people be able to feel sure
of obtaining certain rights at the hands of public officials, and be
able not to feel dependent on the arbitrary good will of those
officials or on their private opinion as to whether or not it is
good to respect those rights on a given occasion. This again is
plausible, given the importance attached in the republican tradition of thought to citizens' not being dominated by governmental
or indeed other powers, not being subject to their arbitrary discretion (Braithwaite and Pettit 1990; Pettit 1997a). But if that is a
value relevant to how officials behave towards citizens – or

indeed citizens towards one another – then it is extremely un-likely that anything an official might expect to achieve in the general furtherance of that value could justify them in breaking role on a particular occasion. It is unlikely that it could justify them, as we say, in taking the law into their own hands and in judging that by denying a citizen their rights in this instance they can thereby increase overall the degree to which citizens enjoy such rights, and enjoy non-domination, at the hands of officials. Let the citizen affected become aware of the line taken by the official and their sense of independence is going to be compro-mised straightaway – and compromised, not just in relation to this official now, but in relation to this and other officials in the future. Let other citizens become aware of how the official behaves, and their sense of independence is going to suffer compromise also; they will see the case as a lesson in how officials generally are disposed to treat citizens. The damage that role-breaking is likely to do to the realization of the value in question is so great that it is hard to see how any contribution it might be expected to make in a particular unusual instance could justify risking that damage (see Hamlin 1989; Lyons 1982 for the issues here).

The point in cases of these kinds is that for many of the values that a consequentialist is likely to recognize as relevant to the exercise of certain roles, there is very little that an agent could realistically expect to achieve in furthering that value by breaking role. The danger to which the objection is meant to point is the danger of zealotry: the danger that if a consequentialist justifies the discharge of a role by reference to a certain neutral value, then the occupant of the role may internalize that justifying value and, becoming a lawless zealot, may find reason often to break role on the grounds that doing so furthers the realization of that value. The considerations just raised, however, suggest that there may be a lot less room for consequentialist zealotry than critics of the approach seem to suggest.

Second Objection

Suppose it is granted that while a consequentialism may require a certain revision of intuitive judgments – this is what we would

expect under an enterprise of reflective equilibration – there is no
ground for worrying that it will be wildly counterintuitive, for-
cing on us an endorsement of rampant role-breaking; there is no
ground for thinking that it will force us to see a lot of intuitively
right choices as wrong, or intuitively wrong choices as right. A
second objection that may still be raised against the approach is
that it would force an agent to choose the right options for the
wrong reasons. Even as it supports ordinary intuition about
which options are the right options to take, so the criticism goes,
it betrays ordinary intuition about why it is that they are the right
options to take and about why it is that they should appeal to a
moral agent.

The idea in this objection is that while ordinary intuition
would have the parent love their child and favor it for that reason,
take their promises seriously and keep them for that reason,
acknowledge the rights of their fellows and respect them for that
reason, the consequentialist perspective would insist that in
each case it is something higher or lower – in any case something
different – that should keep the agent on track. It is considerations
to do with what is likely to leave the world a better place in
the wake of their intervention, in particular, a better place in
neutral terms. The consequentialist agent should live among
ordinary people and even do what ordinary people do but,
so this objection goes, the consequentialist perspective requires
that the agent do this for other than ordinary reasons; it
requires that the agent should maintain alien habits of mind and
thought.

The objection holds that the consequentialist perspective
requires a reconstruction or rescripting of the ordinary psychology that we described in the first section as non-atomistic, non-
moralistic, and non-actuarial. But that shows precisely why we
need not be troubled by it. We accept that human beings are
indeed the non-atomistic, non-moralistic, and non-actuarial lot
described and that this is a very good, or at least a very firm,
aspect of our make-up. Whatever values we find compelling,
then, and potentially determinative of rightness, they cannot be
values which would require a reconstruction of that psychology.
They cannot be values that would counsel a rethinking of our
involved attitudes towards others, of our particularistic sources of

motivation, or of our deeply non-calculative habits of deliberation.

But are there likely to be many neutral values that can satisfy
this constraint? Are there likely to be many values such that their
promotion requires that people generally maintain the non-atomistic, non-moralistic, and non-actuarial stance associated with
ordinary psychology? There is no problem with neutral values
that are themselves explicitly invoked in our ordinary habits of
thought: values associated, for example, with helping the needy,
behaving fairly, telling the truth. What of values that do not figure
in everyday deliberation, however, but that are thought, nonetheless, to be relevant for assessing various patterns of behavior?

What of the value of encouraging confidence in children, for
example, that we invoked as a possible justifier of caring for your
own children? And what of the value of developing people's
sense of independence – a core republican value (Pettit 1997a) –
that we mentioned in connection with the official's treating a
citizen properly? How can the consequentialist justify a pattern
of behavior in terms of such a neutral value and at the same time
hold that the agent ought not to think in terms of that value, but
ought rather to think as a loving parent or as an official who has no
option but to discharge their brief in a certain way?

The answer is that with certain values, the very habit of thinking in terms of them, the very habit of allowing them delibera-
tively to dictate what one does, may be inimical to the furthering
of that value. Consider the feeling that a child must have if it
becomes salient, as it surely will, that their parent does not spon-
taneously and more or less unconditionally respond to their
needs but rather that the parent always first considers whether
the response is indeed the best way in which they can serve the
general value of children having confidence in their parents.
Whatever that child is led to feel it won't be the sort of confidence
desired. Or consider the feeling of the citizen as they recognize
that officials do not acknowledge their rights under the law as a
matter of course but that they always first consider whether
acknowledging those rights in this particular case is the best
way of promoting non-domination of citizens overall. Whatever
this citizen experiences at the hands of such an official it will not
be a robust assurance of their independence.

In cases like this it should be clear that the best thing an agent can do to promote the value in question is to forswear the habit of deliberating about their actions by reference to that value. The agent should adopt a self-restrictive attitude of thinking only in the more concrete, other-centred fashion that the neutral value serves to justify. They should put themselves on – better, leave themselves on – the more or less automatic pilot associated with that mode of thinking, secure in the knowledge that that represents a habit of mind which is justifiable, indeed uniquely justifiable, in the consequentialist currency to which they pay allegiance. They should be self-restrictive consequentialists, not consequentialists who always and everywhere keep their eyes on the ultimate values that they embrace (Pettit and Brennan 1986; see too Railton 1984).

This consideration bolsters the claim in response to the first objection, that the values relevant to the general justification of roles will only rarely justify role-breaking. Suppose that there is some scenario where the value that generally justifies the existence and discharge of a certain role does serve to justify breaking role. Does it follow that the the agent should be disposed to take the role-breaking option in such a situation? No, it doesn't. We may allow that it would be right for the agent to take that option, did it present itself as the way to promote the value in question. But it does not follow that it would be right for the agent to be of a cast of mind that would make that sort of option a salient, and saliently superior, alternative in that sort of scenario. The disposition always to take an optimific role-breaking option might not be itself an optimific disposition; on the contrary, its existence might seriously compromise the agent's ability to promote the very value in question.

The upshot, then, is that the fact that consequentialists find a justification for certain patterns of behavior in their promoting relevant neutral values does not mean that they have to recommend that agents should think and make their decisions by reference to those values. There are many values whose promotion requires precisely that the agent not think in terms of them. The examples we have given of children having confidence in their parents, or of citizens having a sense of independence in face of officials, are two of many that we might have used. Others include the value of being spontaneous, which is certainly not going to be promoted by thinking in terms of spontaneity (Smart 1977); the value of being generous, which is not going to be advanced by the habit of reckoning about whether an option scores high in generosity terms (Williams 1981); the value of saving time, which will be usually be better served by following a given routine mechanically than by always thinking about which sort of routine will save most time (Pettit 1984); and so on (Pettit and Brennan 1986).

The sort of consequentialism that satisfies the constraints identified in the first section – the sort that allows the recognition only of values that will not deeply disrupt our ordinary psychology – is bound to be restrictive in my sense. Among the values it acknowledges as determinants of rightness we may expect to find many whose promotion is best served by the habit of not thinking in terms of them but rather of following other routines of deliberation and decision.

Such a restrictive consequentialism need not be conceived of as a strategic philosophy that encourages attitudes of cunning and even self-deception in the agent. My picture of the approach is rather this. The agent who espouses a consequentialist disposition recognizes that they are a human being with a certain more or less inflexible psychology and that for good or ill – but surely, in most circumstances, for good – they are devoted to particular people, motivated by certain contingent concerns, and in the unrevisable habit of making their decisions without excessive calculation. The question which the consequentialist commitment raises for that agent is how far they are justified in continuing on the paths along which that psychology would lead them in the circumstances they face; in particular, how far they are justified in the court of judgment that acknowledges only the justification of best promoting the presumptively relevant neutral values.

That question of justification will arise, willy-nilly, for agents whenever they are challenged, as they will certainly be challenged, about how they can devote themselves so whole-heartedly to this or that cause, about how they can ignore the claims of so-and-so, about how they can sleep at night when they know that such and such, and so on. But in any case agents will recognize themselves that they ought to consider the question of justification: that it is right for them to do so. They ought not to consider it continually, of course; that would be entirely inconsistent with preserving our familiar moral psychology and indeed with promoting any plausible values. But they ought to consider it sufficiently often to ensure the justifiability of what they do, so the consequentialist commitment will force them to recognize. And where the consideration of the question leads to a recognition that there is no justification for this or that aspect of their performance, then they clearly ought to try to reform their habits.

The mental set that I associate with being a consequentialist might be described as one of virtual consequentialism. Agents are not expected to inspect their behaviour continually, or guide their decision-making, by reference to how well it promotes the neutral values that they countenance. But agents are expected always to be ready to go over to such a self-examining, and potentially such a self-reforming, mode. They will be expected to do so whenever they are challenged by their fellows about their behavior; they will be expected to recognize the validity of such challenges and the requirement to respond. And they will be expected to do so, more generally, whenever there is reason to think that their behavior may not indeed be optimific. Such reason will be available so far as agents have not thought about the matter for some time, or have not thought about it since the appearance of some change in their circumstances, but it will often be presented exogenously, for example, by the recognition of some need or cause which they are doing nothing to service or by the appearance of someone who offers a model of behavior that is clearly superior to their own.

This mental set of preparedness to self-examine and self-reform represents a virtual consequentialism. While agents do not actually make decisions by reference to the values they acknowledge in consequentialist adjudication – do not do so even in a tacit or implicit way – they do virtually make decisions by reference to such values. If things are going well, and agents are neither backsliders nor weak of will, then we may expect the decisions actually made to conform to the requirements of consequentialist justification. And we may expect them to conform for non-accidental reasons. It is as if agents made their decisions on the basis of consequentialist reasoning; the consequentialist reasoning has a virtual though not an actual presence in their mental life (cf. Pettit 1995).

In conclusion, one further comment. Any decent moral theory must enable defenders to sustain the ordinary sort of moral psychology described and the strength of non-consequentialist theories has traditionally been that they seem better equipped to do this than any teleological view. I hope that that strength may no longer seem to give non-consequentialism the edge, and that consequentialism, through being cast in a virtual mould, can assume in this regard an equally appealing aspect. But what I now wish to point out is that there is also a second way in which any decent moral theory must serve defenders and that our virtual consequentialism, like consequentialist theories generally, obviously scores well above non-consequentialist alternatives on this front.

Any decent moral theory must not only enable defenders to sustain an ordinary moral psychology, it must also give them a perspective from which they can judge and rank the various institutional ways in which civil, economic, and political life may be structured and that very psychology formed. The theory must facilitate not just the moral life of participants in everyday roles but the political thought of those who want to argue for a reshaping and recasting of the roles. Should we have an insulated family sphere or expose that sphere in greater measure to initiatives within civil society? Should we encourage certain forms of civic virtue or try not to make our institutions dependent on moral dispositions? Should we allow a market that tolerates free-for-all profit-seeking or should we look for various regulatory constraints? Should we have a punitive criminal justice system or seek one that relies more on having offenders make up to their victims? Should we have a bill of rights that gives the judiciary greater control over the legislature or should we embrace populist democracy more whole-heartedly? These questions from political theory are just as important as the day-to-day questions of moral life and any half-credible moral philosophy must give us a basis on which to deal with them.

The great thing about virtual consequentialism is that while it does as well as any non-consequentialist theories in sustaining the possibility of an ordinary moral life, it does as well as any other sort of consequentialism in serving the needs of political theory. Let the virtual consequentialist be clear about the neutral values that are relevant and the way is open straight away to begin to practice political theory. As moral choices are justified in the light of such values – justified, not necessarily selected – so political and constitutional proposals can be defended on their basis. The best institutions will be those that promise to maximize the relevant expected values. For a liberal consequentialist the best institutions will be those that maximize the expectation of freedom as non-interference, for the communitarian they will be those that maximize the expectation of cohesive community, for the republican they will be those that maximize the expectation of freedom as non-domination (Pettit 1997a). And so on.

Things are different, however, on the non-consequentialist front. For suppose that a non-consequentialist celebrates acting on a universalizable principle, or acting in a virtuous or contractually compelling way – and this, even when such courses of action are non-promotional in character – or acting so as to further some relativized value, for example, acting according to attachment or duty, or acting out of a recognition of certain rights. It may be clear what such a non-consequentialist will require of institutions, say the state, in a perfect, compliant world; he or she will require that whatever ends it tries to further the state should always meet the relevant constraint. But that is the easy case; that is the case where the satisfaction of the constraint by the state is going to contribute to maximizing overall satisfaction of the constraint. The telling question is, what will the non-consequentialist say about the shape that institutions ought to take in an imperfect world, say, in a world where the fact that the state acts in conformity to a certain constraint is bound to mean that the constraint is less widely satisfied in people's behaviour generally?

What will the non-consequentialist say, for example, about the shape that a state ought to take if the fact of committing itself to respect for people's rights of free speech – and to respect, therefore, for the rights of racists and bigots in this regard – is bound to mean that sooner or later a fascist movement will come to power and eliminate free speech altogether? Confronted with such a question, non-consequentialists face a dilemma. If they stick with their non-consequentialism, then they will have to support politically self-defeating policies. If they go for more reasonable policies – if they recommend, for example, that the state should be able to put a limit on the rights of racists or bigots – then they will have to move closer to the consequentialist camp; they will have to move towards the claim that what the state ought to do in the example envisaged is act so as to promote the expectation of free speech.

Third Objection

And so to the last objection that I want to consider to the teleological perspective. The first objection was that any consequentialist theory is going to support what are intuitively bad options in many choices. And the second was that even where it supports good options, it is going to support them for the wrong reasons. The third objection is that any consequentialist theory is going to mislead us in representing some good options as obligatory and uniquely justifiable when intuition tells us that good though they are, they are not obligatory or uniquely justifiable; they are acts, rather, of supererogatory merit. In this sense, it is said, any consequentialist theory is going to be intuitively overdemanding.

This is a powerful objection, for it is indeed a matter of irresistible intuition that while it would be heroic of someone to emulate a Francis of Assisi or any moral saint, such a course of action cannot often be represented as something that an agent is morally required – morally required in the only available sense of requirement – to do. Let us assume that for many agents in many situations there will be a possible course of action that is heroic in this fashion. And let us assume that under many views of the relevant neutral values, that course of action will count as best, doing most to promote the expected realization of such values. The problem raised for consequentialists – or at least one of the problems that may be raised for consequentialists in this area – is that it seems they will have to countenance the heroic option as the best option, as the right option, and as the one and only option that agents can justify themselves in doing.

If we cannot find a way around this objection, we may not feel obliged to give up on the consequentialist perspective. But we will have to acknowledge that becoming a consequentialist involves rejecting a fairly central presumption about rightness: the presumption according to which a number of options in a choice, some of which are better than others, may be equally unobjectionable. The best option, whether or not it is taken as the right option, may not be the only one that can be justified to others. We will have to recognize that consequentialism is a deeply revisionary theory in relation to folk morality, though we may justify the revision on the ground that folk morality is inconsistent; on the ground, in particular, that the justifiability presumption does not fit well with the presumptions that consequentialism seeks to save (Kagan 1989; Singer 1972).

The traditional response to the overdemandingness objection begins from the observation that the consequentialist has to have regard, not just to what it is best to do, but also to what it is best in relevant situations to denounce, to hold up for public condemnation. Consider the situation where you have three options: be amoral; look after your family; go and work for the poorest people in the world. Even if we suppose that the third option is the best in consequentialist terms, we may not think that it is good for us – good in relevant consequentialist terms – to denounce you for not taking it (Sidgwick 1966: 469). We may be disposed to denounce you if you take the first, amoral option but we may not want to denounce you for taking the second, family-directed option; this might be for fear of demoralizing you and perhaps driving you back to the amoral choice. The approach saves the justifiability presumption by associating justifiability, not with the best option alone – not with the option that can claim to be the uniquely right one – but with any option which it would not be good to denounce.

This response does not look very appealing on the face of it. Suppose I am won over to a consequentialist perspective. Doesn't that mean that I should want, above all, to satisfy the demands of neutral values and that it should be a matter only of secondary concern that I not fall so far short as to attract public condemnation? Doesn't it mean that there is really no room for me to feel satisfied with less than the best; no room for me to regard myself as justified in achieving anything that falls short of that? But while the traditional response is unsatisfactory in this respect I believe that it points us in the right direction. There is a distinction between what it is best to do and what you cannot reasonably be denounced for doing which is not so tied to considerations of the utility of denunciation.

This is the distinction between what I can justify in a context where other agents are treated as parametric, as given aspects of nature with which I cannot expect to engage, and what I can justify in a context where other agents are treated as being on a par with me; in particular, they are treated as subject to exactly the same sort of interrogation and the same demand for justification. If other agents are treated as parametric, then I must see their failure to contribute to the good, even their evil-doing, as just one among the many different factors that shape my choice-situation and determine which option will contribute most to the realization of relevant values. Thus I must see myself as challenged in the demand for justification to show that the option I choose does indeed represent the best I can do, in those circumstances, for the promotion of the relevant values. If other agents are treated as persons who may be engaged by any demands that engage me, however – if they are treated as potential interlocutors (Pettit and Smith 1996) – then I may see their failure to contribute to the good as being on a par with mine and I may see myself as called upon in the demand for justification to show that I am doing at least my bit. Whatever shortfall has to be made up, the onus falls on those others, not on me.

What the traditional response suggests is that there is a second concern engaged in moral thought apart from the concern to do what is best and right; this second concern is to do what I cannot usefully be denounced for doing. I think that the tradition is right about there being two concerns but that the distinction should be drawn in different terms. What we have is a distinction between the best that can be asked of me in a world where I am the only relevant agent, the only relevant decision-maker, and the best that can be asked of me in a world where the demand is addressed simultaneously, and for similar reasons, to certain others (cf. Murphy 1993). This may still be described as a distinction between doing what is best and doing what I cannot be denounced for doing but the latter category is identified now in a distinctive way: not by reference to what others cannot usefully condemn but by reference to what I can justify in a context in which certain others are equally called upon to justify themselves.

The new way of understanding what I cannot be denounced for doing enables us to remedy the fault that we found in the traditional response to the overdemandingness objection. We argued in finding that fault that as a consequentialist I should want to satisfy the demands of neutral values and that it should be a matter only of secondary concern that I not fall so far short as to attract public condemnation. But this argument is now blocked. It is quite understandable that in some contexts I will want to see what option the promotion of value calls upon me to perform, period, and that in others I will want to see what option it calls upon me in the context of other similarly situated agents to perform. In some contexts, after all, I will be the only relevant agent, while in others I will be only one of many equally relevant agents.

Consider how I may think as a consequentialist about what I should do for the relief of hunger in the Third World. It is possible for me to give away much of what I have so that while I significantly sacrifice the interests of me and mine I do so in a measure that is more than made up by the good I do abroad. As a consequentialist I am bound to think of this option as the best thing that I can do, assuming that doing it does indeed improve matters, and to see myself as very far less than perfect for not doing it. But as a consequentialist I am not forced to think of myself as utterly immoral, if I fail to be so heroic; I am not forced to see myself as subject to censure under every heading countenanced in the annals of morality. For, recognizing that I am not the only affluent member of the human race, I can see that short of doing the very best possible, there is a second ideal which I may aspire to meet: the ideal of doing the best that can be asked of me in a context where the demand is simultaneously addressed to those other agents. The contribution to which this directs me, and it is bound to be relatively vague at the limits, may not be the best that I can do for the relief of Third World hunger – some other affluent individuals will certainly fail to do their bit – but it is a limit below which I cannot fall without becoming unable to justify my behavior in any terms whatsoever. It represents a moral demand that I as a consequentialist have to countenance, even if it is not the primary demand of morality.

This distinction between primary and secondary categories of moral assessment makes for a connection between consequentialism and certain non-consequentialist approaches. When contract theory identifies the right option with that which no one could object to in a certain context of contract, for example, we can see it as focusing just on our secondary category. And when the honoring approach says that the right thing to do in any option is that which honors the relevant neutral values, not necessarily that which promotes them, we can see it equally as directing our attention to the option that is satisfactory on that secondary count. Consequentialists do not say that the be-all and end-all of morality is achieving this secondary sort of justifiability; on the contrary, they think of morality as prescribing that agents each do the best that is accessible to them. But consequentialists can admit that there is a question as to whether an agent who fails to do the best available succeeds at least in doing that which enjoys this secondary justifiability. And they can recognize that the demand to act in a way that ensures such justifiability may often be quite a substantive requirement.

The overdemandingness objection, as I have taken it, suggests that consequentialism cannot represent an attractive theory of rightness because it would find, in any situation, only one option that has any moral credentials: the option which best promotes relevant values. It cannot be an attractive theory, so the line runs, because it would demoralize those of us who fail to live up to such a demanding theory; it must leave us without any accessible moral standards by which to assess our sub-heroic performances. We can now see that that objection is not a telling one. As a consequentialist I must recognize the standard of what best promotes value as the supreme moral ideal. I must equally recognize, however, that there is a less demanding but even more pressing standard by which to orientate. This is the standard of doing the best that can be asked of me in a context where the demand is simultaneously addressed to other, similarly placed agents. The primary ideal will reveal whether my behavior leaves a moral deficit in place; the secondary ideal will show whether my behavior discharges an even more basic moral debt.

One last thought. I have considered the overdemandingness objection in a context where it is both feasible and desirable for the agent to act in a way that treats others as parametric and that aims, in the context of what others are expected to do, to maximize expected value. But it is worth noting that in many contexts there will be lots of problems – lots of disvalue – associated with treating others as parametric. In many situations there will be lots of problems associated with forming predictions about how far others will fail to comply in response to a certain demand and then trying to compensate for the expected shortfall. Such a course of action will be condescending in character, representing not just a prediction about others but a way of pre-empting their decisions; it will involve treating those others like instrumentalities, not interlocutors (Pettit and Smith 1996). In such a case it goes without saying that treating those others as parametric and going for what otherwise might be the optimal result may very well not be the course of action that is best by the consequentialist's lights.

This observation is important because it gives the lie to a charge that is sometimes associated with the overdemandingness objection. This is an allegation of hubris or immodesty: a charge that according to consequentialists ordinary agents should systematically transcend their own partial perspective and the demands that are salient there, striving always for a god's eye view and putting themselves in the service of a cosmic vision. It is true that according to consequentialists it is never enough just to satisfy yourself that you are doing your part in some idealized scheme of compliance; there is always a question as to whether, given the non-compliance of others, there is more that you can and ideally should try to achieve. But it is also true, and certainly worth emphasizing, that taking up a shortfall left by others may often involve treating them as less than yourself and may often generate counterproductive results. Consequentialism argues against the complacent attitude of minding only your own moral business – your own intuitive part – and never asking after the overall effects of that posture. But it does not offer support to the attitude of those busybodies who would systematically anticipate the failures of others and take upon themselves responsibility for compensation: responsibility for seeing that, assuming such failures, the world still goes as well as it can.

Notes

1 This section draws heavily on material from Pettit 1994a.
2 I assume that "right" is not taken as the word that tags that actual property which I may use a certain description to make salient without stipulating that the property does indeed satisfy – satisfy, as distinct from just appearing in current circumstances to satisfy – the description. Under such a tagging theory, the word would not have any meaning, strictly speaking; it would conform to a certain, traditional image of proper names. And while the word would have a referent, assuming that the world supplies a suitable property, those who used the term might be in total ignorance about the character of the referent. A tagging theory may work with some referring expressions but it looks quite counterintuitive with a predicate like "right." It is not as if there is a candidate property for the referent of "right" that is salient independently of things that users assume to be true of the property.
3 Or, if it is not that descriptive property itself, it is the higher-order property of having that property. But this possibility I shall ignore here. It would make no difference to our argument and, in any case, it is a less plausible candidate: network connections would seem to direct us to the realizers of the network roles, not to anything higher-order.
4 According to universalizability theory the judgment that something is right may be taken to be the judgment that it is universally prescribable or it may recast as something other than a judgment: say, in Hare's way, as the act of universal prescription itself, an act that is not true or false and that does not aspire to express a cognitive state like a belief. I shall assume that the theory is better taken in the first, cognitivist manner, in line with my general approach, but nothing hangs on this assumption here.
5 Perhaps I may seek to honor human happiness while allowing myself to take measures that deny happiness to me, since the value I honor in honoring happiness may well abstract from my own fate (McNaughton and Rawling 1992).

6 If it seems I should naturally favor promoting the relativized end of my own self-sufficiency, consider a parallel decision between whether to promote or honor the relativized end of my discharging my duties.

7 I picked up this test from a conversation with Frank Jackson and Michael Smith.

8 I should mention one response that a contract theorist or virtue theorist might make to the line of criticism that I have run here. This would say that as an account of rightness the theory takes values as given – in another role it may also offer a theory of value – and that it should be seen as a theory about what is the suitable response to value. The suitable response, on this approach, would not be identified as promoting or honoring values or anything of that substantive kind but as whatever response would prove compelling to contracting parties or virtuous agents (Swanton 1995). But this response runs foul of the same line of objection. For when the contracting party or the virtuous agent appeals to certain values to justify a choice, they must be able to say why the values do indeed justify it; they must be able to show that the choice serves the values in the promotional or honoring way, for example. It will hardly do for them to say that the choice serves the values well just to the extent that it serves them in the manner that they find compelling. It will not do to say this, as they will have to say it, without being able to describe the character of the service – the promotional or honouring character – that makes it compelling for them.

9 Of course it remains equally possible, for all we have said, that non-consequentialist approaches will fail in this respect, as we have found that they fail in others.

10 This paper was first presented at a conference at Monash University, Melbourne in June 1995 and an excerpt was delivered at the University of North Carolina Colloquium in Chapel Hill, October 1996. I learned an enormous number of lessons from comments that I received at both events. I also learned a great deal from independent comments by individuals who read or heard the paper and I must express my gratitude to Marcia Baron, Brad Hooker, Frank Jackson, Rae Langton, David McNaughton, Liam Murphy, Tim Mulgan, Jerry Postema, Geoff Sayre-McCord, Michael Slote, Michael Smith, Christine Swanton, and Chin Liew Ten. Some of my best friends are non-consequentialists and some of those best friends have been my most dedicated (and constructive) critics. Ironic offering though it may seem to be, I dedicate this essay to two of them: Doug MacLean and Susan Wolf. I owe Susan an extra debt, since she was a very helpful commentator at the UNC colloquium.

References

Anderson, Elizabeth (1993) *Value in Ethics and Economics*, Cambridge, Mass.: Harvard University Press.

Austin, John (1832) *The Province of Jurisprudence*, London (new edn 1954, by H. L. A. Hart, London: Weidenfeld).

Baron, Marcia (1995) *Kantian Ethics Almost Without Apology*, Ithaca, NY: Cornell University Press.

Beiner, Ronald (1983) *Political Judgment*, London: Methuen.

Blackburn, Simon (1984) *Spreading the Word*, Oxford: Oxford University Press.

Bradley, F. H. (1962) *Ethical Studies*, Oxford: Oxford University Press.

Braithwaite, John and Pettit, Philip (1990) *Not Just Deserts: a Republican Theory of Criminal Justice*, Oxford: Oxford University Press.

Dancy, Jonathan (1993) *Moral Reasons*, Oxford: Blackwell Publishers.

Dreier, James (1990) "Internalism and speaker relativism," *Ethics* 101: 6–26.

Foot, Philippa (1985) "Utilitarianism and the virtues," *Mind* 94: 196–209.

Freeman, Samuel (1995) "Utilitarianism, deontology and the priority of the right," *Philosophy and Public Affairs* 23: 313–49.

Frey, R. G. (ed.) (1984) *Utility and Rights*, Oxford: Blackwell Publishers.

Gaita, Raymond (1991) *Good and Evil: an Absolute Conception*, Basingstoke: Macmillan.

Hamlin, Alan (1989) "Rights, indirect utilitarianism, and contractarianism," *Economics and Philosophy* 5: 167–88.

Hare, R. M. (1981) *Moral Thinking*, Oxford: Oxford University Press.

Herman, Barbara (1993) *The Practice of Moral Judgment*, Cambridge, Mass.: Harvard University Press.

Hooker, Brad (1990) "Rule-consequentialism," *Mind* 99: 67–77.

——(1994) "Rule-consequentialism, incoherence, fairness," *Proceedings of the Aristotelian Society* 95: 19–35.

Hurley, Susan (1989) *Natural Reasons*, New York: Oxford University Press.

Hursthouse, Rosalind (1991) "Virtue theory and abortion," *Philosophy and Public Affairs* 20: 223–46.

Jackson, Frank (1991) "Decision-theoretic consequentialism and the nearest and dearest objection," *Ethics* 101: 461–82.

Jackson, Frank and Pargetter, Robert (1986) "Oughts, options, and actualism," *Philosophical Review* 95: 233–55.

Jackson, Frank and Pettit, Philip (1995) "Moral functionalism," *Philosophical Quarterly* 45: 20–40.

——and ——(1996) "Moral functionalism, supervenience, and reductionism," *Philosophical Quarterly* 46: 82–6.

Kagan, Shelly (1989) *The Limits of Morality*, Oxford: Oxford University Press.

Kant, Immanuel (1966) *The Moral Law: Groundwork of the Metaphysics of Morals*, ed. H. J. Paton, London: Hutchinson.

Korsgaard, Christine (1996) *The Sources of Normativity*, New York: Cambridge University Press.

Kymlicka, Will (1988) "Rawls on teleology and deontology," *Philosophy and Public Affairs* 17: 173–90.

Lewis, C. I. (1969) *Values and Intentions*, Stanford, Calif.: Stanford University Press.

Louden, Robert B. (1992) *Morality and Moral Theory: a Reappraisal and Reaffirmation*, New York and Oxford: Oxford University Press.

Lyons, David (1982) "Utility and rights," *Nomos* 24: 107–38.

McCloskey, H. J. (1957) "Restricted utilitarianism," *Philosophical Review* 66: 466–85.

McDowell, John (1979) "Virtue and reason," *Monist* 62: 331–50.

——(1981) "Non-cognitivism and rule-following," in S. Holtzman and C. Leich (eds) *Wittgenstein: To Follow a Rule*, London: Routledge.

McDowell, John and Pettit, Philip (1986) Introduction to Pettit and McDowell (eds) *Subject, Thought and Context*, Oxford: Oxford University Press.

McNaughton, David (1988) *Moral Vision*, Oxford: Blackwell Publishers.

McNaughton, David and Rawling, Piers (1992) "Honoring and promoting values," *Ethics* 102: 835–43.

Murphy, Liam (1993) "The demands of beneficence," *Philosophy and Public Affairs* 22: 267–92.

Nagel, Thomas (1986) *The View from Nowhere*, New York: Oxford University Press.

Nozick, Robert (1974) *Anarchy, State, and Utopia*, Oxford: Blackwell Publishers.

Oakley, Justin (1996) "Varieties of virtue ethics," *Ratio* 9: 128–52.

O'Neill, Onora (1975) *Acting on Principle*, New York: Columbia University Press.

——(1989) *Constructions of Reason: Explorations of Kant's Practical Philosophy*, Cambridge: Cambridge University Press.

Parfit, Derek (1984) *Reasons and Persons*, Oxford: Oxford University Press.

Pettit, Philip (1984) "Satisficing consequentialism," *Proceedings of the Aristotelian Society*, Suppl. vol. 58: 165–76.

—— (1987) "Universalisability without utilitarianism," *Mind* 96: 74–82.

—— (1991a) "Consequentialism," in Peter Singer (ed.) *A Companion to Ethics*, Oxford: Blackwell Publishers.

—— (1991b) "Realism and response-dependence," *Mind* 100: 587–626.

—— (1993a) *The Common Mind: an Essay on Psychology, Society and Politics*, New York: Oxford University Press (paperback edn with new postscript, 1996).

—— (ed.) (1993b) *Consequentialism*, London: Dartmouth Press.

—— (1993c) "A definition of physicalism," *Analysis* 53: 213–23.

—— (1994a) "Consequentialism and moral psychology," *International Journal of Philosophical Studies* 2: 1–17; originally appeared as "Consequentialisme et psychologie morale," *Revue de Metaphysique et de Morale* 99(2) (1994): 223–44.

—— (1994b) Review of John Rawls, *Political Liberalism*, *Journal of Philosophy* 91: 215–20.

—— (1995) "The virtual reality of Homo Economicus," *Monist* 78: 308–29.

—— (1997a) *Republicanism: a Theory of Freedom and Government*, Oxford: Oxford University Press.

—— (1997b) "Embracing objectivity in ethics," in Brian Leiter (ed.), *Objectivity in Law and Morals*, Cambridge: Cambridge University Press.

—— (forthcoming) "Practical belief and philosophical theory," *Australasian Journal of Philosophy* 76.

Pettit, Philip and Brennan, Geoffrey (1986) "Restrictive consequentialism," *Australasian Journal of Philosophy* 64: 438–55.

Pettit, Philip and Smith, Michael (1990) "Backgrounding desire," *Philosophical Review* 99: 565–92.

—— and —— (1996) "Freedom in belief and desire," *Journal of Philosophy* 93: 429–49.

Rabinowitz, Wlodzimierz (1979) *Universalizability*, Dordrecht: D. Reidel.

Railton, Peter (1984) "Alienation, consequentialism and the demands of Morality," *Philosophy and Public Affairs* 13: 134–71.

Rawls, John (1971) *A Theory of Justice*, Oxford: Oxford University Press.

—— (1995) "Reply to Habermas," *Journal of Philosophy* 92: 132–80.

Scanlon, Tim (1982) "Contractualism," in Amartya Sen and Bernard Williams (eds) *Utilitarianism and Beyond*, Cambridge: Cambridge University Press.

Scheffler, Sam (1982) *The Rejection of Consequentialism*, Oxford: Oxford University Press.

—— (ed.) (1988) *Consequentialism and its Critics*, Oxford: Oxford University Press.

Sen, Amartya (1982) "Rights and agency," *Philosophy and Public Affairs* 11: 3–39.

Sen, Amartya and Williams, Bernard (eds) (1982) *Utilitarianism and Beyond*, Cambridge: Cambridge University Press.

Sidgwick, Henry (1966) *The Methods of Ethics*, New York: Dover.

Singer, Peter (1972) "Famine, affluence and morality," *Philosophy and Public Affairs* 1: 229–43.

Slote, Michael (1989) *Beyond Optimizing*, Cambridge, Mass.: Harvard University Press.

—— (1992) *From Morality to Virtue*, New York: Oxford University Press.

Smart, J. J. C. (1967) "Extreme and restricted utilitarianism," in Philippa Foot (ed.) *Theories of Ethics*, London: Oxford University Press.

—— (1977) "Benevolence is an overriding attitude," *Australasian Journal of Philosophy* 55: 127–35.

Smart, J. J. C. and Williams Bernard, (1973) *Utilitarianism: For and Against*, Cambridge: Cambridge University Press.

Smith, Michael (1994) *The Moral Problem*, Oxford: Blackwell Publishers.

Stocker, Michael (1976) "The schizophrenia of modern ethical theory," *Journal of Philosophy* 73: 453–66.

Swanton, Christine (1995) "Profiles of the virtues," *Pacific Philosophical Quarterly* 76: 47–72.

Timmons, Mark (1996) "Outline of a contextualist moral epistemology," in W. Sinnott-Armstrong and M. Timmons (eds) *Moral Knowledge*, New York: Oxford University Press.

Van Roojen, M. (1996) "Moral functionalism and moral reduction," *Philosophical Quarterly* 46: 77–81.

Williams, Bernard (1981) *Moral Luck*, Cambridge: Cambridge University Press.

Wolf, Susan (1982) "Moral saints," *Journal of Philosophy* 79: 419–39.

3

Virtue Ethics

Michael Slote

Although what is today called virtue ethics was the pre-eminent form of ethical theorizing in the ancient world, this way of approaching ethics has been largely ignored during the modern era. But in recent years – and beginning perhaps with Elizabeth Anscombe's article "Modern moral philosophy" (Anscombe 1958) – there has been a revival of interest in virtue ethics to the point where today it stands as one of the major ways of doing substantive philosophical ethics. The new interest has come about in part as a result of dissatisfaction with the way moral philosophy has been done in modern times, and, especially, recently. For modern moral philosophy has emphasized moral obligation and moral law at the expense, some have felt, of the sources of morality in the inner life and character of the individual. And virtue ethics in recent times has sought to make good that deficiency while at the same time adapting ancient ideas of virtue to the requirements of current-day ethical theory and to practical issues of applied ethics.

In this essay, I shall describe what virtue ethics is and attempt to explain what I believe to be its advantages over other currently influential forms of substantive ethical theorizing, most notably, the consequentialism and Kantianism defended by my co-contributors to this volume. In the course of its revival, virtue ethics has largely been inspired by the Aristotelian model of ethics, but the present essay will draw both on Aristotelianism and on other traditions of virtue ethics in its attempt to describe currently promising approaches. Also, virtue ethics during much of its recent revival and present prominence has attracted to its banner many ethicists who are critical of the whole idea of ethical theorizing. Aristotle notably held that a proper understanding of what is admirable and right in human action cannot be captured in general rules or principles, but is a matter, rather, of sensitivity and fine discernment incorporated into good habits of moral thought, desire, and action. And many notable recent thinkers who invite classification as virtue ethicists have tended to infer that ethical *theory* is fundamentally misguided: the moral life, they have held, is too rich and complex to be captured by utilitarian/consequentialist, Kantian, or social-contract approaches of the sort that seek to ground ethics in unifying first principles. (See Baier 1985; McDowell 1979; Nussbaum 1985; Rorty 1988; and Williams 1985. I should also mention Alasdair MacIntyre (1984), who defends a form of virtue theory, but is rather dismissive of the tradition of "ahistorical" analytic ethics that the contributions of the present volume belong to.)

More recently, however, many virtue ethicists have begun to see their approach as representing a distinctive and advantageous way of engaging in ethical theorizing. I shall just below mention some of the reasons why I favor treating virtue ethics as a form of ethical theory, rather than as a rejection of theory altogether. And I hope to show in what follows that in the role of theory rather than anti-theory, certain forms of virtue ethics represent promising alternatives to consequentialism and Kantianism.

1   What is Virtue Ethics?

Before we go any further with the defense of virtue ethics, I should first say something about what virtue ethics actually is. The recent calls for a revival of virtue ethics are in fact somewhat ambiguous. Some ethicists have simply wanted to see one or another preferred set of moral principles supplemented or complemented by an account of virtuous traits and actions. Others have sought a genuinely *free-standing* ethics of virtue, and the idea of virtue ethics is today widely understood as involving an ethical approach independent of other major traditions. But what, then, distinguishes virtue ethics from other ways of doing ethics?

As in so many other places in philosophy, exact definitions are difficult to come by, but the main contrast, as I have already suggested, is with forms of ethics based in moral laws, rules, principles. In virtue ethics, the focus is on the virtuous individual and on those inner traits, dispositions, and motives that qualify her as being virtuous. (Some forms of virtue ethics do allow for general moral rules or even laws, but these are typically treated as derivative or secondary factors.) Many modern philosophers think of the moral life as a matter of relating properly to moral rules, but in the virtue ethics of the ancient world and in those few instances of virtue ethics one finds in modern or recent philosophy, the understanding of the moral or ethical life primarily requires us to understand what it is to be a virtuous individual or what it is to have one or another particular virtue, conceived as an inner trait or disposition of the individual. So the first thing we can say about virtue ethics in an attempt to distinguish it from other approaches is that it is *agent-focused*.

But another important feature needs to be mentioned. An ethics of rules will typically characterize acts as morally right or wrong, morally permissible or obligatory, depending on how they accord with appropriate rules. Such moral epithets are called "deontic" (from the Greek word for necessity), and they contrast with another class of ethical epithets where there is less immediate or ultimate connection with rules, namely, "aretaic" (from the Greek word for excellence or virtue) ethical terms like "morally good," "admirable," "virtuous." Virtue ethics makes primary use of aretaic terms in its ethical characterizations, and it either treats deontic epithets as derivative from the aretaic or dispenses with them altogether. Thus an ethics of virtue thinks primarily in terms of what is noble or ignoble, admirable or deplorable, good or bad, rather than in terms of what is obligatory, permissible, or wrong, and together with the focus on the (inner character of the) agent, this comes close enough, I think, to marking off what is distinctive of and common to all forms of virtue ethics: both the ancient virtue ethics of Plato, Aristotle, the Stoics, and the Epicureans, and the modern virtue ethics, for example of the nineteenth-century British ethicist James Martineau (1891). (Once we have these two features of virtue ethics clearly in view, we can also see that neither of them characterizes consequentialism, with its traditional focus on *obligatory actions* rather than on goodness of character.)

However, among the forms of virtue ethics that meet the above conditions, some are more radical than others, and since I plan, in what follows, to discuss the merits and indeed the promise both of the less radical and of the more radical kinds of virtue ethics, I would like to say something about this further distinction. It will help to consider the example of Aristotle's ethics. In the *Nicomachean Ethics*, Aristotle focuses more on the inner traits and character of the virtuous individual than he does on what makes actions good, or noble, or right, and so his theory is *agent-focused*, rather than *act-focused* in the manner of modern consequentialism and of views based on moral rules that are supposed to govern human actions. Nonetheless, his view as it is frequently interpreted is in an important sense *act-based*. For Aristotle, the excellence or rightness of an action doesn't essentially depend on the motives or habits that gave rise to it, or on the character of the person who did it. Rather, the virtuous individual is someone who, without relying on rules, is sensitive and intelligent enough to perceive what is noble or right as it varies from circumstance to circumstance, but this metaphor of perception seems to indicate that being virtuous involves being keyed in to facts independent of one's virtuousness about what acts are admirable or called for.

A more radical kind of virtue ethics would say that the ethical character of actions is not thus independent of how and why and by whom the actions are done. Rather, what is independent and fundamental is our understanding and evaluation of human motives and habits, and the evaluation of actions is entirely derivative from and dependent on what we have to say ethically about (the inner life of) the agents who perform those actions. The more radical kind of virtue ethics is thus *agent-based*, not merely, like Aristotle's views (on one common interpretation), agent-focused. And perhaps not very surprisingly there are very few clear-cut examples, whether in the ancient or the modern world, of such a more radical approach. Arguably, though, the philosopher James Martineau, mentioned above, has this kind of radical view, and Plato in the *Republic* comes quite close to such a radical view.

I mention both sorts of virtue ethics here, because I think both sorts have contemporaneous relevance. And what I shall be doing in what follows is first, show how well and plausibly a merely agent-focused neo-Aristotelian view can fare in comparison with present-day alternatives like utilitarianism/consequentialism, Kantianism, and moral commonsensism; and then discuss the contemporary interest and the promise of certain radical, agent-based forms of virtue ethics. I am not sure which form of virtue ethics is likely to fare best and make the greatest contribution in the current climate of ethical theory, because in comparison with consequentialism and Kantianism, virtue ethics has *in recent times* so far had little chance to spread its wings. Best, then, to discuss two or three alternative approaches to virtue theory, rather than only a single version, if two or three approaches really do have promise, as I hope to show.

But this still means giving preference to some versions of virtue ethics over others – there are far more than three kinds of virtue ethics discussed in the growing recent literature of the subject. Along the way, I shall sometimes give my reasons for preferring certain approaches to virtue theory over others, but perhaps the largest choice at issue here is in the preference for theory itself. So let me say something at this point about my reasons for not allowing myself to be carried along on the strong current of anti-theory that runs through much of the recent revival of virtue ethics.

2   Theory versus Anti-theory

Notable recent anti-theorists such as Annette Baier (1985) and Bernard Williams (1985) have been very critical of ethical theory's quest for hierarchically ordered, exceptionless, and universally applicable moral principles. They have said that the theorist's preference for impartiality and simplicity has led moral theories to posit an underlying unity to all moral thought and conceive all moral disputes as resolvable by decision procedures that see all moral complexities as reducible to and measurable in terms of some single commensurating moral consideration or factor. But it is far from clear that everything that deserves the name of moral theory has all these tendencies. Many think of Aristotle as a moral theorist *par excellence*, but he denies the possibility of exceptionless universal principles and has no place in his philosophy for the idea of a single kind of moral consideration in terms of which all moral issues can be resolved. Nor is Aristotle's view impartialist, if by that one means a view that requires one to treat all people equally and without partiality or preference. One might, then, conclude that Aristotle is no moral theorist, but my own preference is to allow a wider understanding of the notion (see Louden 1992). Indeed the kind of neo-Aristotelian contemporary version of virtue ethics I shall be presenting shortly has none of the supposedly objectionable features mentioned above. Moreover, it is worth mentioning that it is not even clear that Kantian ethics and the kind of consequentialism presented in this volume exemplify all or most of the theoretical tendencies decried by the anti-theorists. And, in any event, it will be no part of my brief against views opposing virtue ethics that they are too theoretical. In what follows I hope to show that we need theory in ethics and thus that theoretical virtues like simplicity and unifying power have some weight in deciding what kind of ethical view to adopt. To be sure, intuitive considerations also have considerable weight, and it is my view that consequentialism in particular has very unwelcome and anti-intuitive implications that hobble it as an approach to morality. But I think the real issue in this volume and in ethics generally is *what kind of ethical theory to adopt, not whether we need theory in ethics*, and I shall shortly explain why I think this and why I think current forms of virtue ethics that rely on theoretical considerations are promising. What I would like to do now, though, and by way of approaching these conclusions is to point out some problems with a purely intuitive, particularistic, anti-theoretical approach to morality. The idea that our moral understanding of things is too rich and complex to be reduced to universal principles or to require, in the name of some inappropriate scientific ideal, any kind of simplifying unification in terms of a single factor or small set of such factors is not *per se* objectionable. Indeed, it has a certain attractiveness. But I want to now show, as briefly as I know how, that our ordinary intuitive moral thought is not just complex, but subject to paradox and internal incoherence, and this is a far less acceptable situation than what the anti-theorists imagine to be the case. In fact, it is what makes moral theory both necessary and desirable.

Consider the problem of moral luck as discussed by Thomas Nagel (1979). A person driving along a lonely country road and paying too much attention to the scenery might swerve into the oncoming traffic lane, incur no accident, and blame herself very little if at all for her inattention or negligence. And our own attitude, thinking of such a case on its own, would normally be quite similar. However, if we imagine the same scenario except that a car in fact is coming in the opposite direction, with the result that an accident occurs and the other driver or a passenger in her own car is killed, the negligent driver will very much blame herself. And our own inclination, say, as observers would be very similar. Yet the difference between the two cases is, from the standpoint of the agent, a matter of luck or accident, and our common-sense moral intuitions (check this in yourselves!) find it implausible and morally repugnant to believe that differences in blameworthiness and other serious moral differences between people should be a matter of luck or accident, beyond anyone's control or advance knowledge. So the moral judgments we make and intuitions we have about cases of negligence are in fact inconsistent, hardly an acceptable state of affairs for the moral philosopher.

Let me mention another area in which our ordinary moral intuitions fail to cohere with one another. Our common moral thinking treats it as sometimes obligatory to do good things for others and almost always obligatory to refrain from harming them. But there is no similar obligation in regard to benefiting oneself or refraining from doing damage to one's prospects or even one's health. This difference is captured by saying that common-sense morality is self–other asymmetric in regard to our obligations. But why shouldn't we have obligations to advance and not to damage our own prospects, our own happiness? Common sense (and again you can check for yourselves) has an answer ready for this question, and it is that it makes no sense to suppose there is an obligation to do things we are already inclined to do and can naturally be expected to do. Since we naturally and expectably do care for our own interests, there can't be – there is no moral need for – an obligation to do so.

But aside from the issue whether people really can be expected to take care of their own interests in a rational way (think of all the self-destructive, lazy, or health-risking people you know), the just-given explanation actually is incoherent or incongruent with other intuitive moral assumptions. For example, we are naturally very concerned to help those who are near and dear to us and typically lack this degree of practical concern for strangers or people we don't know. Yet according to common sense we have obligations to near and dear that we *don't* have toward others. And that is the very opposite of what one should expect given the above rationale for the absence of an obligation to pursue and advance our own well-being. Common-sense thinking turns out to be subject to other paradoxes or incongruities of this sort, and that means there is something wrong with common sense. Our intuitions turn out to clash among themselves, and if we are to attain to full coherence in our ethical thinking, we are forced to reject at least some intuitions. But which ones? Well, to decide *that* issue, we need to look for a way of understanding ethics that allows us to avoid incoherence or paradox, and that task requires us to be philosophically and morally *inventive*.

Similar problems have notably occurred in other areas of philosophy. When naive set theory turned out to be self-contradictory, different theorists began proposing different ways of grounding arithmetic in set theory, and the validity and success of those different approaches was measured in terms of theoretical considerations like simplicity, scope, explanatory power. Likewise, when it turned out that our intuitive assumptions about what statements scientifically confirm what others were inconsistent, the desire for a coherent understanding of scientific confirmation led philosophers of science to propose different ways of formally understanding confirmation, and, again, the success or promise of their proposals was judged partly in terms of how much ordinary thinking they preserved, but also partly in terms of theoretical desiderata like simplicity, scope, etc.

Why should it be any different in ethics? Given that intuitions clash, ingenuity is needed to come up with something that avoids paradox, and if moral intuitions cannot settle everything, then theoretical considerations, philosophical considerations, seem relevant to our task, given the analogy with what happens in other areas of philosophy and *the desire to come up with some kind of coherent ethical view of things.*[1] Bernard Williams (1985: 116f.) has criticized ethical theorizing for simplifying and unifying what seems rich and complex. We have, he thinks, not too many ideas, but too few. And to be sure (and I shall make something of this in criticizing utilitarianism/consequentialism below) a moral theory *can* oversimplify ethical phenomena, leave too many things we believe or feel out of account. But Williams misses the point that at least in some respects our ethical thought has too many ideas, rather than too few; for if our intuitive thought contains contradictions or paradoxes, something has to be eliminated in order to attain the kind of ethical understanding we are looking for. He overstates the case, then, against moral theory. A theory that blurs intuitive ethical distinctions and phenomena has a strike against it, but we do need some sort of theory in ethics and have to abandon some intuitions, if we are to gain the sort of paradox-free understanding in that domain that has been and is being sought in set theory, confirmation theory, and a host of other areas in philosophy.

3   Virtue Ethics versus Kantian and Common-sense Morality

In attempting to revive virtue ethics and make it worthy of consideration in the current climate of ethical debate and theory, I think we have to do more than simply brush off and polish up ancient Aristotelianism. Many central Aristotelian ethical views appear to us nowadays to lack plausibility or force, and although the agent-focused (but not agent-based) virtue ethics that I want to discuss and defend first may properly, and for reasons I shall shortly describe, be deemed neo-Aristotelian, it is a view squarely anchored in recent ethics-theoretical debates among Kantianism, common-sense morality, and consequentialism, and it would be demanding too much even of Aristotle to expect his views to have such a contemporaneous thrust. The virtue ethics I want initially to propose is based in our current common-sense ethical thinking, and although Aristotle's ethics is in great measure based in the

ordinary ethical thinking of his own day, times have greatly chan-
ged. For example, the notion of guilt and our modern-day emphasis on kindness and compassion (influenced, no doubt, by the
historical example of Christ and Christianity) are not really to be
found in Aristotle or, as a rule, in Greek philosophy generally.
And Aristotle's common-sense-based account of ethically good or
right action assumes a doctrine of the mean that simply cannot
account for what we in modern times consider to be some of the
most important aspects of the ethical evaluation of actions.

According to the doctrine of the mean, noble, good, admirable,
right actions (they coincide for Aristotle) lie in a mean between
extremes. The courageous and hence admirable thing to do in a
situation of danger will be neither cowardly nor foolhardy, but
somewhere in between; and even though Aristotle agrees that courage lies closer to foolhardiness than to cowardice, still each of the
Aristotelian virtues involves acting (and desiring too) in a way that
lies at some point, intuitively, between two extremes of vice. This
model of moral action may fit courage and justice and temperance
(not taking too much, not taking too little food, for example), but a
great number of commentators have noted that it has no natural
application to certain areas of the moral life we nowadays think of
as very important. Honesty and truthfulness are not a matter of
telling neither too much nor too little of the truth, nor a matter of
hitting a mark between *understatement* and *overstatement*. The
attempt to conceive the virtue of truthfulness in such terms distorts
our real and committed moral thinking about that virtue, and similar points can be made about the virtue of loyalty to people and
about promise-keeping. Modern moral philosophy puts considerable emphasis, therefore, on virtues that don't fit the Aristotelian
model of the mean, and a modern-day virtue ethics has reason to
resist taking over that doctrine from Aristotle.

Aristotle also believed in a doctrine of the unity of the virtues,
according to which in order to have any single important virtue
one must possess all the important virtues. This view also grates
against much of our modern way of seeing things, and I believe
there is no reason to adopt it. I would propose instead that if
we are seeking a virtue-ethical theory that has the kind of intuitive
plausibility for our time that Aristotle sought for his own theory,
we do best to consult and draw upon our current-day thinking

and intuitions about what is ethically admirable and what counts as a virtue. It will turn out that those intuitions support an overall ethical view that is in important respects structurally similar to Aristotle's views, but I think it best to begin by structurally comparing Kantianism, common-sense morality, and consequentialism with our common thinking about the virtues.

What do I mean by structure? Well, consider the asymmetry with regard to self and other that we earlier noted as a feature of common-sense morality: we seem to have moral obligations in regard to the happiness of others that we lack in regard to ourselves. This feature of the intuitive moral landscape yields paradox, we saw, when combined with other features of that landscape, but it is also interesting to note that common-sense morality is similarly self–other asymmetric with respect to the *moral goodness* of actions and traits of character. Other things being equal, we ordinarily think that it is morally better to give more rather than less help to another person who needs help; but doing more rather than less for oneself (helping oneself, e.g., to more generous portions of a free lunch) is not typically regarded as morally more meritorious. Perhaps it is smarter or wiser or more prudent to provide oneself with a better lunch or take pills to relieve one's headache, but "morally better" is not a phrase that naturally comes to mind in connection with such actions. Similarly, although we might admire someone for having been prudent on her own behalf, we wouldn't usually consider the possessor of such a trait morally better than someone lacking the trait; but if one becomes kinder or is kinder to people than some other person, then one is normally regarded as to that extent morally more praiseworthy or better. So with regard to well-being there is a self–other asymmetry in our common thinking about what is morally better and worse.

The same self–other asymmetries also exist in and for Kantian morality. For Kant says we have duties to benefit, i.e. promote the well-being of, others that we lack in connection with the promotion of our own well-being, and also that promoting the well-being of others is virtuous and morally meritorious in a way that benefiting oneself is not. (Perhaps there is virtue in seeking one's own happiness *as a means to* benefiting others or fulfilling other duties, but the virtuousness of benefiting others is *not* derivative or conditional in this way.) By contrast, act-utilitarianism and act-consequentialism more generally are self–other symmetric with regard to the promotion of human well-being: it is as morally good and obligatory to advance one's own well-being (when there is no one else around to help) as it is to advance the well-being of another person (when there is no one else around one can help).

Interestingly enough, our ordinary thinking about what is admirable and counts as a virtue is also self–other symmetric in the sense just specified. We admire resourcefulness, sagacity, prudence, and circumspection (both the traits and most instances of them), even though these virtues are primarily beneficial to those who possess them rather than to others. Yet of course we also admire (instances of) primarily other-benefiting traits like kindness, benevolence, and honesty; these too count as virtues in our ordinary thinking. This shows that what we ordinarily regard as virtues doesn't necessarily march with what we think of as morally good or as moral virtues. Self-regarding resourcefulness or prudence may be admired and count as a virtue, but, intuitively speaking, it is not morally good nor a moral virtue. (Nor yet does being resourceful or prudent count as being "virtuous," because the latter concept, unlike the notion of *a* virtue, has moral connotations and is roughly the same as the concept of being morally good.) Our common thinking about the virtues, then, includes much that lies outside the sphere of morality, and even if common-sense morality is self–other asymmetric, therefore, a virtue ethics that relies on common-sense thought about the virtues and what is admirable will not be.

The reason for all this emphasis on symmetry and asymmetry is that such structural issues bear on the merits of different ethical theories. We have already seen that the self–other asymmetry of common-sense moral obligation leads, when taken with other common-sense judgments, to incongruity and paradox. That is a reason for rejecting ordinary moral thought as it stands and looking for something better. (For reasons too complex to enter into here, but that include the immense difficulties that arise for ethics in connection with the problem of moral luck, it seems unlikely that such a better theory or view can be reached simply by making a few minor adjustments in common-sense thinking; see Slote 1992, chs 3 and 7.) But Kantian moral theory faces exactly similar difficulties because it offers the same explanation as our common sense as to why there is no obligation to promote one's own well-being and yet also holds that we have obligations concerning the welfare of those near and dear to us that we lack toward strangers.

However, there is a further point to be made about both Kantian and common-sense morality in connection with their asymmetric character. As I pointed out just above, both views say that it is virtuous and morally good to benefit others, seek others' happiness, in a way that it is not virtuous or morally good to promote one's own well-being. And it seems to me that such views (unlike utilitarianism and our ordinary thought about what is *admirable* or *a virtue*) in some sense devalue or downgrade the well-being of moral agents and thus the agents themselves. Kantianism and common-sense *moral* thought of course *permit* us to seek our own well-being (within moral limits); but they treat that permission as a mere *concession* to agents' well-being, rather than as a source of positive moral value analogous to promoting the happiness of others. And it seems to me invidious and somewhat downgrading of the status of agents if one treats the agent's pursuit of her own well-being as lacking the kind of positive moral value one assigns to her pursuit of others' happiness. (To be sure, Kant, and less clearly common sense, assigns us an independent duty to develop our talents, and the setting of such moral tasks does assume and perhaps assure a certain dignity and value on the part of moral agents, but it seems to me that one at the very same time also detracts from that dignity and somewhat devalues the agent if one morally devalues her pursuit of her own self-interest as compared with her pursuit of other people's interests or welfare.)

One might object here that moral value is not the only kind of value and that in common-sense terms it is rational, and so has value from *that* standpoint, if one pursues one's own self-interest. But even if this reply somewhat blunts the claim that common-sense morality devalues the moral agent by pointing up other areas of evaluative thought that may restore the evaluative balance, so to speak, between agent and other, it won't work in behalf of Kantian moral theory because the latter assigns an inferior *rational* standing and value to the pursuit of self-interest, as compared with the moral and rational standing of helping others (we are under a categorical or inescapable moral requirement to help others, but there are no such requirements of rational prudence). So I don't think Kant's view can easily escape the charges mentioned above,[2] and since, in addition, both common sense and Kantian morality incur the above-mentioned paradox concerning our obligations to those near and dear to us, both sorts of approach to morality face at least one problem *that consequentialism and our ordinary thought about admirability and the virtues simply avoid*. Indeed, having seen that both Kantian and common-sense morality face a number of serious difficulties, we are *left* with consequentialism and our ordinary thought about what is admirable or counts as a virtue as so far relatively unscathed, and we thus now need to consider the comparative merits of these two ways of approaching ethics. We also need a name for that part of our ordinary evaluative thinking that speaks of what is admirable or counts as (an instance of) a virtue without using specifically moral terminology like "obligation," "morally good," or "blameworthy." We get into trouble using the latter terminology in accordance with our ordinary intuitions, and what I propose now is to avoid such language in favor of the symmetric but not specifically moral terminology of admirability and the virtues, using the latter in accordance with the full complexity and richness of our ordinary intuitions about these matters. And I propose to use the phrase "common-sense virtue ethics" to apply to the view that thereby emerges. Common-sense virtue ethics doesn't fall into the paradoxes that attend self–other asymmetry and it also doesn't devalue the agent or virtue-possessor. (Since we are speaking about value language that is not specifically moral but talk about admirability and the virtues can be said at least to be *ethical* in some broad sense, I shall drop the phrase "moral agent" in connection with my own theory of common-sense virtue ethics.) It is time to see how it compares with consequentialism.

4   Common-sense Virtue Ethics versus Consequentialism

Consequentialism and its most well-known species, utilitarianism, evade the paradox and inconsistency we find in ordinary moral thought and if they are open to the charge of devaluing (the well-being or happiness of) moral agents, that cannot be because they never place ethical value on acts or traits promoting (solely) the well-being of the agent. So if there is some reason for preferring common-sense virtue ethics to consequentialism, we have not yet mentioned it, and that will be the task of the present section of this essay.

Consequentialism evades the paradox mentioned earlier in connection with our intuitively stronger obligations to near and dear ones, through denying any such ground-floor differences in our obligations to people and, of course, also denying that we lack moral obligations to advance our own welfare. And it doesn't fall victim to the inconsistencies of our thinking in the area of moral luck, because it simply denies the intuition that blameworthiness and moral goodness cannot be a matter of luck or accident. It says blameworthiness is simply a matter of what it is *right to blame*, and since it understands rightness in turn in terms of good consequences and good consequences are frequently unpredictable and a matter of luck, it clearly allows moral blameworthiness to depend on factors of luck or accident. In saying this, consequentialism of course makes a somewhat paradoxical assumption of its own, namely, that blameworthiness is not a moral quality internal to the agent and what she has done, but a matter of whether it will be socially useful to blame her. But the consequentialist could argue that such an unintuitive conclusion might be a price worth paying for the elimination of outright inconsistency in the area of moral luck.

However, consequentialism in many or most of its prevalent forms does seem open to a charge of devaluing agents, though from a slightly different direction from the way that accusation applies to Kantian ethics. Consequentialism says that at the most fundamental level we ought to be no more concerned with any one person's happiness than with that of any other. So when consequentialism (more precisely, act-consequentialism) tells us we ought morally to produce the best overall results we can, it seems to lead to an obligation on our part to sacrifice ourselves or our self-interest whenever an objectively better state of affairs would result from our doing so. Now some forms of consequentialism treat cultural achievements as valuable in their own right rather than, like utilitarianism, solely as means to overall sentient or human happiness, and these anti-utilitarian forms of consequentialism might deem it permissible or not wrong for many professors or students of philosophy or scientists or artists to pursue their interesting careers, rather than go off to help the sick and starving people of this world. For it might be claimed that the world is a better place because of such cultural efforts than it would be if given people sought mainly or solely to alleviate human misery. But if one holds a utilitarian version of consequentialism or is simply not convinced that one has an important cultural contribution to make, it seems necessary to conclude that one has a moral duty to abandon one's professional or business career, if (one thinks) one can do more good in the world by going to help the sick and starving at home and abroad than one could do by pursuing one's career, being kind to those near and dear to one, and even giving generously to charity (all while living in relative comfort).

As a result, consequentialism and utilitarianism seem to require more self-sacrifice on the part of (many) moral agents than, intuitively, it seems fair to require of them. For most of us think the Albert Schweitzers and Mother Teresas of this world go *beyond the call of duty* and that we are not morally wrong, but simply less morally praiseworthy than they, if we lead career-oriented "decent" lives. And so the criticism that standard act-consequentialism and, especially, act-utilitarianism are unfairly demanding or too demanding of moral agents can lead one to say that these theories devalue moral agents and their interests: not because they place no moral value on (the agent's pursuing) those interests, but because the agent's interests count as a mere drop in the bucket in relation to the total human or sentient well-being that utilitarianism and plausible versions of consequentialism all direct us to promote. And it in no way mitigates this charge to point out that the moral agent's interests will be more adequately cared for if *other* moral agents do their consequentialist duties; for the consequentialist requires sacrifice of one's welfare in the name of overall optimality of results even if no one else *is* doing her duty, her share. In such cases, consequentialism's demand of sacrifice seems especially to devalue the agent's natural concern for her own projects, her own well-being.

Now there are some forms of consequentialism that avoid this form of criticism by laying less stringent requirements upon moral agents. Rather than demand that one produce the best results one can, these forms of consequentialism require only that one do enough (or a considerable amount of) good in and for the world. These so-called "satisficing," as opposed to optimizing or maximizing, forms of consequentialism and utilitarianism would allow people more time for their own personal interests and careers in a world where more good, objectively, could be done by sacrificing them. The sacrifice is then beyond the call of duty and praiseworthy, just not morally required, and it is thus only the maximizing/optimizing forms of consequentialism generally defended within that tradition that seem mostly likely to fall prey to the objection concerning the devaluation of the agent.[3]

However, there is a further feature of consequentialism that can be elicited from our previous discussion and that allows an important distinction to be made between the ways consequentialism and common-sense virtue ethics treat the happiness of agents. Consequentialism is *agent-neutral*. One's obligations to oneself are basically no weaker or stronger than those to any other single person, and this is true whether one accepts an optimizing or a satisficing form of consequentialism. But the relation between self and other plays out differently in an ethics of virtue based in our common-sense thinking about the virtues, even though both consequentialism and common-sense virtue are self–other symmetric in the broad sense defined earlier. This requires a good deal of explanation, but the explanation will in fact help us for the first time to gain a picture of the overall structure and distinctive merits of the common-sense virtue-ethical approach.

Our ordinary thinking about what is admirable and deplorable treats it as inherently more deplorable to refuse help to those near and dear to one than to refuse similar help to strangers, and this already entails a difference from consequentialism's requirement of agent-neutral ethical judgment. But even if agent-neutrality requires a kind of symmetry of fundamental moral concern as between any two individuals (where one of these can be the agent herself), common-sense virtue ethics exemplifies its own distinctive form of overall ethical symmetry, and that form is not only compatible with but entails our having differing fundamental concerns regarding different individuals. In particular, I think there is reason to believe that our implicit thinking about what is admirable and a virtue favors some sort of balance of concern as between oneself (the agent) and *other people considered as a class or category.*

What may begin to move us toward such a conclusion is a feature of our ordinary thinking I have not yet mentioned. Some commonly regarded virtues are mainly other-directed and other-benefiting, like truthfulness, kindness, fairness, and compassion; others are mainly self-directed and self-benefiting, like prudence, fortitude, resourcefulness, and circumspection; and still others, like courage, wisdom, and self-control, seem to be "mixed" of both sorts of elements. But it seems in no degree a tenet of our common thought that the other-benefiting virtues are greater or more important virtues than the self-benefiting or mixed virtues: fair dealing is certainly admired, but, from an intuitive standpoint, not necessarily any more admired than fortitude or courage or resourcefulness, and if we take a mixed virtue like courage, the importance we place on its other-regarding usefulness is by no means greater than that we place on its self-regarding usefulness. All this gives us reason to think that common thinking about the virtues is symmetrical or balanced as between the aretaic value placed on self-regarding virtues and that placed on other-regarding virtues.

But notice further that the whole notion of an other-regarding or other-benefiting virtue treats other people, in regard to the person who possesses a given trait, *as a class, rather than one on one.* So unlike act-utilitarianism and act-consequentialism, which assume some sort of equality or balance between the possessor of any good trait and each and every other person, the balance or symmetry that common sense seems to subscribe to is between any given agent or trait possessor and others as a class. Using terminology from the medieval scholastic philosophers, we can say that utilitarianism thinks in terms of some sort of balance between self and others, understanding "others" *in sensu diviso,* whereas common sense seems to understand the idea of balance between self and others *in sensu composito.*

What I now want to argue is that, together with some further features of our thought about the virtues, the just-mentioned balance yields an overarching general principle that can serve as an action guide for common-sense virtue ethics. The principle, to a first approximation, is that one should in one's life balance concern for oneself with concern for other people taken as a class. But there are two problems with such a principle. First, it makes use of the term "should" ("ought" would have done just as well), and virtue ethics is supposed to be grounded in the use of aretaic terms, not deontic terms like "should" and "ought." So I need to show how the use of such a regulative and action-guiding terminology can be derived from aretaic talk about what is admirable, deplorable, good, or bad. But before I do this, there is perhaps a more pressing second problem in the fact that the symmetry I have just been talking about does not on its own entail a general principle of the sort just enunciated.

Why not? Well, because from the fact that the self-regarding and other-regarding aspects of the virtues are, intuitively speaking, equally important, it doesn't follow that we should take both aspects into account in our actions *rather than specialize within the field of virtue*: i.e. cultivate and exhibit either self-regarding or other-regarding virtues, *but not both*. After all, even if we feel being an architect and being a professor are equally significant and valuable roles or careers, we wouldn't want to recommend a dual career somehow in both fields over specializing in either area.

But another feature of our contemporary thinking can take us beyond this impasse. The self-benefiting traits we ordinarily think of as virtues are not singly or as a group *incompatible* with other-benefiting virtues and vice versa: e.g. kindness is not incompatible with fortitude, nor resourcefulness with fairness (or courage). Given the two categories of self-regarding and other-regarding traits, it seems plausible to hold that any trait falling into either one of those categories that is (largely) incompatible with admirable traits of the other category should not itself count as a virtue. And this supposition, if true, is evidence that our common-sense thought commends or recommends some measure of balance, rather than specialization, with regard to self- and other-regarding virtues.

Why don't we think of selfishness as an admirable trait of character, a virtue? It might enable one to do good things for oneself, so given that fortitude and prudence are primarily self-beneficial too, why do we think the latter are virtues, but selfishness isn't? I think largely because selfishness precludes other-regarding and other-benefiting virtues as fortitude or prudence does not. A selfish person may incidentally or as a means to self-advancement do things for others, but fortitude and prudence are compatible with a *fundamental concern* for (one's treatment of) others. In that case, the fact that selfishness is not generally considered a virtue (hence the title of Ayn Rand's *The Virtue of Selfishness*) is evidence that thoroughgoing specialization in the self-regarding direction is by our common lights deplorable, the very opposite of admirable.

But something similar can also be said about *selflessness*. Selflessness is incompatible with many or most self-regarding self-benefiting virtues, and even if it was highly admired in Victorian times, nowadays – perhaps because we are less priggish and high-minded, perhaps because we think we know more about human psychology and are less willing to take things at face value – selflessness is a practically automatic object of suspicion. The person who not only shows a great concern for others but who, in addition, seems to deprecate or ignore his own needs whenever there is the slightest good he can do for others, would typically be thought to have something wrong with him, would be suspected of masochism or of being burdened by inordinate and misdirected guilt (possibly as a result of having been stifled or harshly dealt with as a child). And our contemporary belief that selflessness (or self-abnegation) is not admirable, together with our similar belief about selfishness, gives us reason to think that self–other specialization is not acceptable to our common thinking. To the extent optimizing utilitarianism morally requires us to specialize *mostly in benefiting others*, it comes very close to what we object to in selflessness, and both, really, can be said to downgrade or devalue the individual (or her well-being). But a common-sense ethics of virtue avoids that charge quite deliberately and has all the reasons given above to promulgate an overarching principle urging us to act or live in such a way as to *balance* self-concern with concern for others taken as a class.

As far as I can tell, no one has explicitly formulated or defended such a principle previously. Aristotle's ethics, with its emphasis on acting from both self-benefiting and other-benefiting virtues, comes closer to this idea than any other historical view I can think of, and to that extent the present approach in not inappropriately viewed as neo-Aristotelian. More recently, Carol Gilligan (1982) has articulated an ethic of caring or responsibility *for both self and other*, but her discussion is (and has subsequently continued to be) vague or neutral as between an *in sensu composito* and an *in sensu diviso* interpretation of that ethic. However, the principle I introduced above is clearly in need of further clarification, and to that end I propose, to begin with, to make use of a distinction that is much employed in Kantian ethics.

Kant distinguishes between *perfect duties* (like the duties not to lie and not to kill the innocent), which we must obey in any and all circumstances, and *imperfect duties*, which bind us in a less stringent or all-or-nothing manner. According to Kant, roughly, a single lie violates the duty not to lie, but a single failure to help others when one is in a position to do so does not automatically count as a violation of our imperfect duty to promote the well-being or happiness of others. One just has to make up or have made up for the failure by helping on other occasions.

Now according to Kant, again very roughly, we have two basic sets of imperfect duties: to promote our own moral (or cultural) self-development and to promote the happiness of other people. And the effect of his juxtaposing our imperfect duties in this way is in fact to urge a kind of balance between the parts. If I tell someone: "plant corn and· plant wheat," she is being urged, implicitly and via the *form* of my utterance, to ensure some degree of proportionality or balance between the corn and wheat she plants. If, in response to what I tell her, the person plants ten acres of corn and only two of wheat, I think she would be regarded as violating at least the spirit of the original recommendation or command. And I think Kant's two-part statement of our imperfect duties is likewise interpretable in that spirit, and so too the overarching common-sense virtue-ethical injunction to be self-concerned and also concerned with other people considered as a class. The latter principle urges at least some degree of balance between these two considerations, and though this is hardly specific, the principle does give general guidelines about how one should act in life. And it can be made somewhat more specific and helpful by saying more about the notion of concern for oneself.

Kant, remember, urges concern for *one's own* self-development and the happiness of *others*, but not for one's own happiness (except when that helps one fulfill one's other duties) or for the moral development of others. (Kant seems actually a bit inconsistent about our duties in regard to the moral development of other people.) So the balance he impicitly urges between self-concern and other-concern is asymmetrical in regard to the objects of that concern. An intuitively based ethics of virtue can and should proceed more symmetrically than Kant does. We have seen how it is possible to admire the way someone advances her own well-being, and we ordinarily think there *is* reason to try to help others to become better or more admirable (in various respects). We deplore a parent who doesn't take on this responsibility with regard to his or her own children and also think less well of a teacher who doesn't try to help students toward (admirable) skills, insights, and accomplishments. Indeed, we even feel there is something deplorable in not caring about or taking some responsibility for the civic, moral, or even artistic virtues of *fellow citizens*; think of the perfectly appropriate concern some Americans felt about the morality of other Americans during the Vietnam War.

So I would urge that our two-part principle be further specified by breaking each part into two parts, so that it reads: one should be concerned to promote one's own well-being and virtues and also concerned to promote the well-being and virtues of other people. (Of course, some actions may promote more than one of these goals.) Again, the symmetry and balance advocated in this principle are to be understood *in sensu composito*, so that the well-being of the agent is not devalued. And the contrast with Kant is instructive. Kant urges a balance of a sort between duties affecting oneself and duties affecting other people (considered as a class), but those duties are asymmetrically related because the fundamentally required practical goal of self-concern is just cultural or moral development, whereas that of other-concern is just happiness or well-being. By urging practical concern for both the happiness and the admirability of oneself *and* others, our over-arching principle is made attractive, so to speak, from the top down through its theoretically desirable thoroughgoing symme-try, but is also supported from the bottom up by the way it accommodates and summarizes our present-day intuitive think-ing about the importance and virtue-status of various character traits.

But someone might want to question the last point, on the grounds that deep down most of us in fact think much more highly of self-sacrifice than of self-preservation and self-assertion at the expense of others. Both Brad Hooker and Robert Young have suggested to me that if we know of a person faced with a choice between saving her own life and saving the lives of many others, we will think much more highly of her if she saves the others. Doesn't that show there to be something wrong with the idea of some sort of balance between self-concern and other-concern?

I don't think so. Remember we are talking about the equivalent, in virtue ethics, of Kantian and other imperfect duties. And such duties spread their force across cases and circumstances in a way perfect duties do not. Even if in some cases it is more admirable to care for others, if there are different sorts of cases, circumstances, times of life, in which the opposite is the case, then the argument for balance can still work. After all, Kant in effect urged a degree of balance between benefiting others and developing oneself, but there are circumstances in which acting in the name of self-devel-opment is clearly much less admirable than helping others, e.g., if it prevents one from saving many lives. However, at other times self-development will take precedence, and this allows one to speak of there being some sort of evaluative balance between self-development and benefiting or helping others. So to defend the idea of balance between *helping oneself* and helping others, we need to find a case where it would be more admirable to assert one's own happiness than to act on behalf of the happiness of (certain) others.

Imagine a dutiful daughter, say, in Ireland whose mother has died and whose siblings are all off at university, so that Sinead, as we may call her, is left with the problem of caring for an ailing father. She finds a job near the family home in Killarney, puts off her own plans to be a fashion designer or architect or whatever, and takes care of the father, who has lost his job. Meanwhile the Irish economy is faltering and Sinead's siblings are not doing well at university. One of them has a cycling accident and has to be sent home in a state of permanent invalidism. One of her sisters marries a man in far-away Dublin and has, rapidly, five children. The man is a drunk who frequently beats her, and the sister finally leaves him and comes back to Killarney. But she can't get a decent job and take care of her children too, and so Sinead ends up carrying the whole burden of the family on her own shoulders, and those at home seem content to let her do so. In the same way, two other siblings still at university now graduate and have jobs, but seem too busy to worry about events at home.

One day, Sinead, thinking about all that has happened, decides she has had enough. Her family had better get itself together; she has done a great deal for them, but now, she feels, it is time for them to take collective care of themselves. She wants to get on with her own priorities, her own life, but she is religious and wishes to consult with her local priest. The priest, however, tells her she is being self-centered, that the family is sacred, that we are sent here to help others, etc. In contrast to previous occasions, this time she finds herself resisting what the priest is telling her; she decides she really must be resolute and not let herself be made to feel guilty or be talked out of taking an apprenticeship as a fashion designer that she has been offered in London by an older friend. Six months later Sinead is living in London, and although her family keep telling her how selfish she was to have left them, she is still in regular contact with them.

I think we would think well of this woman and her decision and less well of her had she obediently listened to the priest and the subsequent remonstrations of her family. In some cases – more cases than one might initially think – we find, or would find, self-assertion more admirable than self-denial, so I think the idea of balance and of self–other symmetry (*in sensu composito*) remains entirely plausible. Such balance and symmetry are not, however, to be understood as involving *equality*, or even *rough equality*, among certain concerns. This degree of precision is foreign to common-sense intuitive thought in this area, and in speaking, as I have, of an ideal that involves *some measure or degree* of balance (or symmetry) among various concerns, I mean nothing more (but also nothing less) specific than that each of those concerns ought to be *substantial* both absolutely and in relation to the others.

5   Further Aspects of Common-sense Virtue Ethics

It is time to make good on our earlier claim that we can derive shoulds or oughts from softer-seeming, and morally-unspecific, aretaic notions like excellence, admirability, and deplorability. We have been making free use of deontic terms such as "should" and "ought," and the claim to be doing virtue ethics depends on ultimately relying only on aretaic notions. The biggest problem here is the fact that deontic terms such as "ought" and "wrong" appear to be more forceful than any aretaic terminology, but I am convinced that this appearance is deceiving.

Consider the difference between the *moral* terminology of badness and of wrongness. Have we condemned an action more strongly in saying that it was morally wrong than in saying that it was a morally bad thing to do? Do we recommend more strongly against an act in saying it would be wrong to do it than in saying that it would be bad to do it? I don't think so. However, even if the aretaic isn't weaker in force than the deontic, one might hold that *moral* claims are stronger than the morally-neutral aretaic evaluations I have been urging us to make use of. But is even this much clear? Is it more forcefully negative to say that an act would be morally wrong than to say it would be a stupid or ignoble or terrible thing to do? Yet "terrible" in particular seems simply to be a strengthening aretaic extrapolation from the terms "criticizable," "deplorable," and "bad." This still leaves us with a problem concerning the moral term "blameworthy," but leaving that aside for the moment, let me suggest that if we have aretaic terms firmly in place, corresponding or analogous deontic terms are automatically applicable and can be derived accordingly.

Thus consider the aretaic, but not specifically moral, claim that a certain act is or was deplorable. Isn't it automatically appropriate to infer that one shouldn't perform, or shouldn't have performed, that act? The latter judgment is deontic, but we don't have to consider it specifically moral, because "ought" and "should" can be used in a very general way to recommend actions based on considerations of prudence, etiquette, aesthetics, morals, or a mixture of such factors. And if we consider, for example, how natural a tie between the aretaic and the deontic is in an area like aesthetics, it will be seen how plausible a similar tie is in regard to our ethical thinking. Thus if a certain way of dancing a certain step or sequence is, in balletic terms, deplorable or terrible, it is automatically natural to infer that one shouldn't dance the step or sequence in that way. And by the same token I think that once we have established aretaic judgments in ethics, deontic ones can readily be derived and justified. In that case, the distinctive principle we are espousing here can most fundamentally be read as saying, aretaically: it is deplorable not to concern oneself with promoting one's own well-being and virtues and also deplorable not to concern oneself with promoting the well-being and virtues of other people. (Perhaps it should be added that when one does these things sufficiently, one is acting positively admirably.) Then the version of this principle stated earlier can be derived as an appropriate deontic analogue.

However, this still leaves the moral notion of blameworthiness out of account in our morally neutral or unspecific vocabulary. But why should this worry us? Mostly, I think, because without some such notion, we seem to have no way to judge social institutions and practices. In society we need to be able to institute and justify various forms of punishments and penalties in order to protect the innocent and vulnerable and preserve social order and community, yet how can we do this if nothing counts as morally blameworthy, as opposed to merely being deplorable and terrible, and if we can't speak of justice or of human deserts?

Well, justice may or may not be a specifically moral notion, but in fact the paradox-instigating self–other asymmetries that beset the common-sense morality of individual action don't seem to affect judgments about the internal justice of large-scale entities like societies. Furthermore, though there may be self–other asymmetries affecting how a given society treats *other* societies, their effect can be absorbed into issues about *international justice* that also seem to give rise to no problem-creating self–other asymmetries. I have in fact elsewhere (Slote 1993 and forthcoming) developed two (competing) virtue-ethical conceptions of justice that apply both to internal issues of social justice and to questions of international justice, and both conceptions use the ideas of an ethically admirable society and of a just society fairly interchangeably.[4]

But once one has framed a paradox-free conception of the socially just or admirable, one is in a position to account for the idea of just penalties and punishments as well. If a society is just and works justly, then we can say that the punishments and penalties it legally establishes and metes out are *ipso facto* just. This contrasts with the common-sense notion that certain punishments are inherently deserved or unfair and that it is the business of a just society to reflect that preinstitutional moral order, but in fact consequentialism, Kantianism, and, now, virtue ethics all – for reasons too complicated to enter into here – reject the latter view in favor of conceiving valid or just laws and punishments as *relative to* an independently specified conception of social justice.

This doesn't yet show us how to introduce and justify the idea of deserving punishment or deserving blame (blameworthiness), but I wonder how significant a loss that really is, given that our virtue ethics can still make use of the ideas of just punishments, just penalties, and just social benefits in order to give an account of how the innocent and the fabric of society itself can properly be protected.

I have been proposing a virtue ethics that eliminates problematic moral terminology in favor of common-sense judgments about act-admirability, virtue-status, and their opposites. It is a common-sense view in what it accepts, not in terms of what it rejects, but the above discussion, I hope, lends credibility to the conclusion that it is capable of accounting for the broad reach of ethical phenomena any good ethical theory has to come to grips with. Common-sense virtue ethics is also *pluralistic*, inasmuch as it insists upon the richness and complexity of the ethical rather than, like utilitarianism, treating all values as ultimately commensurable and of a single kind. Utilitarianism is *monistic* about the grounds for status as a virtue: a trait is a virtue if and only if it has overall, in its various instances, good (or optimal) consequences for human (or sentient) happiness or well-being. But our common-sense thinking about what traits of character are admirable, are virtues, allows scope for a variety of bases for status as a virtue. As we saw earlier, some traits seem to count as virtues not because of their usefulness for humankind generally, but because they serve the self-interest of the (perhaps rare) individuals who possess them. Resourcefulness like Prince Talleyrand's may be rarely met with and not be particularly useful to people *other than* Talleyrand, but still come in for our admiration. But in addition to self-benefiting, other-benefiting, and humankind-benefiting virtues, there intuitively seem to be virtues whose status doesn't rest on the conferral of benefits.

An incurable cancer victim may benefit from his ability to deceive himself about the evidence that he has terminal cancer, but we commonly regard such a person as less admirable than someone who has the courage to face similar facts squarely, who is less dishonest with herself, even if we are willing to concede that the latter may suffer more and be worse off for the knowledge she refuses to evade. So some virtues appear not to benefit those who possess them. Now of course the person who faces the facts of her cancer may spare her relations the effort of maintaining a deception and to that extent benefit other people. But it may also be more difficult to avoid states of depression or panic if one admits to having terminal cancer, and to that extent one may cause more hardship and heartache for others if one *doesn't* deceive oneself or allow oneself to be deceived about one's condition. In any event, it seems clear enough that our comparatively greater admiration for the person who is honest with herself (in this kind of case as with other kinds) is not based on supposed facts about the comparative benefits, either to oneself or to others, of courageously facing the facts versus anxious self-deception. Given the value we tend to place on strength of mind and courage, we are inclined to *think better of* the person who faces her cancer or other facts squarely, even while agreeing that neither that person nor anyone else may be *better off* for her having done so. The factors that underlie virtue-status according to our common thinking are simply more various than a monistic theory like utilitarianism, which treats human welfare as the common coinage of all value, can allow.

But there is another far more widespread form of evaluative monism that also clashes with our common thinking and

intuitions. (Since after the uncovering of paradox, intuitions are
no longer sacrosanct, that may count as only *one strike* against
such monism.) Throughout the history of western philosophical
ethics, most moral thinkers have regarded virtues as *forms of
rationality*. For Aristotle, our rationality is what is most distinctively human, and as practical beings we achieve and exemplify
excellence – virtue – through the possession and exercise of practical rationality (aided by theoretical or intellectual rationality in
various ways). And similar views have also been held by thinkers
as diverse as Spinoza, Kant, the Stoics, and the Epicureans. But the
traits we commonly and persistently tend to regard as virtues are
not all naturally regarded as forms of practical rationality.

Consider the trait of fortitude, the ability and tendency,
roughly, to remain unperturbed or at least active in the face of
adversity. Are people with this trait more *rational* than those who
take adversity harder? Certainly, we may be better off for having
fortitude in certain circumstances, but it is also true that one may
sometimes be better off for being happy-go-lucky, yet we hardly
think of that trait as a form of rationality nor, particularly, as a
virtue. Perhaps the best argument for considering fortitude a kind
of rational excellence is that the trait embodies an attitude of
hopefulness that is a condition of practical rational effectiveness
in salvaging whatever good one can from otherwise adverse situations. But this seems to be "reaching" a bit. Wouldn't it be more
straightforward and plausible to say that we admire fortitude
because of the personal strength and resilience it demonstrates?
Indeed, we now have two examples of virtues – courage to face
facts and fortitude – that connect with the idea of strength of mind
more closely than with the other, more familiar philosophical
bases for attributing virtue-status. Later, I shall briefly discuss a
kind of virtue ethics that centers itself on the notion of inner
strength, but for the moment, though, the point is that our ethical
admiration can be paid out in coinage other than the familiar
categories of rationality and beneficial effect, and thus our common-sense virtue ethics is quite pluralistic in regard to the
sources it allows for status as a virtue.

But paying heed to common sense doesn't as a result lead to
chaos or blinding complexity, given the kind of self–other balance
earlier described as summarizing and encapsulating the overall

tendency of our common-sense virtue thinking. Indeed, if we pay sufficient attention to the idea of self–other symmetry, we may come to see that a common-sense virtue ethics actually allows for more pattern, more symmetry, and to that degree more unification in our thought about the virtues than is allowed for or at least noticed by other moral approaches.

Remember first that there are virtue-ethical analogues of Kant's perfect duties, and certain kinds of killing, maiming, negligence, disloyalty, untrustworthiness, and the like are intuitively deplorable, or even terrible, ways of acting (and feeling). This means that our common-sense virtue ethics can cover the familiar range of individualistic moral phenomena without having to invoke specifically moral vocabulary, but it is also worth noting that even if (perhaps a big "if") there is nothing morally wrong or immoral with killing, maiming, or negligently damaging oneself, our notions of admirability and deplorability are broad enough to allow us to criticize various self-inflicted harmings as deplorable, even terrible, ways to act or fail to act (toward oneself). Trustworthiness and loyalty, however, have standardly been taken as other-regarding, moral virtues, but once the idea of self–other balance and symmetry with regard to the conferring of benefits and refraining from harming is firmly before our minds, it becomes easier, I think, for us to notice that there are also important self-regarding instances of traits like trustworthiness and loyalty.

A person who through weakness of will or purpose often fails to act on his (best) intentions displays a kind of self-regarding untrustworthiness or unreliability that may be open to severe criticism from others and may especially *berate himself* for being the way he is. Indeed, a person who has vowed to stop drinking may be deeply shaken by his own frequent backslidings and deplore his own largely self-regarding untrustworthiness, inconstancy, unreliability in terms *just as bitter* as those with which he would criticize other-regarding untrustworthiness, etc., either on his own part or on the part of others. And similar points can be made about loyalty. When Wordsworth, late in life, said that he would be willing to give up his life for the (established) Church of England, many people regarded him as having betrayed his own earlier social, political, and personal ideals –

and are such self-betrayals always automatically less ethically serious than the betrayal of other people?

Because of the asymmetric character of common-sense morality and the previous emphasis in ethics on morality rather than self-regarding ideals and standards, such self-regarding examples have been ignored or given less than their proper place in our understanding of ethics, but a common-sense ethics of virtue, even as it calls attention to these neglected phenomena, effects a greater symmetry and systematic order within our ethical thought by treating other-regarding trustworthiness and the like as analogous to, of a piece with, self-regarding trustworthiness, etc., in a way that other ethical theories have not noticed or even allowed for. Common-sense virtue ethics allows us to talk of trustworthiness as a general trait of which the self-regarding and other-regarding kinds are particular instances, and instances, indeed, related within our total thought via considerations of balance or symmetry. The unity we thus gain is, however, based in our ordinary ethical intuitions rather than, as so often with utilitarian unification, existing at the *expense* of intuitiveness. But these are intuitions that, as I have suggested, have long been slighted and that we have had to *unearth and place, or at least reconfigure.* And it is worth pointing out, finally, that commonsensism is in this fashion able actually to *add* to our theoretical ethical knowledge, rather than being simply *conservative and predictable.*

We see, therefore, that the idea of balance has numerous ramifications. But that idea isn't imposed upon ethical thinking in the view I have proposed, but rather grows out of a close examination of our ordinary thinking about admirability and the virtues. Indeed, common-sense virtue ethics consists of three different levels, proceeding from the most specific to the most general, of ethical evaluation. Aristotle allows that one can evaluate particular actions or desires on their own as admirable or noble, and to that extent he treats aretaic evaluation as starting with actions rather than with individuals. All along we have been implicitly doing the same, but in speaking so much of various traits as virtues or their opposite we have in effect also allowed ourselves to summarize and encapsulate our intuitive thinking about particular cases into more general claims about the ethical character of certain *kinds* of action and even desire. (E.g. a benevolent person

not only helps others but does so without *begrudging* the help.)
More generally still, our talk of balance between the self-regarding
and other-regarding and the specific overarching principle proposed earlier in effect summarize and encapsulate our intuitive
thinking about what traits are or are not virtues, or ethically
admirable.[5]

I wouldn't be urging common-sense virtue ethics unless our
intuitive moral thought and the main theoretical alternatives
appeared to run into problems and paradoxes that our view can
avoid. Beyond that, there is the fact that such virtue ethics allows
for a rich understanding of what we normally think of as important moral phenomena, and the restrictions on vocabulary it
imposes on itself are done with a mind to avoiding the problems
of alternative views, but also allow us to see a symmetry and unity
in our ethical thinking that an emphasis on the specifically moral
encourages us to ignore or deny. But now it is time we turned to
another promising way of pursuing virtue ethics. The view
advanced so far has been, in the terminology introduced above,
agent-focused rather than agent-based. But I shall now attempt to
show that a radical agent-based approach (or set of approaches) to
virtue ethics that avoids the paradox-inducing intuitions of common-sense morality can also be viewed as a plausible contemporary competitor of Kantian and consequentialist moral theories.
However, given our earlier definition of agent-basing, the whole
idea of such a radical approach to ethics may seem suspect, and it
will be the first task of the following discussion of agent-based
views to explain why the idea of agent-basing is neither as odd
nor as implausible as it may initially appear to be.

6   Making Sense of Agent-based Virtue Ethics

Recall our earlier statement of what it means for a virtue ethics to
be agent-based. It must derive its evaluations of human actions,
whether aretaic or deontic, from *independent and fundamental
aretaic characterizations of the inner traits or motives of individuals or of the individuals themselves.* Neither Aristotle's ethical
theory nor the neo-Aristotelian common-sense virtue ethics

articulated in previous pages is agent-based in this sense, and it should be clear that agent-basing involves a radical move for virtue ethics, because it entails that the agent and her inner life are not fixed on any external or independent action-governing moral standard, but rather constitute in some sense the basis and measure of all moral activity. Such a claim naturally seems suspect for a variety of reasons that I shall be discussing in what follows, but before we concentrate our attention on agent-based theories, it is worth noting another kind of virtue-ethical view that is in some respects transitional or intermediate between (merely) agent-focused and agent-based forms of virtue ethics.

Rosalind Hursthouse (1991) has proposed a form of virtue ethics that treats act-evaluation as derivative from the (aretaic) evaluation of character traits and motives, but regards the evaluation of the traits and motives as based in further ethical facts about human well-being or flourishing, rather than as fundamental and in need of no further ethical grounding. In particular (but speaking roughly), acts are said to be right if they accord with or exercise virtue(s) and a trait is said to count as a virtue if people need it in order to flourish or have good lives; and although such a view can be described as an *agent-prior* form of virtue ethics, it is clearly not agent-based. Hursthouse also regards her view as a gloss on Aristotle's account of ethics, but if, as most commentators suggest, Aristotle says that human flourishing largely *consists in* acting virtuously from a virtuous character over a sufficiently long life, then Hursthouse's link-up with Aristotle is threatened with circularity. How can the idea of flourishing independently ground the idea of virtue if talk of virtuous living is supposed to clarify and give content to the notion of flourishing?

Notice too that Hursthouse's view allows that a trait may be necessary to the flourishing of its possessor and count as a virtue, even though acting in accordance with it on a given occasion could fail to promote and even work against her flourishing or well-being. Benevolence, for example, may be a trait that usually or on the whole, given the way society is, benefits its possessors. People find it difficult, after all, to hide a lack of benevolence, and selfish people are likely to be shunned as friends and as participants in interesting and profitable enterprises that require co-operation and trust. So benevolence may count as a virtue on

Hursthouse's view, but that doesn't mean that when on a particular occasion someone exercises benevolence, she isn't *sacrificing* her own well-being for the sake of another person or other
persons. In other words, even though Hursthouse gives a self-
interested account of what makes something a virtue, her stated
view *avoids standard ethical egoism* by allowing acts to count as
admirable and right even when they are known to run counter to
the agent's self-interest. In that case, however, Hursthouse's
agent-prior virtue ethics faces the difficulty of explaining why,
if being necessary to the agent's happiness, well-being, or flourishing constitutes the basis for a trait's counting as a virtue, that
same criterion shouldn't also count as the basis for the admirability of particular actions.

This is a familiar kind of argument within ethical theory, and it
most notably features in a standard and widely influential criticism that has been made of rule-utilitarianism. Rule-utilitarians
say that rules are to be evaluated in terms of the consequences of
accepting or following them, but acts are to be morally assessed in
terms of whether they accord with the best set of rules. But
utilitarians and anti-utilitarians alike have frequently argued
that if the having of good consequences is the proper criterion
for the evaluation of rules, it also makes sense for the evaluation
of actions, and in that case the rule-utilitarian (and the rule-consequentialist more generally) is mistaken to claim that we should
perform an act that accords with the rules that have best consequences *even when the act itself has and is known to have worse
consequences than some available alternative act.* The latter
claim, or so at least it has widely been argued, seems to go against
the spirit of the original idea (shared by rule-utilitarians and act-
utilitarians) of basing the evaluation of rules and practices in their
consequences for human or sentient happiness.

We have already seen that a similar criticism can be made of
Hursthouse's view. Why should being necessary to the agent's
flourishing be the criterion for goodness or admirability in traits
and motives *but not in actions*? Hursthouse offers us no further
reason that I am aware of, but if we attempt, on her behalf, to iron
out this inconsistency or disuniformity in her account of ethical
value, we run into other difficulties. For if we treat some sort of
necessity to well-being or flourishing as the criterion both

of admirable character traits *and of right or admirable actions*, we
have to say that self-sacrificing actions that *run counter* to the
agent's well-being are not admirable and perhaps not even permissible. That then leaves us with a familiar form of ethical egoism that I believe all three participants in the present debate
would regard as unacceptable, because it is so much out of keeping with our modern-day moral consciousness.

In addition, there is the problem of why status as a virtue
should in the first place depend, as Hursthouse assumes it does,
on what is necessary to the flourishing of given individuals,
rather than on what is necessary or conducive to the flourishing
of the larger community. As Philippa Foot (1978: 159f., 168)
indicated some time ago by way of repudiating an earlier view
of her own that closely resembles Hursthouse's, making virtue
status depend on what benefits just the possessor of a trait seems
an overly egoistic view of what is required of a trait or general
motive in order for it to count as a virtue.

However, if we make conduciveness to the well-being of people
generally the criterion of virtue-status, while continuing to judge
rightness in terms of accord with virtue(s), we end up with a view
that is practically indistinguishable from *some indirect forms of
utilitarianism*, in particular, from Robert M. Adams's (1976) "conscience utilitarianism." And if we iron out the inconsistencies in
this view by making contribution to general happiness or well-
being a criterion both of virtue status and of right action, we end
up with something like act-utilitarianism. This would in substantial measure deprive virtue ethics of its distinctive character as a
view opposed to consequentialism and to Kantianism, and in the
light of all these points, therefore, I think it is time we began
exploring a more radical form of virtue ethics that *is* genuinely
distinctive and that avoids the criticisms we have just been directing at happiness-based agent-prior approaches to virtue ethics.

Agent-based theories of the kind I want to propose treat the
admirability of traits and motives as ethically fundamental and
derive moral judgments of actions from evaluations of traits and
motives. Precisely because these views are not commonsensical,
they can allow themselves to make specifically moral judgments
about actions without getting into the oddnesses and paradoxes
we saw attaching to our intuitive moral thinking (and to Kantian

views as well). Indeed, the agent-based views I shall examine attempt to unify the moral sphere in something like the manner of consequentialism, but in contrast both with most consequentialism and with Hursthouse's agent-prior approach, agent-based views don't bring in claims about what constitutes human happiness or well-being in order to ground judgments about the aretaic goodness of inner traits and the deontic or aretaic status of actions as well. Rather, claims or theories about human well-being are themselves derived from claims about virtue and rightness (as with the Stoics; see Long and Sedley 1987) or (perhaps more plausibly) treated as partly or wholly independent of such claims.

In the latter case, aretaic evaluations of the inner life and claims about what constitutes human well-being *both* count as fundamental and occupy the ground floor of ethics *together*. But precisely because agent-basing can proceed with moral evaluation separately from any particular theory of human well-being (and human good in the sense of human well-being, not of *moral* goodness), I won't be saying very much from now on about the specific character of human well-being or happiness. The whole idea of agent-based virtue ethics probably seems odd enough at this point just because of the way it allows us to ignore theories of human well-being and base all moral evaluations of actions on the inner life, so the most important thing now, as I see it, is to show why such an approach to ethical theory *isn't* really odd or irrelevant and is in fact very promising.

Given all that I have said, we should not be surprised to find that there have in fact been very few instances of agent-based virtue ethics in the entire history of philosophy (clearly, any agent-based view will count as a form of virtue ethics). In fact, the only absolutely clear-cut example of agent-basing I have found is that of James Martineau, the British ethicist of the nineteenth century who is perhaps today best known philosophically as having been the object of a great deal of critical attention from the great British utilitarian, Henry Sidgwick. Other potential historical examples of agent-basing – notably Hume, Abelard, Augustine, Leslie Stephen (father of Virginia Woolf), Spinoza, Nietzsche, and Kant – offer various forms of resistance to such interpretation. And even Plato, who in the *Republic* insists that we evaluate actions by reference to the health and virtue of the individual soul, is perhaps better conceived as offering (only) an agent-prior view, since he also seems to think that (appreciation of) the nature of the Form of the Good represents a level of evaluation prior to the evaluation of souls, with souls counting as virtuous when properly appreciating and being guided by the value inherent in the Form of the Good.

However, I believe there may be a way of freeing the Platonic approach from its dependence on the Forms, and the first way of agent-basing I want briefly to sketch has its ultimate inspiration in Plato. The other way or ways of agent-basing that I shall go on to describe at greater length can be seen as more plausible simplifying variants on Martineau's moral theory. But before I say more about these approaches, there are some very worrying objections to the whole idea of agent-basing that must first be gotten out of the way.

One thing that can seem wrong in principle with any agent-based (or even agent-prior) conception of moral evaluation is that it appears to obliterate the common distinction between doing the right thing and doing the right thing for the right reasons. The well-known example of the prosecutor who does his duty by trying to convict a defendant, but who is motivated by malice rather than by a sense of public duty (Sidgwick 1907: 202) seems to illustrate the distinction in question, and it may well seem that agent-based virtue ethics would have difficulty here because of the way it understands rightness in terms of good motivations and wrongness in terms of the having of bad (or insufficiently good) motives. If actions are wrong when they result from morally bad motives, doesn't that mean that the prosecutor acts wrongly in prosecuting someone out of malice (assuming that malice is morally criticizable)? And isn't that a rather unfortunate consequence of the agent-based approach?

I am not sure. Sidgwick himself seems to grant a certain plausibility to the idea that the prosecutor acts wrongly if he prosecutes from malice. What *is* implausible, rather, is the claim that the prosecutor has no duty to prosecute (or recuse himself and let someone else who is less biased prosecute). And that doesn't follow from the agent-based assumption that he acts wrongly if he prosecutes from malice.

But how can such a duty (or obligation) be understood in agent-based terms? Well, consider the possibility that *if he doesn't prosecute or let someone else prosecute*, the prosecutor's motivation will *also* be bad. Those who talk about the malicious prosecutor case often fail to mention the motives that might lead him *not* to prosecute. With malice present or even in the absence of malice, if the prosecutor doesn't either prosecute or recuse himself and allow someone *else* to prosecute, one very likely explanation will be that he lacks real or strong concern for doing his job and playing the contributing social role that that involves. Imagine that, horrified by his own malice, he ends up not prosecuting and unwilling even to think about letting someone do so. This action too will come from an inner state that is morally criticizable, namely, one involving (among other things) insufficient concern for the public (or general human) good or for being useful to society.

So the idea that motives or inner traits are the basis for evaluating actions that they underlie or that express them doesn't have particularly implausible results. And it allows us something like the distinction between doing the right thing and doing it for the right reason. In particular, it allows us to say that the prosecutor has a duty (or obligation) to prosecute or else recuse himself in favor of another prosecutor, because if he doesn't, we shall in the normal course (barring his having a heart-attack, nervous breakdown, religious conversion, or the like) be able to attribute to him defective or deficient motivation of a kind that makes his action wrong. Yet we can also say that if he prosecutes, he acts (will act) wrongly, even if another person, with different motivation, would have acted rightly in doing so. This allows us then to distinguish between doing one's duty for the right reasons and thus acting rightly, on the one hand, and doing one's duty for the wrong reasons and thus acting wrongly. And this is very close to the distinction between right action and acting rightly for the right reasons, except for the fact that it supposes that when the reasons aren't right, the action itself is actually *wrong*. But we have already seen that this idea in itself is not particularly implausible, and so it turns out that the above-mentioned complaint against agent-basing turns on a faulty assumption about the inability of such views to make fine-grained distinctions of the sort we have just succeeded in making.

However, there is a group of further objections to the whole idea of agent-based ethics that may more fundamentally represent what seems objectionable and even bizarre about any such approach to morality. If the evaluation of actions ultimately derives from that of (the inner states of) their agents, then it would appear to follow that if one is the right sort of person or possesses the right sort of inner states, it doesn't morally matter what one actually *does*, so that the admirable person, or at least her actions, are subject to no genuine moral requirements or constraints. In this light, agent-basing seems a highly autistic and antinomian approach to ethics, one that appears to undermine the familiar, intuitive notion that the moral life involves, among other things, *living up to* certain *standards* of behavior or action. Furthermore, agent-basing also seems to contravene the maxim that "ought" implies "can," for if badly motivated people have obligations but everything such people can do counts as wrong, they have obligations that they are unable to fulfill.

However, none of these damning conclusions in fact follows from the character of agent-basing (nor indeed from Hursthouse's agent-prior view, about which it is possible to raise similar objections). A view can be agent-based (or agent-prior) and still not treat actions as right or admirable simply because they are done by a virtuous individual or by someone with a good or admirable inner state. Nor does an agent-based theory have to say, with respect to each and every action a virtuous individual is capable of performing, that if she were to perform that action, it would automatically count as a good or admirable thing for her to have done.

Thus consider a very simple view according to which (roughly) benevolence is the only good motive and acts are right, admirable, or good to the extent they exhibit or express benevolent motivation. (We can also assume actions are wrong or bad if they exhibit the opposite of benevolence or deficiently benevolent motivation.) To the extent this view treats benevolence as fundamentally and inherently admirable or morally good, it is agent-based. But such a view doesn't entail that the virtuous individual with admirable inner states can simply choose any actions she pleases among those lying within her power, without the admirability or goodness of her behavior being in any way compromised or dismissed. For a benevolent person is typically *capable* of choosing many actions that *fail to express or exhibit* her benevolence.

At least, this is possible if, as many ethicists assume, free will is compatible with universal determinism. This is hardly the place to enter into a full-scale discussion of the problem of free will, but let me just say that many philosophers nowadays think freedom of choice is entirely compatible with one's choice's being predictable (from one's character). Even if perfectly benevolent people always, just because they are so benevolent, do benevolent things, the choice of whether, on any given occasion, to act benevolently still *lies with them.* Thus if one is entirely benevolent and sees an individual needing one's help, one presumably will help and, in doing so, exhibit inner benevolence. But it would also have been within one's power to refuse to help, and if one had refused, one's actions *wouldn't have exhibited benevolence and would therefore presumably have been less admirable than they would or could have been otherwise, according to the simplified agent-based view just mentioned.*

So it is not true to say that agent-basing entails that what one does doesn't matter morally or that it doesn't matter given that one has a good enough inner character or motive. The person who exhibits benevolence in her actions performs actions that, in agent-based terms, can count as morally superior to other actions she might or could have performed, namely, actions (or refrainings from action) that would *not* have demonstrated benevolence. Acts therefore don't count as admirable or virtuous for agent-based theories of the sort just roughly introduced *merely because* they are or would be done by someone who is in fact admirable or admirably motivated; they have to exhibit, express, or further such motivation or be such that they *would* exhibit, etc., such motivation if they occurred, in order to count as admirable or virtuous. And we may conclude, then, that it is simply not true that agent-based theories inevitably treat human actions as subject to no moral standards.

Furthermore, the idea of agent-basing is also entirely consistent with the maxim that "ought" implies "can." Presumably, one cannot change one's motives or character at will. But a malevolent individual who sees a person he can hurt may still have it within his power to refrain from hurting that person, even if we can be sure he won't in fact exercise that power. And the act of refraining would fail to express or exhibit his malevolence and would therefore not count as wrong. Given agent-basing, such an individual has an obligation not to act in ways that express inferior motives, but if the above is correct, he has it in his power to fulfill that obligation. Thus agent-basing is consistent with "ought" implies "can" and allows genuine moral standards to govern our actions, but the standards it advocates operate and bind, so to speak, *from within*.

However, even this metaphor must be taken with caution, because it seems to imply that for agent-based views the "direction of fit" between world and moral agent is all one way: from agent to world. It seems to imply, that is, that, on agent-based views, the moral life is a matter of securing good motivation and acting on it, independently of ascertaining facts about what is needed out in the world around one. If such were the case, then agent-basing would entail a kind of autism or isolation from the world that would make one wonder how any such ethics could possibly be adequate. But agent-basing doesn't in fact yield isolation from or the irrelevance of facts about the world, and one sees this if one considers how the kinds of motivation such theories specify as fundamentally admirable invariably want and need to take the surrounding world into account. If one is really benevolent or wants to be socially useful, one doesn't just throw good things around or give them to the first person one sees. Benevolence, for example, isn't benevolence in the fullest sense unless one cares about who exactly are needy and to what extent they are needy, and such care, in turn, essentially involves wanting and making efforts to know relevant facts, so that one's benevolence can really be useful. Thus someone acting on that motive must be open to, seek contact with, and be influenced by the world around her. Her decisions will not be made in splendid isolation from what most of us would take to be the morally relevant realities, and for an agent-based view, therefore, the moral value of a motive like benevolence isn't free-floating, but depends, rather, on the *kind* of internal state it is and, in particular, on the *aims and hopes it has, and the efforts it makes*, vis-à-vis *the world*. The worries mentioned above, then, really have no foundation; and everything we have just said about benevolence also applies to the foundational motivations of other agent-based views.[6]

However, I think I need to mention one further potential worry before we launch into our account of particular agent-based virtue-ethical views. For it might be thought that if one regards certain motives as fundamentally admirable and seeks to explain the rightness and wrongness of actions ultimately in terms of motives, one is treating the claims about motives as certain and immune to correction, and such overconfidence offends the spirit of rational ethical inquiry and theorizing. Such a thought, however, would be mistaken. If judgments about the ethical status of motives ground claims about right and wrong action, then *the claims about right and wrong action that a given agent-based view yields can be used to test the validity or reasonableness of its grounding assumptions.* Thus if an agent-based view has implications for the evaluation of actions that we find intuitively unacceptable, if many of the things it tells us are right seem, for example, terribly wrong, then that agent-based view becomes at least somewhat questionable and we are given reason to question what it says about the fundamental admirability of certain motives.

Most ethical theories make some sort of ground-floor ethical assumptions, assumptions used to explain or derive other ethical judgments or facts, but not themselves based on any further ethical assumptions. Hedonism (the view that all and only pleasure is intrinsically good for people) is just such a ground-floor explanatory assumption in many forms of utilitarianism, but these forms of utilitarianism and the hedonism they assume are both at least open to question if they yield particular moral judgments we find intuitively (or theoretically) unacceptable or absurd. And something exactly analogous also holds for agent-based moral conceptions. As in science, the use of fundamental or ground-floor explanatory assumptions doesn't require us to treat certain ethical assumptions as sacrosanct and is entirely in keeping with intellectual open-mindedness.

7   Morality as Inner Strength

Having now, I trust, quelled the charges of autism, antinomianism, and theoretical overconfidence or close-mindedness that it is initially tempting to launch against agent-based approaches, I would like to consider some interesting and even promising examples of agent-based ethical theories. Looking back over the history of ethics, it strikes me that there are basically two possible ways in which one can naturally develop the idea of agent-basing: one of them I call "cool," the other "warm." We saw earlier that Plato's agent-prior view relates the morality of individual actions to the health and virtue of the soul, but in the *Republic* (Book IV) Plato also uses the images of a strong and of a beautiful soul to convey what he takes to be the touchstone of all good human action. And I believe that ideas about health and, especially, strength can serve as the aretaic foundations for one possible kind of agent-based virtue-ethics. Since, in addition, it is natural to wonder how any sort of altruism, any sort of *humane concern for other people*, can be derived from notions like health and strength, agent-based approaches of this first kind can be conveniently classified as "cool."

By contrast, James Martineau's (1891) agent-based conception of morality treats compassion as the highest of secular motives, and some of the philosophers who have come closest to presenting agent-based views – Hume (1739), Hutcheson (1738), and nowadays Jorge Garcia (1990) – have placed a special emphasis on compassion or, to use a somewhat more general term, *benevolence* as a motive. I believe the latter notion can provide the focus for a second kirtd of agent-based view (actually, as it turns out, a pair of views) that deserves our attention, and since such views build altruistic human concern explicitly into their aretaic foundations, it is natural to speak of them as "warm."

Since Plato's discussion of health and strength is older than any discussion of benevolence I know of, I would like first to discuss agent-basing as anchored in the idea of strength. But metaphors or images of health and strength also play an important role for Stoicism, for Spinoza, and for Nietzsche, though none of these offers a perfectly clear-cut example of an agent-based òr even agent-prior account of ethics. Still, these views cluster around the same notions that fascinate and influence Plato, and I believe they can naturally be extrapolated to a modern-day version of the virtue-ethical approach of the *Republic* and, in particular, to a genuinely agent-based "cool" theory that regards inner strength, in various of its forms, as the sole foundation for an understanding of the morality of human action.

For Plato, good action is to be understood in terms of the seemingly consequentialistic idea of creating or sustaining the strength (or health, etc.) of the soul, but to me it seems more promising to explore the idea of actions that *express* or *exhibit* inner strength, and so *morality as inner strength*, as it seems natural to call it, should proceed on that basis. And remember too that the attempt to anchor everything in the Form of the Good led us to characterize Plato's view as agent-prior, but not agent-based. An agent-based morality that appeals to the notion of inner strength must therefore treat strength (in various forms) as an ultimately admirable way of existing and being motivated as a person and must show us how to frame a plausible morality of human actions on that basis.

Now the idea that there is something intuitively admirable about being strong inside, something requiring no appeal to or defense from *other ideas*, can perhaps be made more plausible by being more specific about the kind(s) of inner disposition and motivation I have in mind in speaking of inner strength. We saw earlier, for example, that the courage, the strength, to face unpleasant facts seems admirable independently of any benefits it may confer, and here, then, is one form of inner strength that might plausibly be said to be justified at a ground-floor level, i.e., in agent-based terms. What *doesn't* seem plausible, however, is the idea that any contemporaneously relevant and inclusive morality of human action could be based *solely* in ideas about inner strength. What does inner strength have to do with being kind to people, with not deceiving them, with not harming them? And if it doesn't relate to these sorts of things, it clearly cannot function as a general groundwork for morality.

The same problem, the same question, comes up in connection with Plato's defense of morality in the *Republic*. That book begins with the problem of explaining why anyone should be moral or just in the conventional sense of not deceiving, stealing, and the like. But Plato ends up defining justice in terms of the health or strength of the soul and never adequately explains why such a soul would refrain from what are ordinarily regarded as unjust or immoral actions. Even the appeal to the Form of the Good seems just a form of handwaving in connection with these difficulties, because even though Plato holds that the healthy soul must be guided by the Good, we aren't told enough about the Good to know why it would direct us away from lying, stealing, and the like. Doesn't a similar problem arise for an agent-based theory appealing fundamentally to the notion of inner strength? It certainly appears to, but perhaps the appearance can be dispelled by pointing out connections between strength and other-regarding morality that have largely gone unnoticed.

Friedrich Nietzsche (1966) points out the possibility of being moved to give things to other people out of a self-sufficient sense of having more than enough, a superabundance of things. Nietzsche claims that this kind of "noble" giving is ethically superior to giving based on pity or a sense of obligation, but what is most important for present purposes is that Nietzsche has pointed out a way in which altruism can be justified in terms of the ideal of inner strength. (This is ironic, because Nietzsche is a self-proclaimed egoist, but he actually seems to be aiming at a view that is "beyond" the dichotomy of egoism and altruism.) Any person who begrudges things to others no matter how much he has seems needy, too dependent on the things he keeps for himself, and pathetically *weak*, whereas the person who generously gives from a sense of superabundance seems both self-sufficient and strong within.

This kind of inner strength seems intuitively and inherently admirable, and because it presupposes that the generous giver is genuinely satisfied with the good things she has, it escapes any suspicion of devaluing the well-being of the agent. Yet such generosity is pretty clearly not egoistic. To give to others out of a sense of one's own superabundant well-being is not to try to *promote* that well-being, and so Nietzsche has given us an example of genuine altruism based in the ideal of strength. I believe we could find other examples of altruism based on (other forms of) inner strength, but even so, there is a general problem with this whole approach that has led me to think there are probably more promising ways to develop an agent-based virtue ethics.

The problem, in a nutshell, is that morality as strength treats benevolence, compassion, kindness, and the like as only *derivatively* admirable and morally good. And this seems highly implausible to the modern moral consciousness. To be sure compassion cannot always have its way; it sometimes must yield to justice or the public good, and, as we saw earlier, a compassion or generosity that never pays any heed to the agent's own needs seems lacking in self-respect, masochistic, ethically unattractive. But still, even if compassion has to be limited or qualified by other values, it counts with us as a *very important basic moral value.* And it seems to distort the aretaic value we place on compassion, benevolence, kindness, and caring for others to regard them as needing justification in terms of the (cool) ideal of inner strength or indeed any other different value. Such a criticism clearly touches the Kantian account of benevolence, which tries to derive its moral value from facts or postulates about our rationality and autonomy; and indeed many philosophers have criticized Kant for treating the value of benevolence as merely derivative and holding, in addition, that benevolence that is not guided by respect for the moral law lacks moral worth altogether. But the same criticism can also be made of morality as strength, and so I would propose at this point to introduce and discuss a form of agent-based virtue ethics that is immune to this problem precisely because it bases all morality on the aretaic value, the moral admirability, of benevolence. However, it turns out that there are two different forms or ideals of benevolence on which one might plausibly wish to base a warm agent-based theory. It is time we discussed them.

8   Morality as Universal Benevolence

Martineau's *Types of Ethical Theory* represents perhaps the clearest example of agent-basing one can find in the entire history of ethics, and I believe that the advantages of a virtue ethics based on compassion or benevolence can best be brought to light by considering in turn the structure of Martineau's theory and the criticisms that Henry Sidgwick made of that theory.

Martineau gives a ranking of human motives from lowest to highest and, assuming as he does that all moral decisions involve a conflict between two such motives, holds that right action is action from the higher of the two motives, wrong action action from the lower of the two. Martineau's hierarchy of motives ascends (roughly) as follows: vindictiveness; love of sensual pleasure; love of gain; resentment, fear, antipathy; ambition, love of power; compassion; and, at the apex, reverence for the Deity.

Sidgwick (1907, bk III, ch. xii) objects to the rigidity of this hierarchy, pointing out that circumstances and consequences may affect the preferability of acting from one or another of the motives Martineau has ranked. Thus *contra* Martineau there are times when it is better for reasons of justice to act from resentment rather than compassion, and the love of sensual pleasure might sometimes prevail over a love of power or gain (especially if the latter were already being given ample play). Sidgwick concludes that conflicts between lower motives can only be resolved by appeal to the highest ranked motive or, alternatively, to some supremely regulative general motive like justice, prudence, or universal benevolence – none of which is contained among the more particular motives of Martineau's hierarchy. That is, all conflicts of Martineau's lower motives should be settled by reference to reverence for the Deity or by reference to some regulative or "master" motive like benevolence. (This would not be necessary if we could devise a more plausible and less priggish hierarchy than Martineau's, but no one has yet suggested a way of doing that.)

Sidgwick then goes on to make one further assumption. He assumes that for a motive to be regulative, it must be regulative in relation to the ultimate *ends* or *goals* of that motive. And this entails that if we confine ourselves to secular motives, take seriously the fact that compassion is the highest secular motive in Martineau's ranking, and as a result choose universal benevolence (i.e. universally directed benevolence) as supremely regulative, actions and motives will be judged in terms of the goal of universal benevolence, namely, human or sentient happiness. Somehow, we have ended up not with a more orderly or unified form of agent-based view, but with *act-utilitarianism*. And this has happened because Sidgwick ignores the possibility of an agent-based view that judges actions from either of two conflicting motives in terms of how well the two motives exemplify or approximate to the motive of universal benevolence *rather than* in terms of whether those actions achieve or are likely to achieve certain goals that universal benevolence aims at.

Thus suppose someone knows that he can help a friend in need, but that he could instead have fun swimming. The good he can do for himself by swimming is a great deal less than what he can do for his friend, but he also knows that if he swims, certain strangers will somehow indirectly benefit and the benefit will be greater than anything he can provide for his needy friend. However, the man doesn't at all care about the strangers, and though he does care about his friend, he ends up taking a swim. In that case, both "actualist" and "expectabilist" versions of act-utilitarianism will regard his action as the morally best available to him in the circumstances. It actually has better consequences for human happiness than any alternative would have had, and its expectable utility is greater than the alternative of helping his friend, since the man *knows* he will do more good, directly and indirectly, by swimming. But there is a difference between *expecting* or *knowing* that an act will have good consequences and being *motivated* to produce those consequences, and if we judge actions in agent-based fashion by how closely their motives exemplify or approximate to universal benevolence, then it is morally *less* good for him to go swimming for the selfish reason he does than to have sought to help his needy friend, and this is precisely the opposite of what standard forms of act-utilitarianism have to say about this situation.

Thus in order to rule out agent-based views making use of the notion of compassion or benevolence, it is not enough to undermine complicated views like Martineau's, for we have seen that there can be an agent-based *analogue* (or "interiorization") of utilitarianism that morally judges everything, in unified or monistic fashion, by reference to universal benevolence as a *motive that seeks* certain ends instead of by reference to the actual or probable *occurrence* of those ends. And this distinctive *morality as universal benevolence* contrasts with utilitarianism in some striking further ways we have not yet mentioned.

Utilitarians and consequentialists evaluate motives and intentions in the same way as actions, namely, in terms of their consequences. (I am here ignoring rule-utilitarianism for reasons given earlier.) Thus consider someone whose motives would ordinarily be thought not to be morally good, a person who gives money for the building of a hospital, but who is motivated only by a desire to see her name on a building or a desire to get a reputation for generosity as a means to launching a political career. Utilitarians and consequentialists will typically say that her particular motivation, her motivation in those circumstances, is morally good, whereas morality as universal benevolence, because it evaluates motives in terms of how well they approximate to universal benevolence, will be able, more commonsensically, to treat such motivation as less than morally good (even if not very *bad* either). Of course, when we learn of what such a person is doing and, let us assume, of her selfish motivation, we may well be happy and think it a good thing that she has the egotistical motives she has on the occasion in question, given their good consequences (and one's own benevolence). But we can intuitively *distinguish* between motives that, relative to circumstances, we are glad to see and it is good to have occur and motives we genuinely admire as morally good, and consequentialism standardly leads to a denial and collapse of this plausible distinction by morally evaluating motives solely in terms of their consequences. By contrast, morality as universal benevolence, precisely because it insists that the *moral* evaluation of motives depends on their inherent character as motives rather than on their consequences, allows for the distinction and comes much closer to an intuitive conception of what makes motives morally better or worse.

As an agent-based analogue of utilitarianism, morality as universal benevolence is, however, open to many of the criticisms that have recently be directed at utilitarianism, among them, the points made earlier in the essay about utilitarianism's and consequentialism's tendency to devalue the moral agent's well-being by demanding too much self-sacrifice. But this last problem can perhaps be dealt with on analogy with the way utilitarianism and consequentialism attempt to deal with the criticism of overdemandingness: namely, either by arguing against it outright or, as I suggested earlier, by accommodating it through an adjustment of its principle(s) of right action. A satisficing version of (utilitarian) consequentialism can say that right action requires only that one do enough good, and it can then offer some agent-neutral conception of what it is, in various situations, to do enough good for humankind considered as a whole. And a satisficing version of morality as universal benevolence can (in a manner already indicated in the way we stated that view earlier) say that acts are right if they come from a motive (together with underlying moral dispositions) that is *close enough* to universal benevolence – rather than insisting that only acts exemplifying the highest motive, universal benevolence, can count as morally acceptable. Someone who devoted most of her time, say, to the rights of consumers or to peace in Northern Ireland might then count as acting and living rightly, even if she were not universally concerned with human welfare and sometimes preferred simply to enjoy herself. So there are versions of morality as universal benevolence that allow us to meet the criticism of overdemandingness, even if we think that criticism does have force against versions of the view that require us always to have the morally best motives or moral dispositions, when we act.

Some forms of utilitarianism are also, however, criticized for having an overly narrow conception of human well-being and in particular for treating all well-being as a matter of the balance of pleasure over pain. This criticism doesn't hold for (certain) pluralistic forms of consequentialism, and neither, interestingly enough, does it apply to morality as universal benevolence. The latter is not committed to any particular conception of human well-being and is quite happy to allow us to admire a person's concern and compassion for human beings without attributing to that person, or ourselves having, a settled view of what human well-being consists in. (Nor does it tell us that it is all right to act paternalistically on behalf of others without considering what they themselves want and believe about reality.)

Finally, utilitarianism has been criticized for its inability to account for certain aspects of deontology, and these criticisms would undoubtedly also extend to morality as universal benevolence. Strict deontology tells us we would be wrong to kill one person in a group in order to prevent everyone in the group, including the person in question, from being killed by some menacing third party. But although Kantian ethics indeed seems to demand that we refrain from killing the one person, it is not clear that our ordinary thinking actually insists on such a requirement. For example, Bernard Williams (1973: 117) says that the question whether to kill one to save the rest is more difficult than utilitarianism can allow, but he also grants that utilitarianism probably gives the right answer about what to do in such a case. Moreover, since benevolence involves not only the desire to do what is good or best overall for the people one is concerned about, *but also the desire that no one of those people should be hurt or suffer*, morality as universal benevolence can explain why we might be horrified at killing one to save many, even if in the end it holds that that is what we morally ought to do. I conclude, then, that although both consequentialism and morality as universal benevolence are open to a good many familiar criticisms, they have ways of responding to the criticisms. Moreover, they have systematic advantages over many other approaches to morality because of their relative systematicity or unified structure. But as I suggested earlier morality as universal benevolence seems to have intuitive advantages over its more familiar utilitarian and consequentialist analogues. Though it is a view that to the best of my knowledge has not previously been explicitly stated or defended, it is in many ways more commonsensical and plausible than utilitarianism and consequentialism. At the same time its reliance on the ideas of benevolence and universality ought to render it attractive to defenders of the latter views and make them ask themselves whether it wouldn't be better to accept an agent-based "interiorized" version of their own doctrines. If consequentialism and utilitarianism have present-day viability and appeal, agent-based morality as universal benevolence does too.

However, we have not yet exhausted the promising possibilities of agent-basing, and at this point I would like to consider one final way of utilizing the idea of benevolence within an agent-based virtue-ethics. Some educationists and philosophers have recently been exploring and developing the idea of an ethic or morality of *caring*, and in the next section I shall push or disambiguate this idea in the direction of a new kind of agent-based view.

9   Morality as Caring

It is possible to ground an agent-based ethical theory in an ideal of *partial or particularistic benevolence*, of caring *more* for some than for others. We find at least the potential for such a view in

St Augustine's *De Moribus Ecclesiae Catholicae* (15.25), where it
is said that all virtue is based in love for God (though Augustine at
least appears to import non-agent-based elements into some of his
arguments). But it is also possible to develop a purely secular
agent-based view that puts a premium on caring for or benevolence toward some people more than others, and it is this possibility that I want to consider in what follows.

Carol Gilligan (1982) has argued that men tend to conceive
morality in terms of rights, justice, and autonomy, whereas
women more frequently think of the moral in terms of caring,
responsibility, and interrelation with others.[7] And at about the
same time Nel Noddings (1984) sought to articulate and defend in
its own right a "feminine" morality centered specifically on the
idea of caring. But when one reads Noddings, one is left unclear as
to whether she intends her ethics of caring to be agent-based. The
notion of agent-basing has only recently become a tool of ethical
theory, and there is no reason to expect Noddings, writing some
years back, to have related her work to that notion. But given
recent developments, especially in virtue ethics, it is perhaps
interesting to consider whether the morality of caring can't be
seen as agent-based and thereby given a firmer or more definite
theoretical grounding.

In her book, *Caring: a Feminine Approach to Ethics and Moral
Education*, Noddings seems to want to relate everything in morality to particularistic caring, rather than bringing in independent
principles of justice or truth-telling or what-have-you, but there is
still a potential obstacle to seeing her ethics as agent-based. For
although she emphasizes the moral goodness of acting from care,
she also says that we should try to *promote* caring in the world,
and this sounds like a consequentialistic and indeed perfectio-
nistic element in her views. (Perfectionism is a form of consequentialism that tells us, roughly, to focus ultimately on whether
our acts produce virtue and excellence, not on their results for
happiness.) If she believes in a fundamental imperative to
produce or promote caring in the world, then Noddings's view
is clearly not agent-based, but I don't think what we know of
Noddings's views settles the issue of whether her views are
implicitly agent-based, because she never says that the promotion
of caring is a fundamental moral value. If it is not, then there is in

fact a way of *deriving* it from an agent-based partialistic ethic of caring.

Consider the reasons one might have for trying to get (certain) people to care more about (certain other) people. Couldn't one's reason be that by getting them to care more, one could eventually bring about more good for humanity generally or for the people one cares about? If one really wants to help (certain) people, working to get them to care for one another's welfare might have a multiplier effect, allowing one at least indirectly to help more people overall than if one always simply promoted welfare directly. A caring person might thus see the promotion of caring as the best way to promote what she as a caring person is concerned about, and in that measure, the concern for and promotion of virtuous caring on the part of others would be an instance of caring itself conceived as a fundamental form of moral excellence and would thus be accommodatable within an agent-based theory of the moral value of caring. Perfectionism and good results as such would not have to come into the matter. But as I say, I am not sure Noddings is best interpreted in this way and only suggest it because the agent-based theory we have just arrived at is at the very least interesting and promising in its own right.

An agent-based moral theory that puts a moral premium on particularistic caring presumably needs to say more than Noddings herself says about self-concern and about appropriate attitudes and actions toward strangers. As we saw earlier, no reasonable ethics should decry or begrudge self-concern and self-assertiveness in moral agents, and as feminists and others have recently noted, it would be ironic and morally counterproductive for any new ethics to focus exclusively on aspects of feminine moral thought and activity that have typically restricted and been used to restrict the freedom and self-fulfillment of women. An ethic of care or concern exclusively or even primarily for favored *others* seems, then, to be morally retrograde, but there is no reason why a feminine or feminist ethic of caring shouldn't, for example, borrow the idea of *in sensu composito* balancing advocated in the earlier sections of this essay, adapting it to the requirements of agent-basing. Perhaps, morality as caring should say, then, that it is best and most admirable to be motivated by concern for others *in balance with* self-concern and that all and only actions and activities that are consonant with and display such balance are morally acceptable.[8]

There is also the problem of appropriate concern for and treatment of strangers. But a partialistic morality that advocated greater concern for near and dear might still deplore *indifference* to strangers (Held 1993: 223); and if the moral floor of non-indifference, of humane caring, is not set too low, an agent-based morality as caring will be able to treat the usual questions of justice and human rights in a plausible, but highly distinctive way.

Defenders of universality and impartiality may object at this point that the ethic of caring doesn't provide *enough* assurance that strangers will be properly treated and so argue for the theoretical preferability of morality as universal benevolence among agent-based doctrines. But partialists can reply that (greater) devotion to particular individuals seems morally preferable to and more admirable than any sort of strictly impartial benevolence, and it is not clear who has the better case here. Note, however, that some partialists claim that particularistic caring is obligatory and admirable because *necessary to important human goods* that are realizable only in close relationships. Such an explanation takes us away from agent-basing, but I wonder how cogent it is. If parental love is obligatory and admirable *because* essential to the good(s) of family life, why isn't a child just as obligated to take things from her parents and accounted admirable for doing so? The difference here seems to depend on a *fundamental difference in admirability* between caring for and being cared for, and that sits well with an agent-based morality that deems caring admirable as such and apart from its helping to realize certain goods. Similarly, the devotion of a tutor to a retarded child can be very admirable, even if it might be *better* if their relationship weren't needed. The admirability of such caring seems not be grounded in the desirability of a relationship, but, again, to stand in no need of further justification, so a morality of caring should have no qualms, I think, about conceiving itself as agent-based.

However, we have still to consider whether agent-based ethics is well adapted to the resolution of practical moral issues. Applied ethics is a very significant part of contemporary ethics, and it if turned out that agent-basing is somehow irrelevant or unhelpful to such issues, that might make us think again about the theoretical attractiveness of such approaches.[9]

10 Agent-basing and Applied Ethics

There is a possible line of thinking that could easily lead one to wonder whether agent-basing isn't incompatible with taking issues of applied or practical ethics seriously. (Similar criticism can also be made of agent-prior views, but we shall keep them to one side.) If one is faced with a difficult moral problem, it some-how seems irrelevant and even objectionable to examine *one's own motives rather than facts about people and the world* in order to solve it. Yet isn't this what agent-basing allows for and even prescribes? Doesn't, for example, morality as (one or another form of) benevolence tell us that whether it is morally good or accep-table, say, to oppose the taking of heroic measures to keep a dying parent alive depends on the motives of the person in question, and is this at all helpful for someone who *doesn't know* whether to advocate or oppose heroic measures for a dying or suffering parent? Looking inward at or for motives presumably won't solve that person's problem, and so where we most need moral gui-dance, it would seem that agent-basing not only is irrelevant but makes it impossible to find a solution to one's moral difficulties.

What answer, if any, can be given to this criticism? (This ques-tion might be worth thinking over before reading further.) I think a convincing reply can be constructed at least in part by reference to what we said earlier about the way that an internal state like benevolence focuses on, and cares about gathering facts about, the world. One doesn't count as genuinely benevolent if one isn't practically concerned to find out relevant facts about (certain) people's needs or desires and about what things can or are likely to make them happy or unhappy. So when one morally judges a certain course of action or decision by reference to, say, the benevolence of the motives of its agent, one is judging in relation to an inner factor that itself makes reference to and takes account of facts about people in the world. One's inward gaze effectively "doubles back" on the world and allows one, as we shall see in more detail in a moment, to take facts about the world into account in one's attempt to determine what is morally acceptable or best to do. But neither, on the other hand, is this doubling back unnecessarily duplicative or wasteful of moral effort, if we assume that motive is fundamentally at least relevant to the *moral* character of any action. For if we judge the actions of ourselves or others simply by their effects in the world, we end up unable to distinguish accidentally or ironically useful actions (or slips on banana peels) from actions that we actually morally admire and that are morally good and praiseworthy.

Consider, then, someone who hears that her aged mother has suddenly been taken to the hospital and who flies from a distant city to be with her. Given morality as benevolence in some form or other and assuming she is her mother's sole living relative, how should she resolve the issue of what morally she ought to do with or for her parent when she gets to the hospital? Should she or should she not, for example, advocate heroic measures to save her mother? Surely morality as benevolence doesn't give her an answer to this question, but what is worth noting is that given the woman's ignorance, as we are assuming, of her mother's particular condition and prospects, there is no reason for most moral theories to offer an answer to that question at this point. But morality as benevolence *does* offer her an answer to the question what morally she should do when she gets to the hospital. It tells her she morally ought (would be wrong not) to find out more about her mother's condition and prospects, as regards quality and duration of life and certainly as regards future suffering and incapacity. And it can tell her this by reference to her actual motives, because if she doesn't find out more and decides what to do or to advocate about her mother solely on the basis of present relative ignorance, she will demonstrate a callousness (toward her mother) that is very far from kind or benevolent. To decide to pull the plug or not allow heroic measures without finding out more about her mother would demonstrate indifference or callousness toward her, and on that basis morality as benevolence can make the moral judgment that she ought to find out more before making any decision.

Then, once the facts have emerged and assuming they are fairly clear-cut and point to horrendously painful and debilitating prospects for her mother, the woman's decision is once again plausibly derivable from morality as benevolence. At that point, it would be callous of her to insist on heroic measures and benevolent not to do so and the proper moral decision can thus be reached by agent-based considerations.

However, Bernard Williams (1985: 10) and others have recently claimed that such a woman won't *herself* think in such terms. She will be worried about whether her mother would have a painful or pleasant future existence, for example, not about whether she herself would be acting callously if she sought to prolong the mother's existence. But is this clear? Couldn't the kind, loving daughter morally justify her decision not to allow heroic measures *either* by reference simply to likely future sufferings if the mother were kept alive *or* by saying, more complexly and richly: it would be (have been) callous of me to try to keep her alive, given her prospects? Surely, there is nothing unusual or untoward about the latter as an expression of moral problem-solving.[10]

Think, for example, about the arguments that were made in advocacy of the North American Free Trade Agreement (NAFTA). Both Vice-President Gore and House Minority Leader Robert Michel defended the agreement on the grounds that to reject it would be to adopt a cringing, fearful, or despairing attitude to the world and America's future. They could have spoken more directly about consequences, but there is nothing unreasonable about the way they addressed the issue, and so I want to conclude that, given the outward-looking character of inner motives, agent-based views have resources for the resolution of moral issues that parallel those available to such practically applicable moral theories as utilitarianism and consequentialism more generally.

Our ordinary thinking in response to difficult or not-so-difficult practical moral issues can invoke either motives or consequences or both. Consequentialism, however, solves such issues by appealing ultimately to consequences and only indirectly and as a method of useful approximation to considerations of motives. (Remember that for utilitarianism and much consequentialism the question of what it is morally right to do is entangled with the question of what an impartially benevolent and omniscient observer would want us to do.) Agent-based morality as benevolence solves the problem in the opposite fashion by appealing ultimately to motives, but taking in consequences indirectly, to the extent that they are considered by (people with) such motives and investigated in response to such motives. Each approach allows for the case-by-case solution of many moral difficulties or problems, and so with regard to the whole question of applied ethics, neither approach seems to have the advantage, and there is no reason to criticize agent-basing for being irrelevant to practical moral problems or making their solution impossible to achieve.

To be sure, there will be times when morality as benevolence won't be able to solve our moral difficulties. For example, if the facts about her mother's prospects can't be learned or turn out to be highly complicated, morality as benevolence will be stymied. But any consequentialism worthy of the name will also come up empty in such a case, and it is a strength of such views, but no less of agent-based morality as benevolence, whether in particularistic or universalistic form, that such views don't presume to know the answers to difficult moral questions in cases that *outrun our human knowledge or reasoning powers*. Any ethical theory that makes it too easy always to know what to do or feel will seem to that extent flawed or even useless because untrue to our soberer sense of the wrenching complexity of moral phenomena.

However, none of the above is intended to deny the capacity of Aristotelian and neo-Aristotelian views to deal with applied moral issues. Such views typically invoke the idea of our being sensitive to the moral qualities and demands *inherent in situations of choice* as they emerge from our knowledge of relevant human, social, and generally causal facts. (Aristotle uses the term *phronesis* or "practical wisdom" for this perception-like sensitivity to situational ethical values.) But agent-basing at first seems incapable of dealing with applied issues, and that is why it has been important for us to see that agent-basing offers us another but by no means obviously inferior model of moral problem-solving according to which moral facts and conclusions aren't to be found "out in the world," but, rather, emerge from moral motivation directed toward and relying upon perceived human, social, and causal facts.

11   Conclusion: Comparisons within Virtue Ethics

The reader may be left wondering, at this point, why I have not chosen and defended some one approach to virtue ethics as preferable to all others. I have advocated a neo-Aristotelian commonsense virtue ethics in the early parts of this essay, but gone on to mention and discuss at least somewhat favorably three agent-based forms of virtue ethics in later sections. Why this ambivalence?

I think at least part of the reason is that I really do believe it is difficult to decide with any certainty what the best way for us now to develop virtue ethics really is. Virtue ethics has just been reviving from a long slumber and, from the standpoint of contemporary ethical theory, is the "new kid on the block." That suggests that we may not yet know enough to be sure how best to develop a contemporaneously relevant and plausible virtue ethics, and it may also mean that the best way for virtue ethics to advance at this point is by pursuing a number of different promising lines of ethical theorizing. Now, of course, I have here argued in a definite fashion against *some* ways of taking virtue ethics: against anti-theory and against agent-prior views that anchor morality in independent conceptions of human happiness. But I do think it unclear whether neo-Aristotelianism or agent-basing is the most promising direction in which to take virtue ethics and also unclear which of the forms of agent-based view discussed here is the most promising.

To be sure, I did argue that morality as inner strength has disadvantages that very much threaten to knock it altogether out of contention. The fact that it treats benevolence/compassion/caring as only derivatively admirable and morally good flies in the face of our modern moral consciousness. But this extreme disadvantage actually implies a certain potential advantage over morality as (universal or partial) benevolence. At least since Plato's *Republic*, philosophers have treated the challenge of answering the egoistic moral sceptic as a major task of ethics; that is, they have sought to respond to the question "why should I be moral?"

in terms convincing enough to persuade egoists of the wrongness of their ways. However, it is clear that any theory which, like morality as benevolence, simply assumes that benevolence is better than selfishness offers us no hope of answering the egoist. But morality as inner strength does offer such a hope because it places primary ethical value on a characteristic, strength, that an egoist might well have high regard for. And then, without making any altruistic *assumptions*, morality as inner strength shows us how an altruistic (i.e. not self-interested) concern to give to and do well by others *follows out of the high moral value of inner strength*.

Morality as inner strength thus offers us a hope of answering the sceptic about morality, the egoist, and some might think this accomplishment important enough to be worth paying the necessary price of treating benevolence and altruism as merely derivatively admirable. But the defender of morality as benevolence, as well as the ordinary deontologist, might seek to turn the tables here, after the fashion of Prichard (1949), and claim that we distort the value and power of the moral by trying to derive it from non-altruistic or non-moral factors. A truly moral person finds an appeal, say, to benevolence inherently forceful and attractive and *in need of no justification by or connection to non-moral motives or considerations*. And such a reply gives us reason, I think, to prefer morality as benevolence to morality conceived in terms of inner strength.

But clearly this still leaves us with a choice among morality as caring, morality as universal benevolence, and the view I earlier called common-sense virtue ethics. (I have not been able to think of a plausible *pluralistic* form of agent-basing.) All three of these views have here been framed in such a way as to avoid the paradoxes and problems that attach to common-sense morality, to Kantianism, and to maximizing or optimizing consequentialism. But they effect their escapes in quite different fashions. Common-sense virtue ethics cuts down on the number of ethical concepts it makes use of to deal with ethical issues generally, but the concepts it does use it applies as intuitively as possible, with the result being a pluralistic account of ethical phenomena. By contrast, morality as universal benevolence (and this is also true of morality as inner strength) makes use of all our ethical concepts but attempts to ground them in a more *unified* fashion, with the result that its moral judgments do not as much correspond to pre-theoretic and persisting moral intuition(s).

Then finally morality as caring, our agent-based version of Nel Noddings's ethics of care, seems to take elements from both common-sense virtue ethics and morality as universal benevolence. From the latter, it takes the simplifying assumption that all moral questions can ultimately be grounded in questions of *concern* rather than requiring separate or (as with Kant) the unique deployment of deontological considerations or allowing (as we saw common-sense virtue ethics do) for forms and sources of admirability that have little or nothing to do with (anyone's concern for) human well-being. It thus has a more unified structure than common-sense virtue ethics, but pays the price of yielding somewhat less intuitive judgments than those made (as opposed to those left unmade) by the latter.

Morality as caring also borrows from common-sense virtue ethics, though, by offering agent-based adaptations both of its idea of self–other balance and of its advocacy of preference for those near and dear to one. This leaves morality as caring with a less unified and unifying structure than morality as universal benevolence, but with a correspondingly enhanced ability to capture moral intuitions about partialistic relationships that morality as universal benevolence leaves dangerously at large. In some sense, then, morality as caring is a compromise between (the strengths and weaknesses of) morality as universal benevolence and common-sense virtue ethics, and since we have had a hard time deciding between the latter two, it is no surprise that it should also be difficult to decide among all three of these views.

Since the revival of virtue ethics, those interested in the subject have focused mainly on Aristotle and on neo-Aristotelian ideas. But at this point and having seen the possibilities and promise of agent-based approaches, we have to take the latter seriously too. Because virtue ethics is just beginning to flex its muscles, it needs a more varied diet than Aristotle or Aristotelianism alone can provide.

Notes

1 Someone might say: no theory is needed if we consider our task simply to be that of *preserving as many intuitions as possible while avoiding paradox.* But this would be a mistake, for clearly some intuitions are more important to us than others and have greater forcefulness or scope; it is not numbers, but weighted numbers that are important to us, and in fact theory is inevitable when one tries to devise ways of assigning such weightings, of figuring out how to weigh, say, scope vs. strength in determining the importance of intuitions (for preservation).

2 Although common sense escapes those charges, it gets into certain difficulties of its own trying to balance rational vs. moral values. On this see my *From Morality to Virtue*, ch. 2.

3 For discussion of satisficing versions of consequentialism and of "scalar" versions that also evade the charges of overdemandingness and devaluation, see *From Morality to Virtue*, ch. 4.

4 At this point I in fact prefer the approach taken in my forthcoming article on justice to that taken in the earlier, 1993 piece.

5 This claim oversimplifies matters, because it leaves out of account the virtue-ethical analogues of perfect duties and the aspects of (the) virtue(s) that correspond to them. *From Morality to Virtue*, ch. 10 argues that perfect duties can also be reconceived in terms of deplorability and admirability, but the distinctive principle I have defended is, as it stands, only overarching and summary with respect to the "imperfect" side of our virtue-ethical thinking.

6 If someone makes every effort to learn about things and is unlucky enough to be foiled by reality or by his own innate lack of intelligence, his benevolence will not have its intended effect. But the personal defect here is presumably cognitive, not moral, and an agent-based view will insist on this distinction. Further issues about how agent-basing handles the problem of moral luck must, however, be left to another occasion.

7 Although Gilligan's methodology and findings have been called into question, it is still important to consider the ethical issues of "justice" vs. "caring" that her book brings to our attention.

8 However, I am not denying that it is often difficult to disentangle self-interest from altruism, as, for example, when the help one has given one's own children or a friend represents a happy achievement of one's own life.

9 In what I follows, I am indebted to Rosalind Hursthouse's ground-breaking discussion of abortion in "Virtue theory and abortion" (1991).
10 However, if the daughter thinks something like "I mustn't keep her alive, because if I do, I won't deserve to be considered – or be able to regard myself as – a kind person," she is self-absorbed and shows herself less than ideally benevolent or kind. But the mere thought that it would be unkind or callous if one were to keep one's mother alive, given her prospects, seems compatible with the highest kindness. The reference to one's own motives required for the practical application of an agent-based morality as benevolence need in no way undercut the benevolence that such a view prizes.

References

Adams, R. M. (1976) "Motive utilitarianism," *Journal of Philosophy* 79: 467–81.

Anscombe, G. E. M. (1958) "Modern moral philosophy," *Philosophy* 33: 1–19.

Augustine (1844–64) Complete Works, in *Patrologia Latina*, vols 32–47, ed. J. P. Migne, Paris (the Maurist Edition, in Latin).

Baier, A. (1985) *Postures of the Mind*, Minneapolis, Minn.: University of Minnesota Press.

Foot, P. (1978) *Virtues and Vices*, Berkeley, Calif.: University of California Press.

Garcia, J. (1990) "The primacy of the virtuous," *Philosophia* 20: 69–91.

Gilligan, C. (1982) *In a Different Voice*, Cambridge, Mass.: Harvard University Press.

Held, V. (1993) *Feminist Morality*, Chicago: University of Chicago Press.

Hume, D. [1739] (1978) *A Treatise of Human Nature*, ed. L. A. Selby-Bigge, 2nd edn with text revised and variant readings by P. H. Nidditch, Oxford: Clarendon Press.

Hursthouse, R. (1991) "Virtue theory and abortion," *Philosophy and Public Affairs* 20: 223–46.

Hutcheson, F. (1738) *An Inquiry Concerning the Original of Our Ideas of Beauty and Virtue*, 4th edn.

Long, A. A. and Sedley, D. N. (1987) *The Hellenistic Philosophers*, vol. 1, Cambridge: Cambridge University Press.

Louden, R. B. (1992) *Morality and Moral Theory: a Reappraisal and Reaffirmation*, New York and Oxford: Oxford University Press.

McDowell, J. (1979) "Virtue and reason," *Monist* 62: 331–50.

MacIntyre, A. (1984) *After Virtue*, Notre Dame, Ind.: University of Notre Dame Press.

Martineau, J. (1891) *Types of Ethical Theory*, 2 vols, Oxford: Oxford University Press.

Nagel, T. (1979) "Moral luck," in *Mortal Questions*, Cambridge: Cambridge University Press.

Nietzsche, F. [1886] (1966) *Beyond Good and Evil*, New York: Vintage Books.

Noddings, N. (1984) *Caring: a Feminine Approach to Ethics and Moral Education*, Berkeley, Calif.: University of California Press.

Nussbaum, M. (1985) *The Fragility of Goodness*, Cambridge: Cambridge University Press.

Prichard, H. A. (1949) *Moral Obligation*, Oxford: Oxford University Press.

Rorty, A. (1988) *Mind in Action: Essays in the Philosophy of Mind*, Boston, Mass.: Beacon Press.

Sidgwick, H. (1907) *The Methods of Ethics*, 7th edn, London: Macmillan.

Slote, M. (1992) *From Morality to Virtue*, New York: Oxford University Press.

—— (1993) "Virtue ethics and democratic values," *Journal of Social Philosophy* 24: 5–37.

—— (forthcoming) "The justice of caring," *Social Philosophy and Policy* 15.

Williams, B. (1973) "A critique of utilitarianism," in J. J. C. Smart and B. Williams, *Utilitarianism: For and Against*, Cambridge: Cambridge University Press.

—— (1985) *Ethics and the Limits of Philosophy*, Cambridge, Mass.: Harvard University Press.

4

Reply to Pettit and Slote

Marcia Baron

My co-authors offer far more intriguing claims and challenges than I can hope to address in my reply. I shall focus on their main objections to Kantian ethics, and more specifically will question some of their assumptions concerning how to assess ethical theory, assumptions on which their criticisms of Kantian ethics rest. I question Philip Pettit's division of ethical theories, and I take issue with Michael Slote's claim that asymmetries in ethical theory are a flaw. There are many other interesting points in their essays that I might have taken up instead; it is tempting, for instance, to sketch, by way of reply to Pettit, what Kantian ethics has to say regarding political issues.[1] But it seems more important to spell out my most fundamental disagreements with my co-authors.

1   Reply to Pettit

The contrast between how a consequentialist thinks about ethical theory and how a Kantian does is quite striking if one compares my essay with Pettit's. But the basis of our disagreements is not plain to view, and has to do with how to think about ethical theory. We disagree at several junctures, but in most instances the disagreements are rather subtle. In what follows I trace our disagreements.

I begin with Pettit's claim that "the question to which consequentialism and its rivals offer different answers" is "the question

of rightness" (p. 92). This sounds uncontroversial enough, except
that it puts the question of rightness into the foreground, privileging it over other questions one might raise and indeed suggest-
ing that it is the only, or the only important, question that
divides consequentialists from their opponents (see also p. 103).
Moreover, it ignores the fact that the question of rightness plays a
very different part in each of the theories under consideration,
since it is far more important to consequentialists to answer the
question of rightness than it is for Kantians and (especially) virtue
ethicists. Zeroing in on the question of rightness as Pettit does tips
the scales in favor of consequentialism, since it suggests that this
is what ethical theory is all about.

But suppose we ignore that, and for the sake of discussion grant
what I have suggested is not true: that Kantian ethics, virtue
ethics, and consequentialism are all equally concerned with the
question of rightness, and that their primary aim is to answer that
question. Even so, I have misgivings about Pettit's classifications
of the answers offered to that question – assuming, that is, that the
classifications are supposed to be mutually exclusive. It seems to
me that one can be in more than one category, so that it won't do
to assess ethical theories by evaluatively comparing a value theory to a universalizability theory (or to a virtue theory or a contract
theory or an ideal observer theory). If I am right, this defends
Kantian ethics against Pettit's objections, for they rest on the
assumption that Kant cannot be said to have what Pettit calls a
"value theory."

My misgivings first arose when I tried to figure out where Kant
fits. Pettit presents him (along with R. M. Hare) as offering a
universalizability theory, a theory holding "that what constitutes
an option as right is the fact that it is uniquely capable of being
prescribed – held up as what the agent ought to do – and prescribed universally" (p. 119). In Kant's specific version, "an
option is right if and only if the maxim involved can be willed
as a universal law that everyone follows" (p. 120).[2] That sounded
fair enough; but I read on and saw that another sort of theory of
rightness is "value theory." A proponent of value theory – a value
theorist – "holds that the fundamental assumption about rightness is that a right option always does better than a wrong option
in regard to acknowledged values like fairness or honesty"

(p.. 124). I don't know that Kant and Kantians have any view regarding what "the fundamental assumption" about rightness is, but unless that bit is crucial, Kant seems to qualify as a value theorist in addition to holding a universalizability theory. (Realizing that that bit may well be crucial, I'll come back to it later.) A right option does better than a wrong option in regard to the *value of humanity* (valued as an end in itself), on Kant's view.

Kant, then, seems to have both a value theory and a universalizability theory. And his theory might be able to qualify as a virtue theory, as well, since what is right is what a person with a good will chooses; but I won't pursue that possibility. Instead, let's consider some other major philosophers. Hume, for instance. Which category best fits him? Of course rightness isn't a big concern of his, but I am trying to set that complication to one side. He speaks quite generically of "merit," "morality," "virtue"; there's no separating rightness from other evaluative qualities (until we get to the artificial virtues, but that is another story). So I take all his remarks about merit, virtue, and everything else that falls under the broad heading of "value" as indicators of which of Pettit's categories Hume falls into. In the *Treatise* he says that "all virtuous actions derive their merit only from virtuous motives" (Hume 1978: 478). I don't think that fits any of Pettit's categories, though it bears some resemblance to virtue theory. In the *Enquiry Concerning the Principles of Morals* (1975), he endorses an ideal observer theory (which for Pettit is in the same category as contract theory and virtue theory): right and wrong, "moral beauty" and indeed "natural beauty" are qualities that do not inhere in the object, but rather emerge when an agent contemplates the object properly. (See also Hume 1978: 471–2.) But his ethics would also count as a value theory, the value being utility. Of course it is clumsy to analyze him in terms of Pettit's categories precisely because he isn't interested especially in the rightness of options. Looking at the most proximate issues he does address, however, we see that he asks what all virtues have in common – or, put differently, what makes a trait a virtue – and the answer he gives in the *Enquiry* is that they promote utility. The answer he gives in the comparatively brief discussion of this matter in the *Treatise* blends a value theory with something that doesn't earn a label from Pettit but which resembles contract theory and virtue theory in that it privileges people's responses. Speaking of the natural virtues, Hume says that a virtue either is immediately pleasing (thus privileging people's responses) or useful (making it at least partly a value theory). And at the same juncture he also endorses an ideal observer theory. See *Treatise* III, 3, i–v. In short, abstracting from some textual concerns that needn't worry us, Hume's seems consistently to qualify as both a value theory and as an ideal observer theory. So once again, we have reason to suspect that Pettit's categories are not mutually exclusive.

Finally, let's consider Aristotle – again someone who is not especially concerned with the question of rightness. Aristotle, I would argue, has both a virtue theory and a value theory, the relevant value being *eudaimonia*. We need to bear in mind that in giving his characterization of value theory, Pettit does not say that the relation of a right option to the value in question is that of *promoting* the value, but only that "a right option always does better than a wrong option in regard to" the value. Clearly a right option would be an option that does better than a wrong option does with regard to *eudaimonia*, and it is also what a virtuous person would choose.

Two replies might be offered by way of defending the distinctness of the categories against my claim that Hume, Aristotle, and Kant all fit into more than one of them.

1.   Maybe these philosophers are all inconsistent. They fit into more than one category because their own views contain inconsistent elements which push them in the direction of two different categories. Perhaps. The hunch that failure to fit Pettit's categories is due to inconsistency would hold greater plausibility, however, if *all* the philosophers I tried to classify hadn't defied classification into just one of Pettit's categories. That they all do should give us some pause. And in fact it really is not all that surprising that each of them would fit into more than one category, simply because it is very hard to imagine someone failing to be a value theorist. Indeed, I suspect that even the anti-theory proponents Pettit dismisses before categorizing the remaining theories would qualify as having a value theory, if all a value theory says is that the right option does better by the values in

question (whatever the important values are taken to be) than does a wrong option.[3] (I said "if"; that it is a big "if" is acknowledged below, in (2).)

2.   Maybe I've got his categories wrong because I set aside the bit about "fundamental" assumptions. This is a distinct possibility and it does matter, for if, say, Kantians have to choose just one of these ways of characterizing rightness and designate it as their fundamental assumption, they won't qualify as having both a value theory and a universalizability theory. Pettit's characterization of what it is to answer the question of rightness will force everyone who wants to provide an answer to be in just one of his categories. So let's see what he says about answers to the question of rightness: must they designate a fundamental assumption?

Early on Pettit writes that the question of rightness "is that of deciding which presumptions are the crucial ones in the determination of rightness: which are a priori for purposes of moral discourse and among those a priori assumptions which, if any, are fundamental; which, if any, serve as axioms from which to derive the others" (p. 112). It seems that an answer to the question of rightness is supposed to involve taking a stand on which assumptions are fundamental though he does leave the door open for answers that don't, since he says "which, *if any*, are fundamental" (italics added). Elsewhere, too, he leaves open the possibility that some answers won't make such designations. Differentiating anti-theory from other rivals to consequentialism, he says, "The anti-theoretical approach dismisses the question that divides consequentialists from its rivals, not acknowledging the validity of the challenge to articulate and perhaps axiomatize the presumptions that fix the meaning and reference of 'right'" (p. 117). All the theorists, by contrast (the "non-antis," as we might call them), acknowledge the validity of the challenge. But the challenge is to articulate *and perhaps axiomatize*. It sounds, then, as if axiomatizing is optional. If so, my claim that Kant, Hume, and Aristotle can all fit into more than one category still stands.

Later, however, axiomatizing is presented as if it is part of what a theorist does in answering the question of rightness. For

although he doesn't mention it in his characterization of universalizability theory, he says the following about contract theory
and virtue theory: "As I take contract theory to be a way of
axiomatixing the presumptions for rightness, and of identifying
the basis on which rightness is fundamentally determined, so I
understand virtue theory in a corresponding manner" (p. 122).
When we get to value theory, it's again prominent: "The value
theorist...holds that the fundamental assumption about rightness is that a right option always does better than a wrong option
in regard to acknowledged values like fairness or honesty or
whatever" (p. 124).

Suppose Pettit's considered view is that axiomatizing is *not*
optional: it's part of what one must do in giving an answer to
the question of rightness.[4] That will meet my objection that Aristotle, Hume, and Kant fit into more than one category – and that
virtually no one fails to have a value theory – but only at the cost
of limiting the "game" to very few players. For it is by no means
clear that Aristotle, Hume, and Kant have views about what the
fundamental assumption about rightness is. And this now con-
nects with my first objection, which was that Pettit speaks as if the
question of rightness is a far more prominent concern than it in
fact is for virtue ethicists, in particular, and also for Kantians; and
he fails to note that the question plays a different role in each
theory. If the question of rightness *does not* ask theorists what
their fundamental assumption about rightness is, then the question is at least a question that is of interest to Kantians and virtue
ethicists (even though it doesn't have the prominence for most of
them that it has for consequentialists). But if it does ask this, then
it is not at all clear that it is a question that virtue ethicists and
most Kantians are interested in. And so it's doubtful that it is a
question answers to which divide consequentialists from others.

2   Reply to Slote

Both common-sense morality and Kantian ethics, Slote thinks, are
deeply flawed because they have an "asymmetric character".
Both views say "that it is virtuous and morally good to benefit

others, seek others' happiness, in a way that it is not virtuous or morally good to promote one's own well-being" (p. 187). Focusing on Kantian ethics, I want to ask just why this is supposed to be a problem.

Slote thinks that the asymmetries are in themselves at least somewhat undesirable; it's preferable, he holds, that a theory not have an asymmetric character. As will become apparent soon, I do not share that view. But since Slote rests his case mainly on two objections purporting to show that some particular asymmetries constitute flaws in Kantian ethics, I'll focus on those objections. First, in virtue of the asymmetric character just described, Kantian ethics (and common sense morality) "in some sense devalue or downgrade the well-being of moral agents and thus the agents themselves" (p. 187). Second, at least some asymmetries lead, when conjoined with other parts of the theory, to incongruity and paradox. The "self–other asymmetry of common-sense moral obligation leads, when taken with other common-sense judgments, to incongruity and paradox" (p. 186); cf. p. 182) and a similar problem arises for Kantian ethics (p. 188).

The first objection has most plausibility when applied to theories where a great deal of importance is attached to happiness, and where we are supposed to be ready to sacrifice our own happiness for the sake of others' happiness. Consider, for example, a theory that says that it is our duty to promote others' happiness even at the great expense of our own – and (though it is not crucial to add this) that this is our sole duty. It is at least somewhat plausible to say that this theory – let's refer to it as "altruism" – in some sense devalues or downgrades the well-being of moral agents; for from the standpoint of the moral agent, it seems that only the happiness of others matters, not one's own. Somewhat, anyway. I am not convinced that the objection holds even here. If I am an altruist – a believer in (as well as practitioner of) the theory of altruism – I believe not only that I have a duty to promote others' happiness even at the great expense of my own, but also that others have a duty to promote the happiness of others even at the great expense of their own happiness. But if I believe that they have this duty, then since I am, for them, one of the others, in some sense I *do* take my own happiness to matter. I think it matters that they promote others' happiness, mine included. It is just that I have to have my happiness furthered by others, and am not morally permitted to attend to it in any serious way myself. This is a weird view and not, it seems to me, at all attractive, but I am not convinced that its problem is that it devalues or downgrades the agent's well-being or happiness (or even that this is among its problems).

Others may disagree. But what does seem clear is that whatever plausibility the objection has derives from the importance placed on happiness and from the fact that I am not even permitted to count my own happiness as a reason for limiting my efforts to promote others' happiness.

The contrast to Kant's ethics is striking. In Kant's ethics, happiness matters, but it certainly does not have pride of place. The importance of promoting others' happiness derives, in fact, from more fundamental elements, namely, from the value of humanity. This is a crucial difference. In addition, I of course am permitted on Kant's ethics to count my own happiness as a reason for limiting my efforts to promote others' happiness. And if we speak of well-being rather than happiness, it is noteworthy that among my duties to myself is a duty to look after *"the basic stuff* (the matter)" without which I cannot realize my ends (*MM* 445).[5] So while I don't have a duty (except indirectly) to keep myself happy, I do have a duty to tend to my health and general well-being, since without it I am severely limited in my pursuit of my ends.

In short, although we may be inclined to say that altruism downgrades or devalues the well-being of agents, it's difficult to see any reason for accusing Kant's ethics of doing so.

I noted earlier that Slote thinks it preferable that a theory not have an asymmetric character. In this connection it may be helpful to trace the differences between altruism and Kant's ethics to a deeper divide: self–other asymmetry is fundamental in a theory of altruism, but is considerably more superficial in Kant's ethics. What is valued on Kant's ethics is humanity: humanity in everyone, oneself and others. *At this level there is no asymmetry.* The asymmetry arises in virtue of the difference between one's relation to oneself and one's relation to others (which I discussed in my main essay). We respect humanity both negatively and positively in ourselves and in others; the asymmetries arise when we ask *how* we are to do that. We develop our talents; we promote others' happiness. (The asymmetry is less marked with respect to negative duties: we refrain from mocking others, from wanton faultfinding, from defamation, from arrogance, etc.;[6] duties to self involve not letting others tread with impunity on one's rights, being no one's lackey, and not degrading one's personality by hypocrisy and flattery (*MM* 435–6).)

There are, to be sure, grounds for questioning the claims that we have no duty to promote others' perfection, and no duty to promote our own happiness. But I see no reason to regard the asymmetry itself as a problem. If asymmetry occurs at the base of the theory, as it does in a purely altruistic theory, it does seem somewhat problematic; and the reason for this is that there appears to be no decent, let alone good, explanation for it. My suggestion, however, is that asymmetries are only a problem if there is no good explanation for them. And even that puts it too strongly, for it suggests that they are a cause for concern, something that needs to be explained. I don't think that they are. Both symmetries and asymmetries may need explaining; neither is more "suspicious" than the other. There is no burden of proof on either side.[7]

So far I have addressed only the first reason for thinking that self–other asymmetry is objectionable in Kant's ethics (along with the view that self–other asymmetry is *ipso facto* objectionable). The second reason Slote brings forth is that "self–other asymmetry leads to incongruity and paradox" in Kant's ethics as well as in common-sense morality (pp. 186, 188). He explains this primarily by reference to common-sense morality and observes a few pages later that Kantian moral theory faces exactly similar difficulties (p. 186). I agree that whatever the difficulty it poses for common-sense morality, it also poses for Kantian ethics. But I don't think that it poses a serious problem for either one.

Here is how the incongruity is supposed to arise for common-sense morality. (A) We hold that we have moral obligations to others that we lack towards ourselves, specifically, the obligation to promote their happiness. (B) The reason why we don't think we have an obligation to promote our own happiness is that (we think) this is something we do naturally. Yet (B) is incongruent with something else we hold, namely (C), we have obligations to those near and dear to us that we don't have towards others. It is incongruent with (C) because (D), we naturally are more concerned to help those near and dear to us than to help others.

This is not, it seems to me, as incongruent as Slote suggests. In holding (B), we don't hold that the *only* reason for x being more of an obligation than y is that y comes more easily to us. To put it differently, it doesn't follow from (B) that if it comes more easily to us to help our friends than to help strangers, we have less of an obligation to help our friends than to help strangers. There can be other considerations that bear on how obligated we are. For example, one rationale for a special obligation to those closest to us might be the great importance of lasting bonds between people, together with the fragility of such bonds.

In sum, I do not see that the asymmetries in Kantian ethics are a mark against it. They do not, as far as I can see, lead to incongruence or paradox; asymmetry is not objectionable in itself; and I don't see that they devalue or downgrade the agent's welfare. As I acknowledge in my essay, there certainly are problems and puzzles regarding Kantian ethics, but asymmetry seems not to be one of them.

I should register at this point a more sweeping disagreement with Michael Slote (and with Philip Pettit as well, though he doesn't develop the ideas in question here).[8] The disagreement concerns the standards by which we evaluate ethical theories. Slote (and elsewhere Pettit) believe that the desiderata for scientific theories are also desiderata for ethical theories, and so they evaluate theories by reference to such criteria as simplicity. It seems to me, though, that the task of scientific theories is, while not radically unlike that of ethical theories, different enough that the desiderata for the two types of theories may diverge. They are different in that scientific theories aim to explain why something happened, why it is the way it is, and they hope to predict similar happenings (if the phenomena in question are happenings), while the aim of ethical theories is first and foremost the practical one of offering guidance as to how we should live. Not that scientific theories lack a practical aim, of course, but it looms much larger in ethics.[9] (Just how large it is within ethics is itself a contested matter. Consequentialists seem less interested in the practical aim than other ethicists, and more interested in offering criteria of rightness which they then recommend that we try to ignore most of the time, and in ranking states of affairs – a task which I find rather alien.)

Notes

1 Those interested in what Kant had to say about political matters are referred to Part I of the *Metaphysics of Morals* and to his *Perpetual Peace and Other Essays*. However, many Kantians look less to what Kant said on such topics as property rights and more to what (Kant's own views notwithstanding) his moral philosophy suggests. See e.g. Van der Linden 1988, O'Neill 1986 and some chapters of O'Neill 1989 and 1996. On the question of how we should act in an imperfect world, see Korsgaard 1996, ch. 5. A number of Kantians see Rawlsian contractarianism as developing a Kantian answer to the questions that Pettit raises. Whereas some contractarianism (e.g. that of David Gauthier) is very far indeed from Kant's ethics, the approach taken by Rawls to political justice bears a very evident Kantian stamp.

   Another matter I was tempted to take up was Pettit's response to the overdemandingness objection. In addition to recognizing the "standard of what best promotes value as the supreme moral ideal," the consequentialist "must equally recognize... a less demanding but even more pressing standard," namely, "the standard of doing the best that can be asked of me in a context where the demand is simultaneously addressed to other, similarly placed agents." Doesn't this appeal to an independent value of fairness? One can avoid that charge by embracing rule-consequentialism, but Pettit rejects rule-consequentialism. It's not clear how he can consistently endorse the standard of "doing the best that can be asked of me."

2 Pettit also says that Kant "assumed that for any option there is a way of identifying a fairly general principle as the unique maxim that the option instantiates and argued, on the basis of that assumption, for his famous Categorical Imperative" (p. 119). I wish to register my disagreement. Kant did not argue on that basis for the Categorical Imperative. (It's also not clear that he made the assumption Pettit states; I don't see any reason to think that Kant assumed that an option instantiates exactly one maxim. It is true, however, that Kant thinks that we can meaningfully talk about the maxim on which the agent acted. So while there isn't just one maxim that the option instantiates,

if we speak in terms of the agent rather than the option, we can speak,
Kant supposes, of *the* maxim.)

3 In her comment on part of Pettit's essay presented at the 1996 annual
   colloquium at the University of North Carolina at Chapel Hill, Susan
   Wolf observes, "virtually any account of rightness must take it as a
   fundamental presumption that to call an action right is to say something good about it, and this seems just to amount to the idea that there
   is some value or values in connection with which we can see right
   actions 'doing well.'" I am grateful to Wolf for sharing her comment
   with me.

4 In correspondence Philip Pettit has indicated, in response to my reply,
   that he did mean that answers to the question of rightness must
   designate a fundamental assumption. He elaborates: "Every theory
   has to decide whether the assumptions associated with rightness and
   endorsed in the theory are all equally fundamental/axiomatic or
   whether some serve as parent assumptions from which the others
   can be derived. Every theory must axiomatize the assumptions in the
   sense of deciding which are fundamental, though not every theory will
   axiomatize them in the more colloquial sense of finding a proper
   subset from which the others can be derived. However, a theory
   which acknowledges a large range of assumptions and treats them all
   as equally fundamental or axiomatic (a theory which does not axiomatize the assumptions in the colloquial sense) will be hard to distinguish from the anti-theoretical positions described in my text."

5 *MM* refers to Kant's *Metaphysics of Morals*. See note 9 to my main
   essay for explanation of my references to Kant's works.

6 The positive side of this is that we have "a duty not to censure [others']
   errors by calling them absurdities, poor judgment and so forth, but
   rather to suppose that his judgment must yet contain some truth and to
   seek this out, uncovering, at the same time, the deceptive illusion
   ... and so, by explaining to him the possibility of his having erred,
   to preserve his respect for his own understanding" (*MM* 463).

7 I emphasize that in denying that asymmetry is in itself a problem, I
   recognize that a particular asymmetry *may* be (just as a particular symmetry might be). In this connection let's consider an asymmetry that
   Slote objects to: the asymmetry that concerns (self-)perfection. Slote
   suggests that instead of denying a duty to perfect others, what we should
   say is that "one should be concerned to promote one's own well-being
   and virtues and also concerned to promote the well-being and virtues in
   other people" (p. 196). He favors, in short, symmetry on both counts.
   Focusing on the part that concerns promotion of virtues, I would maintain that responsibility for oneself mandates concerning oneself with

one's own virtue and concerning oneself extremely little with promoting virtue in anyone else except one's children and, if one is a teacher of children, in one's pupils. Even promoting the virtues of one's close friend is questionable, and at the very least would need to be carefully circumscribed. Slote reminds us of the concern and responsibility some Americans felt about the morality or decency of other Americans during the Vietnam War. But the concern, surely, wasn't for their virtue or their character. It was about *what they were doing.* Our concern was with their actions – especially insofar as their actions reflected our government, and thus in some sense, our collective policy.

8 See Pettit 1991.

9 I am grateful to Fred Schmitt for helpful discussion of this issue.

References

Hume, David [1777] (1975) *Enquiry Concerning the Principles of Morals*, in David Hume, *Enquiries Concerning Human Understanding and Concerning the Principles of Morals*, 3rd edn, ed. L. A. Selby-Bigge and P. H. Nidditch, Oxford: Clarendon Press.

—— [1739] (1978) *A Treatise of Human Nature*, ed. L. A. Selby-Bigge, 2nd edn with text revised and variant readings by P. H. Nidditch, Oxford: Clarendon Press.

Kant, Immanuel (1983) *Perpetual Peace and Other Essays on Politics, History, and Morals*, trans. Ted Humphrey, Indianapolis, Ind. Hackett.

—— (1991) *The Metaphysics of Morals* trans. Mary J. Gregor, Cambridge: Cambridge University Press.

Korsgaard, Christine (1996) *Creating the Kingdom of Ends*, Cambridge: Cambridge University Press.

O'Neill, Onora (1986) *Faces of Hunger: an Essay on Poverty, Justice and Development*, London: Allen & Unwin.

—— (1989) *Constructions of Reason: Explorations of Kant's Practical Philosophy*, Cambridge: Cambridge University Press.

—— (1996) *Towards Justice and Virtue*, Cambridge: Cambridge University Press.

Pettit, Philip (1991) "Consequentialism," in Peter Singer (ed.) *A Companion to Ethics*, Oxford: Blackwell Publishers.

Van der Linden, Harry (1988) *Kantian Ethics and Socialism*, Indianapolis, Ind.: Hackett.

5

Reply to Baron and Slote

Philip Pettit

1 Rival Theories?

Ethical theory starts from reflection on our ordinary ethical thought and aims at understanding and, if necessary, redirecting that thought. But the topics to which we give attention in ethical thinking are many in number and kind. And so, unsurprisingly, ethical theory is an area of philosophy where we find diverse concerns and commitments.

Among the things which we consider in the course of ethical thought are decision-making questions about what I should do here and now or about how I should generally treat someone; more reflective questions that bear on the deliberative reasons that should guide me in decision-making; questions of motivation and character such as what sort of person I should try to be and what kinds of habits and motives I should encourage in myself; and issues of justification to do with whether I am or was justified in taking a certain course of action or in endorsing certain deliberative or motivational patterns. For each such topic of ethical thought, there is a corresponding area of ethical theory. There are theoretical or philosophical positions, for example, on how decision-making should be conducted; on what considerations are good deliberative reasons, answering directly or indirectly to real goods or values; on what sort of motives and habits and traits it is good to cultivate in oneself; and on what it is that makes a certain decision – or a commitment to certain decision-making or deliberative or motivational patterns – the right one to endorse.

The diversity of ethical theory shows up in the three contributions to this volume. I disagree with Marcia Baron when she suggests that there may not be anything that consequentialism, Kantianism, and virtue ethics are all theories of. For there are certainly some questions to which the approaches offer different answers and that is enough to make them rival theories. But what is undoubtedly true is that the approaches vary in which questions they concentrate on and in how they rank those questions for importance.

Among the three approaches in question, consequentialism is by far the narrowest and, as a result, the best defined. Where Kantianism and virtue ethics suggest positions, and often not very tightly connected positions, on different types of question – decisional, deliberative, motivational, justificational and so on – consequentialism explicitly offers a line on one type of question only: the question as to what sort of thing is involved in justifying a particular decision or commitment; the question as to what it is that ultimately makes a certain choice the right one to take or to have taken. This, as I described it in my contribution, is the question of rightness.

The consequentialist focus on the question of rightness means that there is a direct conflict with Kantianism and virtue ethics only so far as those approaches offer rival answers to that question. In my contribution I identified one type of answer to the question as Kantian in character – this was a version of the universalizability theory of rightness – and one as virtue-ethical. This was the theory, akin to radical contractualism, according to which what makes an option right is just that it is what a virtuous agent would choose. But I mentioned that virtue ethics means many different things in the literature – it identifies answers to many different kinds of questions – and clearly I might have said much the same of Kantianism.

In their contributions to this volume, Marcia Baron and Michael Slote consider the Kantianism and virtue ethics that they respectively defend, not in the relatively narrow guise of answers to the question of rightness, but in broader compass, as approaches to a range of ethical questions. That is quite proper but it means that many of the things they defend are points on which I as a consequentialist can feel open and uncommitted.

Consequentialists have much to learn from other approaches, not because of taking mistaken lines on various ethical questions, but because of not taking any line at all on those questions.

There are two ways, in particular, that consequentialists may expect to learn from opponents. They are committed to holding that in any choice the right option is that which promotes expected value but this position is silent on two crucial questions. First, the issue as to what is truly of value. And second, the issue as to how different options are likely to serve the cause of promoting value. The one issue bears on the ends to be promoted, the second on the means by which to promote them. The question of ends is pretty clear: it arises because of the familiar point, emphasized in my contribution, that a consequentialist theory of the right needs to be complemented by a theory of the good. But it may be useful if I say something more on the question of means.

Human agents do not face just choices that bear now on this action, now on that. Apart from such act-centred choices, they also confront choices, for example, of whether in certain areas they should unthinkingly follow a particular decision-making rule – always say "yes" to a friend, never think about breaking the law – and of whether they should indulge certain habits of response: habits like generosity, or devotion, or spontaneity. This complexity means that even if they are clear about the goods or ends that justify choices, consequentialist agents face the further question of how far they should try to further those ends by considering them act by act, and how far they should eschew such calculation, allowing certain rules of thumb or certain habits of thought to guide them unreflectively. One of the most important choices to be settled by consequentialist agents, in other words, is the choice between the different modes of control that these alternatives represent.

The discussion of our ordinary moral psychology in my earlier contribution suggests that any plausible consequentialist position is going to allow and indeed require the eschewal of act-by-act calculation. Taking the fact of how we are psychologically constituted as given, and acknowledging the way that constitution serves in the development of relationships and identities and personalities, it is bound to recognize that if we are to leave the world better off in the wake of our lives – and this, no matter what values are relevant to assessing those lives – then we had better not go for act-by-act calculation. Our consequentialist reflections, as I put it earlier, should have a virtual presence only; they should play a role, not in our actual day-to-day responses, but only in occasional consideration of whether our actions and lives are truly justifiable, a form of consideration to which we should be willing, as appropriate, to have recourse. Because consequentialism is unlikely to counsel act-by-act calculation, it cannot fairly be described, in the way Michael Slote describes it, as an "act-focused" theory (pp. 177–8) that devalues agents (p. 190). Consequentialism is option-focused, for sure: it is relevant to every choice between options and it is not restricted, for example, to choices between rules. But the best option in the most important choice of all – the decision between different modes of agent-control – may be to eschew act-focused calculation and to espouse a variety of control that privileges principle or motivation or personality.

I mention the silence of consequentialism on the two issues of ends and means in order to highlight the fact that consequentialism may have much to learn from the Kantianism and the virtue ethics defended by my co-authors. Kantianism emphasizes that other people matter to us in such a way, for example, that we do not compensate for killing one by creating another; this is a point mentioned by Marcia Baron (pp. 24–5). It would be extraordinary if consequentialism precluded endorsing such an intuitive observation on the nature of value and on the means of promoting it.

The observation need not mean – it had better not mean – that it is always wrong to take a life for the sake of saving lives; otherwise, as many thought-experiments emphasize, it would have wildly counterintuitive results. But it surely does mean that any mode of behaving towards people that treats them as substitutable, one for another, would undermine properly interpersonal relationships. I meant to register just this sort of point when I argued that in our ordinary relationships we care for others in their particularity. When we help someone out of friendship, we do so because Mary, a friend, is in need, not because we help friends in need and Mary happens to qualify under that heading.

The first thing I want to emphasize in this commentary, then, is that the competition between consequentialism, Kantianism, and virtue ethics is not a competition on all fronts. From the consequentialist point of view, Kantianism and virtue ethics may have much to teach. All that it necessarily opposes is any suggestion that the right option is sometimes fixed on some basis other than that it is the option that maximizes expected value.

This opposition, I note finally, need not be a particularly sectarian commitment. If an action is adopted under the optimific policy of following some rule of thumb, for example, or if it imposes itself under the pressure of some optimific habit or motive, then it may do less well by the maximization of expected value than some actually available alternative. It will still be the right choice in that situation, provided that a presupposition of taking the alternative is the absence of the rule of thumb or the motive or habit in question, and provided that the presence of that general disposition is indeed essential for the promotion of expected value in the person's life as a whole.

2   Comment on Slote

Given this general point of view, it will not be surprising that consequentialism as such does not have much to fault in Michael Slote's claims. As I understand the forms of virtue ethics that attract him, they represent contributions to the theory of the good rather than the theory of the right. Slote is certainly a non-consequentialist, as I shall argue, but his non-consequentialism is not distinctively virtue-ethical in the manner of the position that I described as a virtue theory of rightness.

Slote distinguishes between two main forms of virtue ethics, one agent-focused, the other agent-based. As I see these, they differ in how they cast the value of the preferred virtues. The agent-focused theory holds that certain virtues are instrumentally valuable: specifically that they are instrumentally valuable in the identification of good and right actions and, so I presume, in the faithful performance of those actions. Aristotle is presented as a virtue ethicist of this kind. For him "the virtuous individual is someone who, without relying on rules, is sensitive and intelligent enough to perceive what is noble or right as it varies from circumstance to circumstance" (p. 178).

I have no essential difficulty as a consequentialist with this claim about the epistemological and practical utility, even the epistemological and practical indispensability, of virtue. It may indeed be the case that virtue enjoys such a status. And it may also be the case that consequentialists in general – for example, utilitarians – have been slow to recognize the utility of virtue, particularly its utility in fostering sensitivity to goodness and rightness. I happily acknowledge these possibilities (see Pettit and Smith 1993).

It is worth noting as we pass that while Slote is well-disposed to the agent-focused account of the instrumental value of virtue, he takes a stand against the different instrumental value recognized in virtue by what he describes as agent-prior accounts. According to these accounts, the value of having virtuous traits and motives consists in their contribution to one's human well-being or flourishing. His objection to such a story is that it is going to have difficulty in explaining why an unvirtuous action that happens to promote a person's well-being is not just as admirable as a virtuous one. If virtues are admirable for promoting well-being, why not actions, including actions that accord with no known virtue?

The second form of virtue ethics that appeals to Slote is what he describes as the agent-based approach. This involves two commitments: first, that certain virtues have intrinsic value, not just value of an instrumental kind; and second that those virtue-values are the only values relevant in fixing which is the right option. The idea is not the counterintuitive suggestion that an action is guaranteed to have positive value by the fact that it is performed by a person of virtue, even performed by a person of virtue under the motivational stimulus of virtue. What Slote claims in explicating the approach is that the value of an action is established by how far it "exhibits" or "expresses" or "demonstrates" an appropriate virtue. Exhibiting a virtue in this sense certainly involves being motivated by it but, so he insists, it also involves ascertaining the "facts about what is needed out in the world around one" (p. 215). No virtuous motive is sufficient in itself to confer value on an act; the virtue in question must also function in a well-informed way.

There are three brief points I would like to make about this position. The first is that there is nothing inherently objectionable, from a consequentialist point of view, in the suggestion that certain virtues may be valuable properties to have realized in the world (Pettit and Brennan 1986). Thus it is mistaken of Slote to suggest, as he does in passing, that there is an inevitable clash between consequentialism and this belief in virtue: that where consequentialism morally evaluates "motives solely in terms of their consequences," this approach "insists that the moral evalua- tion of motives depends on their inherent character as motives rather than on their consequences" (p. 223). It may be a neutral and intrinsic good, from a consequentialist point of view, that people in general should act out of certain motives and display certain virtues.

The second point to make is that what agent-based theories appear to value, strictly speaking, isn't just the presence of the virtues in question but the presence of those virtues only in people who try – and perhaps only in people who manage – to ascertain the facts about what the world needs of them. This makes the theories much more plausible and it gives the lie to an earlier, more casual suggestion by Slote that according to an agent-based theory "the agent and her inner life are not fixed on any external or independent action-governing moral standard, but rather constitute in some sense the basis and measure of all moral activity" (p. 207).

The third point I want to make about agent-based theories is that if they are unlikely to attract consequentialist approval, this is because of the implausibility of claiming that the value of the virtues in question – or even of the well-informed exercise of the virtues – is the only value of which account needs to be taken in morally evaluating action. That really is an extraordinary claim. Surely there are always likely to be cases where the right option, the option that is guided appropriately by value, does not happen to correspond to the exercise, however well-informed, of any virtue in the agent-based theorist's list. Think of the moral cata- strophe where the only way to save life on earth is by killing an innocent child. Isn't it at least possible that the right option in this horrible scenario is to kill the child?

The agent-based theorist may respond that if killing the child is the right option in such a case, that is because it would demon- strate benevolence or such some virtue. But this is a dangerous line for the agent-based theorist to take. For if the theory guarantees itself the ability always to provide such an answer, then it becomes vanishingly distinct from a straightforward consequentialist account. It appears to assume, in axiomatizing style, that wherever the best consequences are produced by a certain option, that option is bound to demonstrate the presence of a suitable virtue.

So much on the two virtue-ethical theories of value canvassed by Michael Slote. But while they are theories of value, and while there is no inherent reason why consequentialists should not be able to entertain the possibility of their truth, Slote himself does not think of them as pointing the way to a consequentialist position. The reason is that he presumes, as almost all virtue ethicists presume, that the point is to instantiate the virtues not to maximize them. Under an agent-focused theory, instantiating the virtues will mean honoring the values that they reveal; under an agent-based theory, it will mean honoring the values that they themselves represent. Slote's position amounts to a non-consequentialist form of the value-theoretic account of rightness, with virtues or the properties signalled by virtues, figuring in the value role.

The points that Michael Slote makes against taking a consequentialist line bear on matters that will already be familiar from my own contribution; thus he concentrates, in defending his agent-focused version of virtue ethics, on the overdemandingness objection (pp. 189–91). The points that I would make against his line will also be familiar from my earlier discussion. The non-consequentialist theory that he defends means that the best we can achieve in vindication of what we do will be explanation and excuse, not justification proper. We will not be able to provide a straightforward, substantive answer in response to the challenge to justify what we do. At best we will be able to reply with a *tu quoque*: "Wouldn't you value the same things, and perform the same action, if you were in my position?" As I tried to show in my contribution, the defender of such a position has to reject the universalizability of rightness or, accepting the universalizability constraint, has to acknowledge that the word "right" is often indexical in significance: "right" as uttered by me in marking the justifiability of what I do will refer to a different property

from what it refers to when you use it to justify your actions. I do
not think that either position is a happy one to have to embrace
and I believe that we should not be attracted to the sort of theory
which it would force upon us.

3   Comment on Baron

Much of what Marcia Baron has to say in her discussion of
Kantianism and virtue ethics is a contribution to the theory of
value and, as with the bulk of Michael Slote's comments, I can be
relaxed as a consequentialist about the consideration of her
remarks. Those remarks may have something important to tell
me about the nature of the good: in particular, something that is
in no way inimical to my consequentialist commitments. I already
illustrated the point in referring to her discussion of why we
cannot compensate for taking the life of one person by giving
life to another.

Baron has explicitly negative things to say about consequentialism, however, and in this brief comment I would like to concentrate on those charges. She makes two criticisms that I particularly
want to address. One is the charge that in supposing that there are
just two main ways of responding to a neutral value – to honor the
value or to promote it – my consequentialism misses out on a lot
of ethical riches. And the other is the related charge that my
failure to see that different values may call for different responses
shows up in the fact that I cannot make good sense of how to
respond to the value that Kant describes as humanity.

In launching the first criticism, Baron maintains that there are
many values – here, of course, a consequentialist can agree – and
that these values often call for a wide range of different responses.
"Some are such that the best response is to exemplify or instantiate them; others are such that the best response is to promote
them; still others call for producing as much of them as possible;
others call for honoring them by refraining from doing anything
that would violate them" (p. 22). But this passage doesn't
yet direct us to responses beyond the two that I distinguish.
Exemplifying or instantiating or indeed expressing a value is a

species of honoring; with an appropriate value it means acting in the way that would promote the value in a suitably compliant world, even if that mode of action does not promote it in the actual world. And producing as much as possible of a value is another description of what it means, by my account, to promote a value: it maximizes the expected realization of the value.

In developing the first criticism, however, Baron goes on to mention a response to value that is certainly distinct from both honoring and promoting. Drawing on work by Christine Swanton (1995), she says that in many cases the point may be neither to honor nor to promote a value but rather to appreciate it. "An appropriate response to such value as the value of a redwood forest is to appreciate it" (p. 22). I would not deny for a moment that it is good to have appreciation of such things as redwood forests but I am not persuaded by this example that we have here a relevant alternative to promoting a value and instantiating – or more generally, honoring – that value.

In discussing the issue on hand, Baron and I are assuming in common that certain neutral values are given and that the right option in any choice is that which responds appropriately to those values. The consequentialist thinks that the appropriate response is to promote the values and the non-consequentialist denies this. So far Baron and I are in agreement. I think of the value-theoretical non-consequentialist, however, as holding that the thing is always to instantiate or honor the relevant values. And the question now raised is whether this is not excessively unimaginative on my part. There may be more ways of responding to values, so it is suggested, than are dreamt of in my austere view of non-consequentialism. I do not have to be particularly defensive on this matter, of course. But as it happens I think that the suggestion that Baron and Swanton make about appreciation stems from a mistake about what is involved in responding to a value.

Suppose that I countenance a value, V, and that I believe that the proper response to such a value – the response that marks out a corresponding action as right – is R-ing V. R-ing V is right, so I maintain. But if R-ing V is right, then R-ing V is a value. And so, if I am not to be launched on a regress of values, R-ing V had better not be a value that is itself distinct from the value, V. In particular, it must not be distinct in such a way that the project of R-ing R-ing

V, if we can put it that way, is distinct from the original project of
R-ing *V*. *R* must meet a certain non-iteration constraint. If *R* does
not meet such a constraint, then a regress looms: *V* will be one
value, *R*-ing *V* a second, distinct value, *R*-ing *R*-ing *V* a third,
distinct value, and so on.

While it can certainly be described as a response to value in the
ordinary usage of that phrase, appreciation does not meet this
constraint and does not count as a response in the sense required
for a theory of rightness. Appreciating a value is one thing. But
appreciating appreciating a value is another. Appreciating a value
is itself a value, in particular a value that is distinct from the
value appreciated. And as a distinct value it can call itself to
be appreciated. We may appreciate redwoods or we may appreciate the appreciation of those redwoods, whether by ourselves or
by others.

There is a salient contrast in this respect between appreciation
on the one hand and honoring and promotion on the other. For to
promote the promotion of a value – or to promote the promotion of
the value – is not distinct from promoting the
value itself. And similarly with honoring. To honor a value is to
act so that it would be promoted in a suitably compliant world.
But to act so that the promotion of the value would be promoted in
such a world is not distinct from acting so that the value itself
would be promoted in that world. Neither honoring nor promoting iterates in the troublesome manner of appreciation. They
represent basic responses to values as distinct from functions
that take us from given values – say the value of redwoods – to
further values: the value of appreciating redwoods.

There are other basic responses to value apart from honoring
and promoting. 'Satisficing' in the sense of non-maximizing promotion (Slote 1989) is one example; at least that is so if providing
enough of providing enough of something is the same as providing
enough of it. Yet further examples appear in more straightforward
variations on the promotional idea: say, the actual-value version of
promotion that I rejected, equally with satisficing, in the characterization of consequentialism. If there are various basic promotional responses, of course, so there will also be various
counterparts in the domain of honoring. But, still, my sense is
that the world is less rich with possible responses to value than

Baron and Swanton imagine. The austerity which marks my view of non-consequentialist possibilities may be well justified.

My reply, then, to the observation about appreciating value is this. For any positive value, V, there is a further, distinct value involved in appreciating V. How to respond to these values of V on the one hand and R-ing V on the other? We return in each case to the familiar question. Should we act so that the values are promoted in my sense, or perhaps in a related sense? Or should we act so that they are instantiated, and more generally, honored? Appreciation has an important place in the consideration of value but it has no place in theory of the demands – the demands for a suitable response – that value makes upon us.

The second criticism that Baron makes of my consequentialism is that, given my commitment to the promotion of value, I am unable to give a persuasive account of how to respond to the value that Kant describes as humanity. She starts from the assumption that there is an unquestionable, unambiguous value here, deserving of the name "humanity," and then she finds fault with my approach on the grounds that the plausible demands of that value are not easily represented as demands to promote humanity. Not only does she find fault with my position, indeed; she has a field day as she runs through the various implausible, sometimes risible, ideals that might be associated with the injunction to promote humanity.[1]

But if the only proper response to value – that is, to ultimate, neutral value – is to promote it, the constraint thereby imposed will be loosened so far as there are many values that call to be promoted, including many values associated with the Kantian injunction to respect humanity. I do not think, as a matter of fact, that there is any intuitive sense in which humanity is a value that calls to be promoted. What I do say, however, is that there are all sorts of values associated with the way humans treat one another that do indeed deserve promotion: the values associated with allowing others to speak, for example, with treating them as worth listening to, and with giving them an active hearing; the values, in short, that are involved in accepting others into the human, conversational community (Pettit 1997a, 1997b). Where a Kantian rightly insists on the importance of respecting humanity, I would insist on the importance of promoting such associated values. I need not be forced to embrace what sounds like the incongruous enterprise of promoting humanity.

Baron comes close to recognizing the availability of this sort of response. "It might be suggested that we view humanity as a goal if we seek to bring about a state of affairs in which everyone respects humanity" (p. 26). "But that won't do," she says. "It conflates humanity with respect for humanity." I reply, of course, that it won't do if the assumption is made that there is one and only one value in play here: that which answers to the Kantian term. Needless to say, I reject that assumption. As a consequentialist, I believe that in the end values demand nothing more or less than their promotion: that we can establish the ultimate justifiability of what we do only by reference to producing the goods. But I also believe that values are various, even the values involved in the treatment of other human beings, and that they cannot be summed up in a single word like "humanity."

This gives me a good note on which to resolve my discussion. Consequentialism is an important doctrine but, to return to the theme with which I began, it is a doctrine that bears only on one sort of ethical question. Admit the truth of consequentialism and there are still a myriad of issues to explore in ethical theory. And among those issues one of the most important bears on the nature of value and on the varieties of value, including the varieties of value implicated in our dealings with one another. I have not written much on the theory of value, not at least in matters that pertain to personal life; the main work that I have done in the area bears on the political value of republican freedom: freedom as non-domination (Pettit 1997a). But this silence should not be taken to express indifference. On the contrary it is here in this area, so I believe, that the most interesting work remains to be done in ethical theory.

Notes

1 Marcia Baron indicates in correspondence that she did not intend this criticism; her aim, in the section I am discussing, was to explain how someone could believe that there are obligatory ends without believ-

ing that one ought to promote them maximally. Still, since her critique does entail this criticism, it is important for me to respond to it.

References

Pettit, Philip (1997a) *Republicanism: a Theory of Freedom and Govern-ment*, Oxford: Oxford University Press.

——(1997b) "Freedom with honor," *Social Research* 64: 52–76.

Pettit, Philip and Brennan, Geoffrey (1986) "Restrictive consequential-ism," *Australasian Journal of Philosophy* 64: 438–55.

Pettit, Philip and Smith, Michael (1993) "Practical unreason," *Mind* 102: 53–80.

Slote, Michael (1989) *Beyond Optimizing*, Cambridge, Mass.: Harvard University Press.

Swanton, Christine (1995) "Profiles of the virtues," *Pacific Philosophi-cal Quarterly* 76: 47–72.

6

Reply to Baron and Pettit

Michael Slote

Philip Pettit and Marcia Baron's discussions, respectively, of consequentialism and Kantian ethics advance our understanding of these two major approaches to ethics and clearly call for some sort of response from the virtue ethicist. However, since virtue ethics in recent times has in large part been reacting to consequentialism and Kantianism, much of what I myself would want to say in answer to the contributions of my collaborators is effectively contained in my original essay. Still, Baron and Pettit do raise some new questions and touch on some very general themes that I think virtue ethicists ought to be responsive to. Let me begin by discussing an issue raised by Baron.

1   Reply to Baron

Marcia Baron thinks that Kantian ethics and virtue ethics may not be as different as many virtue ethicists and also Kantians have imagined, and with this I certainly agree. For example, it is often claimed that Kant provides us with a legal or legislative model of the moral life that is entirely antithetical to virtue ethics, but I tend to think that the idea of universal or universalizable law implicit in the Categorical Imperative ultimately rests for Kant on a strongly held conception of what it is for an act to have moral worth, and moral worth is an aretaic, not a deontic, concept. (I have here been influenced by discussions with my colleague Sam Kerstein.)

Kant holds, I believe, that the ultimate criterion for distinguishing right from wrong must allow moral worth (or merit) to attach to morally required actions done from a sense of duty, and he also thinks that when our morality is determined ("heteronomously") by some some "material" end like our own or others' happiness, conscientious action will lack such worth. Only if we are responsive to and guided by the form of morality, the universality and universalizability implicit in any genuine moral or rational principle, does he think our acting from duty will have moral worth, and in its most familiar form the Categorical Imperative (CI) treats the distinction between right and wrong in precisely such formal terms.

So Kant's defense of the CI arguably appeals to foundational aretaic judgments. But, of course, those judgments would be disputed by agent-based and other virtue ethicists. If Kant holds that (acting from) concern for others has moral worth only if it derives from a sense of duty defined by the CI, the defender of morality as (partial or impartial) benevolence will insist, to the contrary, that (acting from) concern for the good of others has moral merit or worth in its own right. Such a virtue ethicist will not only not be afraid of heteronomy, but will want to bring the fight into the Kantian camp. For although Kant believes that the CI entails a moral obligation to concern ourselves with the good of other people, many a virtue ethicist will say that a self-conscious application of the moral dictates of benevolence (of the kind Kant finds most worthy) can in some cases be morally less meritorious that a spontaneous act of generosity or compassion.

In addition, Marcia Baron suggests that Kant's ethics may be agent-based insofar as it ultimately rest on the category of the good will. But if the interpretation of Kant mentioned above is on the right track, such a characterization will be difficult to justify. For although the notion of a morally worthy or good action is aretaic, it applies to actions, not to inner states. Moreover, even if the will, or acts of will or choice, are inner, they correspond one-to-one to actions, and if moral choice or willing has worth under precisely the conditions that also determine the moral worth of actions, then it seems gratuitous to suppose that "morally worthy or good (act of) will" is the ultimate grounding notion and "morally worthy or good action" merely derivative from it. (If "good will" is supposed to refer not to willings, but to a long-term inner disposition to choose or act worthily or well, then the notion is clearly derivative and thus incapable by itself of providing any sort of agent-based foundation for ethics.) However, I am no Kant scholar, and the question whether Kant's views are agent-based may well be worth further consideration; we owe Baron a debt for raising this issue in such clear terms.

Virtue ethicists would want to question the Kantian view of (the conditions of) moral worth, but, perhaps more significantly, not only virtue ethicists but philosophers of many other ethical persuasions have (over the past two centuries) wanted to question the capacity of (one or another version of) the CI to distinguish right from wrong, to function as a criterion of right and wrong (apart from questions about moral goodness or worth). For one thing, the Formula of Universal Law version of the CI has notorious difficulty accounting for the permissibility of various kinds of morally accepted human activity. Can the maxim, for example, of someone whose deepest desire is, simply, to be a postman be appropriately universalized? Can the maxim of someone who wants to marry a particular person (whom others also want to marry) or of someone who simply wants to win an Olympic medal be universalized in accordance with the Universal Law version of the CI? Quite possibly not, and this is a point that Baron herself seems willing to grant. Yet the maxims just alluded to don't seem immoral, or to give rise to immoral behavior. When someone tries to persuade another to marry him or trains hard in order to gain the glory of an Olympic medal, his actions aren't perhaps morally good, but it seems morally prissy to condemn his actions as morally wrong or contrary to moral duty, and so Kantian views have a problem with this version of the Categorical Imperative.

Perhaps that is why, more and more, Kantians seem to be relying on other versions of the CI. But there are also problems with the application of these other versions to moral questions. The Formula of Humanity version of the CI says, roughly, that we must treat people as ends-in-themselves (or self-existent ends) and never solely as means – because unlike everything else in the world, human beings can set ends for themselves and thus have a dignity that is beyond the mere "price" that attaches to things that can be ends of action but cannot set ends. However, the force of Kant's argument from the fact we uniquely set ends to the conclusion that people are and ought to be ends-in-themselves (*vis-à-vis* one another) strikes me as far from obvious, and the conclusion itself is difficult to make clear sense of.

Moreover, it in no way obviously follows from the fact that we should treat others as ends-in-themselves that, as Kantians claim, we mustn't make (or allow?) trade-offs in human lives, that we mustn't ever kill (or maim?) one innocent person in order to prevent a catastrophe to a whole country or to humanity as a whole. The refusal to kill even one innocent person has been said by Kantians and certain other deontologists to be an expression of our respect for human dignity, a way of acknowledging and showing the supreme value we place on human beings and human lives. But critics have responded that the willingness to sacrifice one person in order to preserve a greater number of human lives is just as good, and perhaps even better, as a way of acknowledging or respecting the dignity and importance of human beings. Kantians want to be able to show that consequentialist and agent-based views favoring, in certain circumstances, the sacrificing, say, of one person to prevent a catastrophe involving others (as well as the person being sacrificed) are mistaken. But at this point it is difficult (for some of us) to see how an argument to that effect making use of the Formula of Humanity can be successfully brought off.[1]

In that case, the reason a virtue ethicist (or consequentialist) has to reject Kantian ethics stems more from the latter's repeated failure to show how the largely intuitive moral judgments it wishes to defend can be justified in its own terms, than from any prima-facie or a priori objectionability in trying to understand moral obligation in terms of the Categorical Imperative. Recent agent-based and agent-focused ethical theories are able, so to speak, to make a fresh start on questions about the nature and justification of morality, and as the arguments offered earlier for agent-based morality as universal benevolence and morality as caring, in particular, demonstrate, we can deliver most (though not all) of our common-sense or intuitive moral judgments by reference to certain motives (other than the desire to do one's independently determined duty). So the superiority, if any, of agent-basing lies partly in the way it focuses on the inner life, but also, and perhaps more importantly, on the way it uses aretaic characterizations of the inner life to deliver more of morality than other views seem capable of doing.

It is also worth noting, however, that warm agent-based views represent a kind of half-way house or compromise between Kantian ethics and (most forms of) consequentialism. Most versions of consequentialism – and certainly the most historically familiar and prevalent form of consequentialism, act-utilitarianism – assign an important methodological role to the motive of (universal) benevolence, holding that moral judgments are most properly made from the standpoint of some form of benevolence. But agent-based morality as caring and morality as universal benevolence give (one or another form of) benevolence an even more central role by regarding it not (merely) as a valid and useful methodological tool, but as the actual basis for all moral judgment.

Thus for the utilitarian consequentialist, what makes an act right is whether it produces best consequences for sentient humanity or sentient beings generally, but universal benevolence focuses on such consequences and gives us a way to check up on what is or isn't right. Accordingly, what is right is either what yields best consequences or what an informed impartially benevolent being would approve, but the latter characterization is derivative from the former, rather than vice versa. In agent-based views, however, things work in just the opposite way. Benevolence is what makes the acts that express it right, but, given a knowledge of relevant facts, a right act will also be one with best or good consequences for the people or sentient beings involved. We saw some of this difference in our earlier discussion of how both consequentialism and agent-based views can be applied to practical moral issues. But my point here is that, despite the differences, consequentialism and warm agent-basing typically give benevolence a far more important role than it has in Kantian ethics.

The latter, to be sure, insists upon an imperfect duty to make the good of others one's end, and, even guided by conscientiousness, the having and acting upon such an end constitutes a kind of benevolence. But for Kant's theory benevolence of this sort enters the picture after all the main arguments for the CI itself have been given and thus merely as an implication of all that has gone before. Consequentialism and, to an even greater extent, agent-basing bring in benevolence much earlier or much more centrally in their attempts to characterize the nature of morality, and to that extent agent-based views resemble consequentialism more than they do Kant.

On the other hand, the stress that Kantian views place on the character of one's maxims and of one's will(ing) yields a similarity to agent-basing that, as we know, neither shares with consequentialism. Consequentialism in its most familiar forms makes the moral permissibility, obligatoriness, and goodness of actions depend on casual or natural factors outside the mind. But Kantian ethics locates permissibility and obligatoriness in the (inner) maxims or policies of an agent and of course treats the moral worth of an action as a function of its conscientiousness and thus, again, as independent of "stepmotherly nature." And agent-based virtue ethics clearly also treats the morality of actions as having to do with the inner life of agents rather than with what actually happens in the outside world.

Given what we have just seen, then, agent-based forms of virtue ethics represent a kind of reconciliation of or compromise between certain central themes or assumptions in Kantian and in consequentialist ethics. But having said as much, it is time I paid specific attention to Philip Pettit's discussion of consequentialism.

2   Reply to Pettit

In the course of his essay, Philip Pettit discusses two forms of virtue ethics. One of these, what he calls "the virtue theory of rightness," holds that rightness is not independent of the virtuous individual: an act or option's rightness rather is constituted by the fact that a certain sort of virtuous person would choose it. But he notes that some virtue ethicists – myself among them – don't rely on this formula, and earlier on he describes, in particular, an alternative, anti-theoretical virtue ethics that treats moral judgment as quasi-perceptual, i.e. as sensitive to moral considerations outside or independent of the virtuous agent.

My own essay attributed such a quasi-perceptual model to Aristotle (while questioning whether Aristotle is really as anti-theoretical as some present-day virtue ethicists would have it). For what Aristotle says about the virtuous agent's ability to perceive the nobility or rightness of actions, together with a number of other Aristotelian views, implies that the nobility or rightness of actions is at least to some degree independent of the virtuous agent and is not simply constituted by the responses or choices of (hypothetical) virtuous agents.[2] In that case, Aristotle doesn't subscribe to the sort of virtue theory of rightness that Pettit describes (and Hursthouse attributes to Aristotle), and indeed the neo-Aristotelian virtue ethics I offer in the first part of my own essay is also not a virtue theory of rightness in Pettit's sense.

Moreover, the agent-based forms of virtue I describe in the last part of the essay hold that for an action to be morally right, it is not enough that a virtuous agent with, say, benevolent motivation would have chosen or wanted one to perform it. The agent of the act must herself have the proper motivation in order for the act to count as acceptable morally. So, despite their highly theoretical character, agent-based views also aren't virtue theories of rightness in Pettit's sense.[3] As a result, Pettit's criticisms of the latter aren't in any way obviously relevant to the views I defended in my own essay, and if one tries to transpose and rework those criticisms so that they apply to the forms of virtue ethics I defended, the argument doesn't seem to work.

Thus Pettit argues that, on a virtue theory of the right, the virtuous individual cannot naturally or plausibly refer to his own nature and decisions in coming to a decision about what act to perform, so that there is a split, for any such view, between what makes an act right and what a virtuous individual will normally consider in determining whether to perform it. However, my earlier quasi-perceptual, neo-Aristotelian view clearly allows one to consider reasons for action that include the very facts that help make an act noble or admirable or right. And the same (though less obviously) holds true for agent-based forms of virtue ethics. For as we saw earlier, a benevolent person can consider whether one of his actions would be benevolently motivated, as a means to determining whether that action would be permissible or should be performed. So given agent-based morality as (one or another form of) benevolence, the virtuous agent can refer to what makes an action right as a means to deciding whether to perform it. The split Pettit refers to doesn't exist for such forms of virtue ethics, and that is well and good, since we would like our ethical views to be relevant to practical moral problems.

However, Pettit also challenges non-consequentialists in the realm of political morality, arguing that distinctively Kantian or virtue-ethical approaches are not likely to be able to say anything as plausible about social justice as consequentialism can. Leaving aside the possible responses of the Kantian, I think Pettit clearly has a point here in regard to virtue ethics.

For one thing, most recent discussions of virtue ethics (though this is also true of Kantian ethics) have concentrated on moral issues concerning individuals and individual relationships to the exclusion of political questions. But since questions of social justice and political morality are important and, arguably (and according to Aristotle), of a piece with individualistic moral issues, any ethical theory has reason to address these larger topics and is open to serious question if it proves incapable of doing so in a plausible fashion.

Virtue ethics is in an especially difficult position in this connection. Most recent virtue ethics has drawn upon Aristotelian ideas, but Aristotle's political philosophy was anti-democratic or at least not pro-democratic, so any ethics that looks to Aristotelianism in the area of political philosophy runs the risk of appearing hopelessly retrograde and outmoded from the standpoint of current-day (liberal) democratic ideals. But if for that reason virtue ethics decides not to offer any account of political morality and social justice, it runs a different risk. If virtue ethics can account only for individualistic or private morality and we need some other form of ethics to deal with larger issues, then the form that can successfully deal with the larger issues will have an advantage over virtue ethics if it can also handle individualistic morality. Any approach that can deal with both individual and social issues has an advantage over any that cannot. Indeed, if virtue ethics cannot deal with larger issues, we perhaps have reason to suspect what it says about smaller ones.

Consequentialism, as Pettit correctly points out, doesn't have a problem of this kind. Consequentialism and utilitarian consequentialism in particular have a long history of dealing with both individualistic and political issues, and as Mill in "Representative government" and a host of other consequentialist political philosophers have emphasized, utilitarian (and other, non-perfectionist) forms of consequentialism have an obvious capacity to justify democratic political ideals and institutions for or under the circumstances of modern life. How can virtue ethics hope to make the same claim for itself?

3   Virtue Politics

The answer, I think, lies in the consideration that Aristotle is not the only prior virtue-ethical figure to whom a virtue ethics can appeal in pursuing political philosophy and trying to work out a conception of social justice. In particular the moral "sentimentalism" of Hutcheson, Hume, and, subsequently, of Martineau and Nel Noddings offers us a way to defend and account for current-day democratic values that is largely independent of Aristotle. Rather, its emphasis, as we know, is on one or another form of benevolence, and not surprisingly, given the role that benevolence also plays in (utilitarian) consequentialism, an agent-based virtue ethics that draws on the British tradition of moral sentimentalism has the capacity to deal with political morality in a manner that is neither retrograde nor conservative.[4]

In fact, there is an agent-based account of social justice that naturally goes with morality as universal benevolence, and another that naturally goes with morality as caring, and though this is not the place to enter very much into the details, I would like to indicate in the space that remains to me how such agent-based political views can be compatible with and even help us to understand the appeal of democratic and liberal ideals. Of course, this seems to leave the neo-Aristotelian ethics I discussed in the first part essay somewhere out in the cold. But the accounts of social justice I am about to sketch could possibly be combined with a neo-Aristotelian ethics of individual or private action, and I believe it is also possible to formulate a democracy-friendly political philosophy that is in the same spirit as the neo-Aristotelian view (which in so many ways differs from Aristotle's own theory). Such a political philosophy would have some of the spirit of Michael Walzer's *Spheres of Justice* (1984), but I haven't worked this out yet and am not sure it can be worked out. Until it is, I feel the best virtue ethics can do is offer an agent-based account of social justice and social morality generally, and as I indicated above, I think there are in fact two distinct agent-based views we can develop: one that naturally accompanies morality as universal benevolence and another that goes well with morality as caring. Let us start with the former, which turns out to be much simpler.

Corresponding to morality as universal benevolence is something we can call justice as universal benevolence, for just as (utilitarian) consequentialism naturally applies to both individual and political questions, the motive of universal benevolence can be used as a criterion both of individual actions and of political and social institutions. This is possible because there is an analogy between the relation the institutions, etc., of a society have to the (membership of the) society and the relation of individual acts to their agents. The laws, customs, institutions of a given society are, as it were, the actions of that society: they exhibit or express the motives (though also the knowledge) of the social group in something like the way actions express or reflect an agent's motives (and knowledge), though in a more enduring manner that seems appropriate to the way societies outlast the individual agents in them. And so just as individualistic agent-based morality as universal benevolence regards individual actions as good if they reflect (a motive sufficiently close to) universal benevolence and wrong if they exhibit a motive that is fundamentally bad or inferior from the standpoint of universal benevolence, the virtue politics (since the title *Politics* is used for the treatise on political philosophy that follows the *Ethics* in the Aristotelian corpus, the designation seems apt) that corresponds to agent-based morality as universal benevolence will in similar fashion treat the justice of institutions and the like as dependent on what they reflect of the motives of the people who found or maintain them and is thus naturally regarded as agent-based as well. A law, for example, will be just (at the time it is promulgated) if it doesn't reflect selfishness, malice, or some other deficiency in universal benevolence on the part of (enough of) those responsible for its existence, which will include legislators and possibly also some of the people who voted for them. At some later point in its existence that law or likewise any institution or practice will be just if its continued existence reflects well (enough) on (enough of) those responsible for that continued existence or at least doesn't exhibit motives that are so far from universal benevolence that they count as morally bad or deficient.

Such an agent-based standard of justice also allows us to say what is unjust about various undemocratic institutions. Where a society's political institutions or laws (mainly) reflect the greed or indifference to humanity of some elite, or its selfish desire to retain its hegemony of power and privilege, those institutions and laws count as unjust according to (what we may call) justice as universal benevolence, and since almost all realistic examples of undemocratic institutions and laws – e.g. the absence of majority rule and laws forbidding certain kinds of speech or the organization of trade unions – do exhibit or reflect the above sorts of defective motives, justice as universal benevolence allows us to explain why democratic institutions are necessary to justice at least under the familiar conditions of modern life. (The argument becomes more difficult and less plausible in regard, for example, to primitive societies.)

However, we have not yet said what (justice as universal benevolence says) makes a society as a whole just. Societies can be thought of as large groups of people living under certain institutions, customs, or laws. So if an agent-based view of individual morality considers any person to be morally good or at least not bad if she has good enough motives, an agent-based view of social justice will naturally treat the justice of a given society as depending on how good the motivation of the people who constitute it is. For justice as universal benevolence, then, the justice of a society will depend on whether enough members of a given society have practical motivation that is close enough to universal benevolence. In that case, societies governed selfishly by some elite will count as unjust and so too, presumably, will meritocratic societies where a 'devil take the hindmost' attitude governs the attitudes of the more successful toward the less successful. Societies that disregard the well-being and security of people in other

nations for the usual reasons will also count as unjust according
to the present view, and so in a manner reminiscent of utilitarianism and consequentialism more generally, agent-based justice as benevolence treats social justice as making demands that
reflect conditions beyond the borders of a given nation or
society.

But the comparison with utilitarianism should make us at this
point curious about how divergent these two foundationally different theories are in their judgments about particular cases. Both
utilitarian consequentialism and justice as universal benevolence
for the most part justify democratic institutions and condemn
undemocratic societies, but they do in fact differ in their judgments about certain particular cases. Attending to the differences
can, I believe, give us reason to favor justice as benevolence over
utilitarian or consequentialist forms of justice – as well, then, as
further reason to prefer systematic agent-basing over any systematic form of consequentialism.

According to (most) utilitarian conceptions of justice (and leaving aside effects on people outside one's society), the utilitarian
will judge social institutions and the motives of those participa-
ting in them in terms of whether they actually or expectably
advance the well-being of the people of that society. And this
allows societies and social institutions to count as just even if
everyone's motives are entirely selfish and greedy. Amartya Sen
has pointed out that on a motive-utilitarian view of the evaluation
of motives, the motive of merciless profit maximization might
turn out to be the morally best of human motives, if, as some
economists have claimed, such mercilessness were necessary to
the maximization of gross national product and overall social
well-being (see Sen 1979). But then on a utilitarian conception
of justice a society governed by and benefiting from such motives
will count as more just than it would have been if its people had
been less selfishly motivated and lesser well-being had thereby
resulted.

By contrast, justice as universal benevolence will treat a society
in which people seek or strive to produce good consequences for
one another and society as a whole as juster than a society in
which better consequences simply occur through the operation of
individual (economic) selfishness. And to a large extent, I think

our moral intuitions favor this way of seeing things over the utilitarian view of justice. Since capitalistically ruthless individuals aim solely at their own power and wealth, it seems morally adventitious and even miraculous (the 'invisible hand' being an almost theological metaphor) that other people should thereby benefit, and when this happens we may well feel that a given society has gained the world at the expense of its moral soul. By making social justice a matter, so to speak, of the moral soul of (the people of) any given society, justice as universal benevolence captures our intuitions about social morality better, I think, than utilitarian and non-perfectionistic forms of consequentialism are capable of doing. But it is time now to switch our attention to the form of agent-based virtue politics that naturally goes with morality as caring.

Matters become more complicated when we try to see what view of justice emerges from morality as caring. The latter is more complicated than morality as universal benevolence, because it engages in and recommends an intuitive moral balancing act between self-concern and concern for others as a class and because it advocates (somewhat) greater concern for near and dear than for other people. Such complexity, however, seems worthwhile, because it allows morality as caring to come closer to our intuitive moral judgments than morality as universal benevolence does, and similar considerations drive the construction of an agent-based theory of justice that naturally goes with morality as caring.

Any attempt to formulate such a theory faces a problem that justice as universal benevolence can avoid. The latter treats the same motive(s) as valuable both in the private and in the public or political sphere, but if we in intuitive fashion say that private morality should be governed by caring motivation as we have described it, we may easily feel that public morality and action require somewhat different motives. Intuitively, people are right to be more concerned with themselves and their families than with other people during the course of their daily lives; but for those of us used to democracy, there is intuitive appeal also in the idea that when we come to vote, say, on national issues or to hold national office, we should put personal favoritism and preferences aside for the good of the country.

The latter attitude embodies what we typically call patriotism, though the excesses associated with this term may lead us to prefer 'love of country' for the kind of public-spiritedness I have just mentioned. Any politically plausible theory of justice that emerges from morality as caring must, then, be sensitive to our sense that different motives are appropriate in the political sphere and in private or personal morality. It must defend the notion that a shift of moral attitude or motivation ideally should occur between these two perspectives, and it has to account for the shift in a plausible fashion; and though there is no space for me here to go into the details, let me just say that the argument has to draw on the motive we invoked just above, the love of (one's own) country. The latter must be taken as consonant with and accompanied by a lesser but substantial regard for (what happens in) other countries, but it is in any case a feeling that can develop and be developed as a kind of counterweight to the motives regarded as appropriate in the private sphere. We think public and political matters – even whom we vote for for national office – should be governed by non-jingoistic love of country rather than by devotion to the special interests of oneself and one's family. Of course, according to morality as caring, even private life isn't *dominated* by the concern for oneself and one's family, but the point is that that life allows and recommends that one give some preference to, have greater concern for, those near and dear to one, whereas political action seems ideally to call for a concern for the good of one's country that involves no special preference for those near and dear to one.

The agent-based view of justice that emerges, then, from morality as caring will judge public institutions and laws as just when they reflect (enough of) the public-spirited motivation that is ideally supposed to govern the public or political sphere, and private institutions, like private activities, will be judged in terms of the more partialistic pattern of motives that morality as caring deems ideal for the personal sphere. Societies, then, too will be just or unjust depending on whether (enough of) their citizens or inhabitants have the indicated combination of personal caring and political public-spiritedness to a sufficient degree. Of course, here as elsewhere, what is enough or sufficient is a matter for judgment and open to debate, but no one ever said political or moral ideals are easy to determine. The vagueness we have inserted above and elsewhere in some sense does justice to the distressing perplexities of moral and political life.[5]

But this is merely a sketch of two new, agent-based approaches to social justice. If they show promise, then virtue ethics is not as stymied in regard to political issues and social justice as has often been thought. Indeed, I hope that in the not-too-distant future virtue politics will be regarded as a plausible, helpful companion to the virtue ethics that has recently undergone such a strong revival.

Notes

1 Above, we briefly discussed some of the consequences of deriving Kantian morality from ideas about the moral worth or goodness of will and action. But if, as some believe, Kantianism is best understood as grounding its view of right and wrong action in the idea of inherent dignity or moral worth of all human beings (as 'ends-in-themselves'), Kantian ethics may, once again, avoid the legal/legislative model of morality, but it will also then clearly not count as a form of virtue ethics. The moral worth all human beings are said to possess is independent of their (acts') moral goodness or badness (of moral worth in the other sense we have been using) and is therefore not the sort of (aretaic) variable excellence to which virtue ethics fundamentally appeals.

2 If we understand matters so, then Aristotle's claim that the virtuous individual is the measure of what is right or noble can and must be read epistemologically, i.e., as saying that virtuous individuals are the best (and perhaps infallible) judges of what is noble in action or desire.

3 By the same token, agent-based views differ from so-called ideal observer theories which treat rightness as a function of what an ideal observer would prefer or approve. For ideal observer theories allow for the possibility that an ideal observer might disapprove of her own motivation. So the characterization of the 'ideal' observer needn't coincide with one's (ultimate) view of what traits are admirable, thus undercutting any similarity to approaches that base act-evaluations in a theory of good inner traits.

4 Although Hume denied both the rational status of morality and the possibility of practical reason generally, agent-based theories based in

one or another form of benevolence can arguably accommodate an agent-based kind of practical rationality and show that such rationality requires us to be moral in our attitudes and actions. But this large topic is best saved for another occasion.

5 For fuller discussion of the theory of justice that naturally emerges from morality as caring, see my 'The justice of caring.'

References

Sen, Amartya (1979) "Utilitarianism and welfarism," *Journal of Philosophy* 76: 463–89.

Slote, Michael (forthcoming) "The justice of caring," *Social Philosophy and Policy* 15.

Walzer, Michael (1984) *Spheres of Justice*, New York: Basic Books.

Index